Spies, Scandals, and Sultans

Spies, Scandals, and Sultans

Istanbul in the Twilight of the Ottoman Empire

The First English Translation of
Egyptian Ibrahim al-Muwaylihi's *Ma Hunalik*

Translated and Introduced by Roger Allen

ROWMAN & LITTLEFIELD PUBLISHERS, INC.
Lanham • Boulder • New York • Toronto • Plymouth, UK

ROWMAN & LITTLEFIELD PUBLISHERS, INC.

Published in the United States of America
by Rowman & Littlefield Publishers, Inc.
A wholly owned subsidary of The Rowman & Littlefield Publishing Group, Inc.
4501 Forbes Boulevard, Suite 200, Lanham, Maryland 20706
www.rowmanlittlefield.com

Estover Road, Plymouth PL6 7PY, United Kingdom

Library of Congress Cataloging-in-Publication Data

Muwaylihi, Ibrahim, d. 1906.
  [Ma hunalik. English]
Spies, scandals, and sultans : Istanbul in the twilight of the Ottoman Empire: The First English Translation of Egyptian Ibrahim al-Muwaylihi's Ma Hunalik / Ibrahim al-Muwaylihi ; translated and introduced by Roger Allen.
    p. cm.
  Includes bibliographical references and index.
  ISBN-13: 978-0-7425-6216-5 (cloth : alk. paper)
  ISBN-10: 0-7425-6216-6 (cloth : alk. paper)
  ISBN-13: 978-0-7425-6217-2 (pbk. : alk. paper)
  ISBN-10: 0-7425-6217-4 (pbk. : alk. paper)
  1. Istanbul (Turkey)—Description and travel—19th century. 2. Turkey—History—1878-1909. I. Allen, Roger M. A. II. Title.
  DR721.M95513 2008
  949.61'8015--dc22

2007026724

Printed in the United States of America

♾™ The paper used in this publication meets the minimum requirements of American National Standard for Information Sciences—Permanence of Paper for Printed Library Materials, ANSI/NISO Z39.48-1992.

Contents

vi   *Contents*

A Note on Transliteration

$\mathcal{I}$n this work I am not resorting to the usual conventions of transliteration, in that I only include the conventional symbol (` ) for the Arabic phoneme `ayn. Faced here with the translation of a work by an Egyptian writer, writing in Arabic for a predominantly Egyptian readership and publishing in an Egyptian newspaper, describing in detail the life and times of the Ottoman Sultan, `Abd al-Hamid, in Istanbul and thus citing all manner of technical terminology and the hierarchy of ranks associated with the Ottoman administration, I confront what is already a complex situation, in that a central part of the modernist agenda of the Turkish leader Mustafa Kamal, renowned as Ataturk, was the decision to convert the writing system of Turkey and its language from Ottoman (i.e., extended Arabic) script to Roman.

Faced with this situation, I have decided to transliterate the terms and names into English as though from an Arabic text but without resorting to the conventional set of diacritical markings above and below elongated vowels and emphatic consonants. In attempting to justify such a decision, I might follow the lead of the great Middle Eastern comic-figure, Nasr al-din Hoja (in Turkish) or Juha (in Arabic), namely of requesting that, if needed, those who know inform those who don't.

The Later Ottoman Sultans

Arabic	Turkish
Mustafa II	Mustafa II
Ahmad III	Ahmet III
Mahmud I	Mahmut I
`Uthman III	Osman III
Mustafa III	Mustafa III
`Abd al-Hamid I	Abdılhamit I
Salim III	Selim III
Mustafa IV	Mustafa IV
Mahmud II	Mahmut II
`Abd al-Majid I	Abdılmecit I
`Abd al-`Aziz	Abdılaziz
`Abd al-Hamid II	Abdılhamit II
Muhammad V Rashad	Mehmet V Reflat
Muhammad VI Wahid al-din	Mehmet VI Vahideddin
`Abd al-Majid II	Abdılmecit II

Introduction

*T*his translation of Ibrahim al-Muwaylihi's renowned, indeed infamous, work is titled *Spies, Scandals, and Sultans*, an apt description of much of its content. However, the original title in Arabic is *Ma Hunalik*, with a literal meaning something akin to "Over Yonder."[1] It was in 1964 that I first read extracts from Muhammad al-Muwaylihi's famous *Hadith `Isa ibn Hisham*, a work that was to become the topic of my DPhil dissertation at Oxford (1968), later published, first in microfiche form in 1974 and then as the book, *A Period of Time*, in 1992.

If correct, the birthdates of the two al-Muwaylihis, father and son—Ibrahim and Muhammad, 1844 and 1858—suggest that, since the age gap between them was a mere fourteen years, they seem to have interacted with each other more as colleagues than as father and son. What is not subject to doubt is that the two men shared a number of variegated experiences during the latter half of the nineteenth century, only coming to an end with Ibrahim's death in 1906. Those experiences involved, among other things, commerce, speculation, newspaper publishing, and not a little political intrigue in Egypt, exile to Italy along with the Khedive Isma`il, periods spent in Paris and London, and then a prolonged stay in the Ottoman capital of Istanbul, before a return to Cairo in the mid-1890s.

It is that stay in Istanbul that is reflected in the present work. While clearly a supporter of the Ottoman role as defender of Islamic interests in the Middle East and in its relationship with the European powers, Ibrahim al-Muwaylihi, the author of *Ma Hunalik*, is equally obviously appalled by the situation that he finds in the Ottoman capital and spares no one in his description of the factors and personalities involved.

As if to prove the efficacy, if not the accuracy, of al-Muwaylihi's acidly critical portrait of Istanbul under the regime of Sultan `Abd al-Hamid, the book version of the work—published in 1896 by the press of the Cairene newspaper, *al-Muqattam* (in which the sequence of chapters had been previously serialized), was immediately banned on orders from the Ottoman capital; all copies were ordered sent to Istanbul. Accounts of al-Muwaylihi's life assure their reader that he carried out the Sultan's orders to the letter, and yet. . . .

In the early 1970s, when I was preparing my study of Muhammad al-Muwaylihi's *Hadith `Isa ibn Hisham*, for publication in book form—a process that, as I noted above, inevitably also involved a study of the life and works of Muhammad's father, Ibrahim, Professor Bernard Lewis informed me that he had found a copy of *Ma Hunalik* in Cairo. He kindly sent me a xeroxed copy and microfilm of the text. Following the completion of my research in Cairo on Muhammad al-Muwaylihi's *Hadith `Isa ibn Hisham*, I was now able to turn to the infamous, banned text of his father and to follow its history through the pages of *al-Muqattam* in the mid-1890s, comparing the original episodes with the published version (as I had previously done with Muhammad's *Hadith `Isa ibn Hisham*). At the same time I also prepared an initial English translation of the text.

Decades have intervened since those times in the early 1970s, and the siren call of the Arabic novel in its more recent manifestations has prevented me from returning to these important earlier texts in the history of modern Arabic prose writing. It was another scholar and colleague, Professor Gaber Asfour, Secretary-General of the Supreme Council for Culture in Cairo, who provided me with the occasion to make this retrospective journey by asking me to edit for publication the complete works of both al-Muwaylihis. Those of Muhammad al-Muwaylihi were published in Cairo (2 vols., 2002), and those of Ibrahim are due to appear in the near future.

It is thus my hope that the publication of the original Arabic text of *Ma Hunalik* (along with its checkered publication history) and other texts by Ibrahim al-Muwaylihi, coupled with this English version, will not only revive an interest in this very early period in the emergence of modern Egyptian prose literature but also, needless to say, be of interest to historians of the later Ottoman period.

In what follows I will provide a history of the author and then briefly compare and contrast the picture of Istanbul and its denizens provided by Ibrahim al-Muwaylihi—hardly an unbiased observer—with other accounts of the same era.

LIFE OF THE AUTHOR: IBRAHIM AL-MUWAYLIHI

The Egyptian political journalist and writer Ibrahim al-Muwaylihi (1844–1906) was born into a wealthy Egyptian family of silk merchants that traced its ancestry back to the town of Muwaylih on the coast of the Red Sea in the Arabian Peninsula. When his father died in 1865, Ibrahim and his younger brother, `Abd al-Salam, took over the administration of the family business. The same year saw the beginning of a long association between Ibrahim al-Muwaylihi and the Egyptian Khedive Isma`il; the latter appointed him to the Council of Merchants and the Court of First Instance. In 1868 Ibrahim was involved in the establishment of a publishing house, the first in a series of such initiatives throughout his career, but in 1872 he suffered a financial setback when he lost the entire family fortune in speculation on the newly established stock exchange. Once again the Khedive appears to have intervened in order to save him from financial ruin.

In 1879 the Khedive Isma`il was forced to abdicate and go into exile. Ibrahim al-Muwaylihi followed him to Italy in order to serve as tutor to his children and continued to publish newspapers, most notably *Al-Ittihad*, whose critical commentaries provoked the anger of the Ottoman Sultan, `Abd al-Hamid. Ibrahim was joined in exile by his son, Muhammad al-Muwaylihi, and in 1884 the two traveled to Paris where they are said to have assisted Jamal al-din al-Afghani and Muhammad `Abduh in producing their influential newspaper, *Al-`Urwa al-Wuthqa*.[2] While in France, Ibrahim al-Muwaylihi published a further issue of *Al-Ittihad* which was so critical of Ottoman foreign policy that his expulsion from France was engineered by the Ottoman authorities.[3] Via Brussels the two al-Muwaylihis made their way to London. There Ibrahim changed his topic and approach to a certain extent, choosing to write articles that attacked the policy of the British government and supporting the Ottoman Sultan. As a result, Ibrahim found himself invited to Istanbul. He sent his son, Muhammad, ahead of him to "test the waters," and, in spite of some initial diffidence, traveled to the Ottoman capital.[4]

Once in Istanbul Ibrahim was given a formal appointment on the Education Council. He made the acquaintance of Munif Pasha, the Minister of Education, a contact that provided both Ibrahim and his son with an entrée to the famous Fatih Library and its collection of manuscripts. However, much of Ibrahim's time in Istanbul was taken up with continuing involvement in political intrigue, both local and international, the results of which are certainly reflected on the pages of *Ma Hunalik*, published in 1896 soon after his return to Cairo.

On 14 April 1898, Ibrahim al-Muwaylihi began publishing his most famous newspaper, *Misbah al-Sharq*, which Muhammad Kurd `Ali in his *al-Mudhakkirat* (Memoirs, 1948–1951) termed "the best weekly." Both Ibrahim al-Muwaylihi and his son, Muhammad, contributed articles, including commentary on current events, political and social issues, and extracts from works of literature transcribed from the manuscripts in the Fatih Library in Istanbul.

The reputation of the newspaper reached its height during the publication (Nov. 1898 to Dec. 1900) of Muhammad's series of episodes, "*Fatra min al-Zaman*," which were published in 1907 as the renowned book, *Hadith `Isa ibn Hisham*.[5] During intervals in the publication of Muhammad's episodes, Ibrahim also contributed to the same genre, writing a series of nine episodes entitled "*Mir'at al-`Alam aw Hadith Musa ibn `Isam*" (June–July 1899, June–Sept. 1900).

Ibrahim now resumed his career as political consultant to the Khedive, and Muhammad gradually took over the editorial functions at the newspaper. However, under his editorship the newspaper's pungent critical articles—the feature that had so contributed to the paper's reputation—diminished in both quality and number. Instead of original articles there were lengthy quotations from Western sources and advertisements. The newspaper suspended publication on 15 August 1902. Ibrahim continued to publish articles in other newspapers and even founded yet another, named *al-Mishkah*, in 1905. However, he fell gravely ill in December of that year and died on 29 January 1906.

Muhammad Kurd `Ali describes Ibrahim al-Muwaylihi as "the greatest writer of his day, someone who could write entertainingly on the dullest subject." Incisive critic, brilliant stylist in the traditional mode, and inveterate political schemer, such is the picture of Ibrahim al-Muwaylihi that emerges from a reading of contemporary accounts, a life story that is often embellished by many apocryphal tales, the dissemination of which he himself often provoked and encouraged.

MA HUNALIK: CONTEXT AND CONTENTS

As was noted above, Ibrahim al-Muwaylihi had written many articles critical of the Ottoman Sultan and of Ottoman policy during the course of his travels in exile. It was only when he wrote in support of the Ottoman government from London that he received an invitation to come to the Ottoman capital. That in itself, of course, when coupled with his earlier expulsion from France, indicates the extent to which the Ottoman authorities kept a close watch on what was being written about them throughout the Middle East and Europe. With all this in mind, we must assume that, while Ibrahim al-Muwaylihi went to Istanbul (following the advice of his son, Muhammad, who had gone there earlier to check on the situation), he was well aware of the fact that part of the purpose of the invitation was to keep a close (or closer) watch on his activities. The fact that he was to be a resident in Istanbul would make that process much easier.

While both al-Muwaylihis clearly made good use of their time in Istanbul to conduct research in the famous Fatih Library—with its collection of Arabic manuscripts, it is clear that Ibrahim was also following his natural talent, namely involving himself in political debates and learning as much as possible about Egyptian-Ottoman relations. The contents of *Ma Hunalik* make it abundantly clear that he managed to learn a great deal, and it seems reasonable to assume that, after a period of several years in Istanbul, Ibrahim al-Muwaylihi's activities were arousing enough suspicion in the minds of the Ottoman security services that it became advisable, if not necessary, for him to leave and return to his native Egypt. It is indeed quite possible that Ibrahim al-Muwaylihi had a manuscript, or at least copious notes, ready before his departure from Istanbul (dangerous though that would have been), since the episodes of *"Ma Hunalik"* in its serialized form began to be published almost immediately after his return to Egypt; indeed they were published weekly and virtually without interruption between July 1895 and February 1896. The book version of *Ma Hunalik* appeared within months of the conclusion of the series of newspaper articles.

The newspaper that Ibrahim al-Muwaylihi chose for publication was *al-Muqattam*. Founded in 1889 by three Syrian journalists, Ya`qub Sarruf, Faris Nimr, and Shahin Makarius, *al-Muqattam*'s purpose was to support the policy of the British occupiers of Egypt (thus opposing the nationalist interests of *al-Ahram* founded earlier). As a natural consequence of this political emphasis, the newspaper was also devoutly anti-Ottoman and it would thus appear that, when Ibrahim had written articles during his stay in London in support of the Ottomans and against British policy, it represented a convenient shift in attitude, a feature of his career that was resented by many of his contemporaries, as the following comment of Muhammad Kurd `Ali makes abundantly clear:

> I actually avoided Ibrahim Bey, for he had so often misquoted my professor, Shaykh Muhammad `Abduh, and attributed to him things for which he was not responsible. Rumor had it however that some higher authority was behind Ibrahim Bey.[6]

A brief survey of articles published in *al-Muqattam* in the period when *"Ma Hunalik"* was appearing in serial form is instructive. Within the Egyptian context the newspaper was consistent in its support of British policy and attacked the "fanaticism" of *al-Mu'ayyad*, the newspaper that advocated the interests of Egyptian nationalism (see, for example numbers 1950, 22 August 1895, and 1962, 5 September 1895). There were regular reports from the Ottoman capital, *"Akhbar min Istana,"* all of them anonymous or attributed to writers with such pseudonyms as *"ahad al-afadil al-`Uthmaniyyin"* (A Worthy Ottoman). The primary topics of *al-Muqattam*'s reporting during the period in which *"Ma Hunalik"* was being published in serial form were the fate of the Armenian people within Ottoman territories and attempts by the authorities to annihilate or at least control the Young Turk movement. There were also regular articles concerning security measures both within the Ottoman capital (number 1864, 11 May 1895) and in Europe (number 2021, 13 November 1895, and number 2025, 18 November 1895). One particularly rich source of scandal was the behavior of the Ottoman Ambassador to Paris, Munir Pasha, who was caught consorting with a French prostitute in the Bois de Boulogne (number 2192, 10 June 1896). On at least two occasions the newspaper carried reports of European journalists who had managed to conduct interviews with Sultan `Abd al-Hamid himself; in each case the primary topic was the unpleasantly oppressive atmosphere created by security measures in Istanbul (the presence of which the Sultan vigorously denied: number 1877, 27 May 1895, and number 2127, 21 March 1896). The miserable state of Jamal al-din al-Afghani, essentially confined under house arrest, was the subject of an article in number 2046, 12 December 1895.

The details provided by these and many other articles on the atmosphere in Istanbul and the conduct of Ottoman domestic and foreign policy in *al-Muqattam* were considerably elaborated when the serialized articles entitled "*Ma Hunalik*" began to appear. The first was published in the newspaper on 28 June 1895, and attributed to "*adib fadil min al-Misriyyin*" (a worthy Egyptian litterateur). The highly critical and sarcastic tone that characterizes the episodes in the series is present from the very opening sentence:

> The Sultans of the Ottoman family were not really conquerors, nor would they be able to boast of any great achievements which might lend an aura of kudos and pride to their history.

The episodes analyze the Ottoman government in vivid, indeed scandalous, detail. The account begins with the status of the Ottoman Sultanate in general, and then proceeds to analyze the bureaucracy, division by division.

The account begins with the Sultan's palace itself (Yildiz, and its bureaucracy, "Almabayn"), the Bab al-`Ali ("Sublime Porte") and foreign policy, and the behavior of the bureaucrats who run each agency of government. The author's policy is to describe the physical layout of the offices that are being discussed, to give details about the functions of each official, and then to provide a whole series of anecdotes about the good and, more frequently, the bad aspects of the position and those who occupy it. There are further sections on the Chief Eunuch (*bash-agha*), the generals in the army—including no less than sixty field marshals (*mushir*). The author then devotes two large chapters to the elaborate spy system which had already been the topic of many earlier articles in *al-Muqattam*; here, of course, there is a total reliance on a large store of anecdotes, since "information," by the very nature of the topic under discussion, is impossible to obtain. These chapters are followed by a number of sections that describe the rituals of the Caliphate in Istanbul: the elaborate procession to Friday prayers and especially details concerning the festivals and rituals of the holy month of Ramadan (number 1876, 21 September 1895). After a discussion of the often corrupt process of appointing officials (including foreign ambassadors), the author concentrates on the senior shaykhs in Istanbul, with the renowned Syrian Shaykh Abu al-Huda from Halab (Aleppo) at their head; this section too includes a generous collection of insulting anecdotes.

At this point in the publication sequence of the newspaper articles we may perhaps detect some indication of the troubles that lay ahead, in that in number 2027, 20 November 1895, the author opens his article with a detailed explanation of his purpose in writing these articles. He has two primary goals, he says: firstly to put a stop to the specific practices currently taking place in the Ottoman capital; and secondly, on a much broader scale, to prevent the imminent collapse of the Ottoman Caliphate and Sultanate altogether. With those goals in mind it is more than ironic that the episodes conclude with a chapter on Sultan `Abd al-Hamid in person and a final article that documents the various depositions of Sultans that have occurred in the past. This final episode appeared in number 2093, 8 February 1896.

Beginning with *al-Muqattam* number 2294, 7 October 1896, we read announcements about the appearance of *Ma Hunalik* in book form. The original episodes are published in the order in which they appeared in the newspaper; two episodes were omitted (numbers 1921 and 1923, 19 and 22 July 1895—they are restored in this translation), and two other articles were added at the very beginning of the book: "*Al-din wa-al-Nasiha*," from number 1960, 2 September 1895, and "*Al-Umma al-`Uthmaniyya*," from number 1898, 22 June 1895. As noted above, the name of *Ma Hunalik*'s author was still listed as it had previously appeared in the newspaper, "Adib fadil min al-Misriyyin," but it is clear that the pseudonym did not succeed in misleading any of the Ottoman Sultan's officials, either in Istanbul or Cairo.

The process that led to the "disappearance" of *Ma Hunalik* is, by the very nature of things, unclear. Obviously, enormous pressure must have been brought to bear on Ibrahim al-Muwaylihi and perhaps his publishers from authorities with close connections to the Ottoman government. All copies of *Ma Hunalik* were said to have been withdrawn from circulation and destroyed. It appears that the procedure was completed with some thoroughness, since little has been heard of the work since 1896. Obviously, at least one copy managed to survive somewhere in Egypt, the one from the copy of which I have prepared this edition (and I dearly wish that I had been able to find out anything about its previous history).

MA HUNALIK AS A PORTRAIT
OF `ABD AL-HAMID'S ISTANBUL

The above sections devoted to the life of Ibrahim al-Muwaylihi and a survey of the contents of *Ma Hunalik* and its publication circumstances are sufficient demonstration, I would suggest, of the fact that the work is written from a very particular point of view, indeed with very particular biases. In the first place, Ibrahim al-Muwaylihi is not merely an Egyptian (albeit one with Arabian Peninsular origins) but a writer who is addressing himself to an Egyptian readership, and a readership of a particular newspaper at that. Thus, while one may read the pages of this translation and observe with a certain amusement its obvious relish for the invocation of all kinds of scurrilous gossip and innuendo, a series of questions will inevitably occur to those who study in detail the later era in the lengthy history of the Ottoman dynasty and from a variety of points of view. What, for example, is the extent to which Ibrahim al-Muwaylihi's description of personalities, offices, events, and ceremonials, and his perception of a process of relentless decline is an accurate reflection of the actual situation? How much veracity can we give to the account of an outside observer whose relationship with the regime has clearly fluctuated considerably (and whose proclivity for political intrigue has already been amply demonstrated before his decision to travel to Istanbul)?

In the following paragraphs I will make use of the categories and subdivisions that Ibrahim al-Muwaylihi himself uses in *Ma Hunalik* to point to both similarities and differences between his account and those of some other commentators on the period and the Ottoman regime of Sultan `Abd al-Hamid. In this context I should make it clear that my aim here is not to write or rewrite a historical account or a political analysis of either the period or its principal figures, but merely to assess the extent to which *Ma Hunalik* may be seen as constituting something more than the spleen venting of a disillusioned and disgruntled Egyptian.

Ibrahim al-Muwaylihi's opening sentence about the Ottoman Sultans cited above already reflects a historical perspective that emphasizes more recent times. As Bernard Lewis notes:

> If the first ten Sultans of the house of Osman astonish us with the spectacle of a series of able and intelligent men rare if not unique in the annals of dynastic succession, the remainder of the rulers of that line provides an even more astonishing series of incompetents, degenerates, and misfits.[7]

Al-Muwaylihi's expression of disillusionment thus seems to be focused on that latter group of the Ottoman Sultanate. What concerns him is not merely the implications and consequences of that process of change that he sees taking place, but the alarming rapidity with which changes that he considers deleterious to the interests of the state and its peoples have been allowed to happen. The centuries during which this latter group of Sultans has ruled and the events and trends that mark them have, more often than not, been discussed by historians within the framework of two particular concepts: those of "decline" and "reform," both of which, needless to say, involve reference to external criteria. The notion of decline, as discussed by Western commentators on the situation in the Ottoman dominions (particularly within the broader framework of the fate of empires), inevitably brings Edward Gibbon's name into the picture, with his invocation of the rise-and-fall model of civilizational history as a mode of analysis applied to the later centuries of the Roman Empire—all penned within the temporal context of the ever-expanding British imperial adventure. It is within the context of a highly developed Ottoman wariness regarding such European imperial ambitions that the debate over "reform" takes place. Thus, Ottoman visitors to Europe show themselves to be well aware of advances in technology (particularly military technology) and other significant factors such as the impact of the influx of Latin-American precious metals and the circumnavigation of Africa on their economy, and yet it is precisely those factors that allow the European powers to exert increasing diplomatic (and, on occasion, strategic) pressure on the Ottoman authorities with a view to demanding the introduction of "reforms." Along with the offers of military know-how come requests for representative government and a greater openness to foreign market forces. The quest for the appropriate and tolerable balance between long-held traditional values and practices and "modern" ideas and methods is an exquisitely delicate one.

European attitudes toward the Ottoman Empire have also gone through different phases. The glory days of Ottoman expansion see Selim ("the Grim") entering Cairo in 1516 and the Ottoman armies laying siege to the city of Vienna in 1529. The Ottoman Empire stretches far and wide, across the northern littoral of Africa to Algeria, into the Arabian Peninsula, and abutting Persia to the east and Russia to the north. For several centuries the proverbial and fabled "East" is known simply as "the Turk." There is a sense however in which the year 1529, besides being viewed as a kind of high point in the exercise of Ottoman military prowess, is also a turning point in that Vienna is not captured. It is the ensuing centuries that are marked by Bernard Lewis's comment above, including the humiliating treaty of Carlowitz (1699)—as a result of which the Ottomans were compelled to cede European territory for the first time, and a series of local rebellions which gradually whittled away the European territories that had formerly been considered part of "*dar al-Islam.*" Since the Ottoman Sultan Selim had accepted the title of "Caliph" from the `Abbasi "shadow-caliph" in Cairo in 1517, this loss of territories was no insignificant matter. Incidentally, it was while fighting in one of these rebellions (with the Greeks) that Lord Byron met his death at Missolonghi in 1824. The naval battle of Navarino (1827) which was part of the same conflict was also a major defeat for the Ottoman navy.[8]

There is then no shortage of evidence to suggest that al-Muwaylihi's comments throughout *Ma Hunalik* concerning the loss of prestige of the Ottoman armed forces and the much-changed relationship with the powers of Europe are founded on widespread perceptions within the Ottoman administration and beyond. The "terrible Turk" who had been beating on the walls of Vienna has now been driven back. Several regions have gained their independence from the authorities in Istanbul, and all kinds of diplomatic pressure are being put on the Ottoman administration to bring about "change" and "reform."

In fact, the forty years or so (1839–1876) before `Abd al-Hamid became Ottoman Sultan, roughly coterminous with the Sultanates of `Abd al-Majid (r. 1839–1861) and `Abd al-`Aziz (r. 1861–1876), had witnessed the implementation of a whole series of reforms known under the general title of "*Tanzimat*." After the traditional power of the Janissary Corps had been crushed in 1826, the armed forces had been reformed and a new officer corps had been trained.[9] Government offices and legislative agencies had been reorganized or instituted, and initiatives in education (colleges) and communications (particularly railways and postal services) had been implemented and enhanced. The primary implementers of this series of changes were Mustafa Rashid Pasha (d. 1858), `Ali Pasha (d. 1871), and Fu'ad Pasha (d. 1869).[10] As Stanford Shaw notes however, "the men of the Tanzimat were not particularly good economists or financial leaders," and the result was what he terms "financial chaos."[11] Added to which was the increasingly fractious political situation in a number of Balkan states and ongoing disputes with Russia over territory. It was precisely at the moment when the European powers were putting pressure on the Ottoman government to implement policies concerning the rights of Ottoman citizens—non-Turks and/or non-Muslims—in these many regions through the promulgation of a "constitution" that a crisis of confidence in the Sultanate placed `Abd al-Hamid on the Ottoman throne in 1876. Virtually every commentator on the situation, its causes, and consequences, notes that it was not an auspicious beginning for any sovereign.

The major flag bearer for this phase of the constitutional movement was Midhat Pasha, one of the most famous figures in this era of later Ottoman history and one of its primary victims in that he was murdered in exile in Saudi Arabia in 1883. Describing the mood of the moment in 1876, he himself notes that "there seemed a feeling of anxiety in the air as of the prescience of future evils," and goes on to state that "the dark gloom of the Hamidian epoch was now about to settle over the land of the Osmanli."[12] The temporal context involved a meeting of representatives of the European powers in Istanbul to advocate further reforms in the light of discussions of the status of both Bulgaria and Bosnia-Herzegovina. Midhat Pasha had already been exerting pressure on the previous Sultan to implement constitutional reform, and the newly installed Sultan `Abd al-Hamid was, it would appear, persuaded of the efficacy of "spiking the Europeans' guns" at the conference by choosing this precise moment to announce the introduction of a new constitution. That indeed happened, one session of the conference being apparently accompanied by the sound of cannon fire in celebration of the announcement. However, the European powers did not reach any agreement with the Ottoman authorities over the issues of territorial dispute, and the conference broke up without reaching any conclusions. The newly installed Sultan was furious and took out his anger on Midhat Pasha who was sent into exile. The parliament of deputies envisioned by the new constitution met, failed to conform to the Sultan's wishes, and was dissolved within weeks.[13] It was not to meet again until 1908 when the Young Turks made its recall one of their principal demands. Instead the reign of Sultan `Abd al-Hamid is depicted as being one of complete autocracy, and, to cite the opinions of Midhat Pasha himself once again, an opportunity that "might have been a day marked in red, the greatest date in Turkish history" was, as it turned out, "only the first act of a stupendous comedy."[14] If indeed it is a major purpose of comedy to make clear to its audiences how not to do things, then perhaps Midhat's characterization may be a valid one, but Ibrahim al-Muwaylihi was certainly one of many people who witnessed the Hamidian decades and viewed them as being anything but amusing, a tragi-comedy perhaps.

Part of the problem in any assessment of this general picture is, of course, the very fact that Sultan `Abd al Hamid gathered so much executive authority to himself. "His Majesty reigns supreme as hitherto, everything and everybody being more than ever under his absolute management and control."[15] After the promulgation of the constitution in 1876, whatever powers were to have devolved on to the shoulders of the newly elected parliament were gathered back into the Sultan's palace, where an enormous bureaucracy was created to deal with the wide variety of economic and political issues, both local and international. What several commentators point out is that the reforms already initiated gathered pace during `Abd al-Hamid's reign, most especially those involving education, communications, and the modernization of the armed forces.[16] However, what also emerged from a combination of factors and, one might almost suggest, from the very nature of bureaucracies, was an atmosphere of interdepartmental rivalry, backstabbing, and intrigue that appears to have been the dominant force in Istanbul by the time that Ibrahim al-Muwaylihi traveled to the capital in order to accept the Sultan's "invitation." It would appear that, following an initial phase during which a number of prominent figures who were regarded as opponents to the Sultan had been exiled—prime among them being Midhat Pasha, as already noted, it was deemed prudent to "invite" a number of them back to the Ottoman capital, not least so that they could be more closely monitored. Such, for example, was the fate of Jamal al-din al-Afghani.

With all this in mind, it is perhaps to be anticipated that Ibrahim al-Muwaylihi's *Ma Hunalik* tends to emphasize the negative aspects of his experiences in Istanbul, almost to the extent of excluding many of the more positive developments that have been noted above. Not only had he already suffered a good deal of harassment from Ottoman dignitaries during his years of exile in Europe, but, as an Egyptian who had witnessed the arrival of British armed forces and civilian bureaucrats in his own country, he also resented the apparent inability of the Ottoman government to resist the intense pressures being exerted on it by the European powers who seemed determined to influence the policies of the entity that the Russian Czar Nicholas the First had declared in 1853 to be "the sick man of Europe." Al-Muwaylihi's attitude thus shows a certain ambivalence toward the phenomena that he observes, in that, while he is at great pains to provide illustration and anecdote about the realities of the Ottoman bureaucracy and its spy system, he also wishes the Sultan, as proclaimed Caliph of Islam, to exert a greater moral role in the latter capacity and to recapture some of the glories of a fabled Ottoman past. With that in mind, I will now attempt in what follows to assess quite how far such ambivalence is reflected in the accounts and opinions to be found on the pages of *Ma Hunalik*.

Lord Kinross finishes his survey of "the Ottoman centuries" with a chapter devoted to "the last of the Sultans." He opens it by pointing out that almost everything about `Abd al-Hamid's upbringing—his acute awareness of the number of assassinations and depositions that had marked the end of his forebears' reigns and his innate wariness of palace intrigue—contributed to his decision not to reside in the Dolmabahce Palace where the previous Sultans had resided after Mahmud II had moved from the fabled Topkapi Palace following a fire in 1826, but instead to make use of the Yildiz (in Turkish, Yıldız) Palace overlooking the Bosphorus.[17] As Carter Findley points out in his study of the Ottoman bureaucracy, "if Abd ul-Hamid stood in personal control of this system, Yıldız Palace formed its center in a larger sense."[18] The complex had been expanded (by knocking down a number of buildings) and a mosque had been built adjoining it, the procession to which on Fridays is the subject of an elaborate description by Ibrahim al-Muwaylihi in

Ma Hunalik.[19] The space between the privacy and seclusion of the Sultan's residence and the public domain was "Almabayn" (literally, what lies in between), and those bureaucrats who functioned in this space were termed the "almabaynjiyya." The chapter titles of *Ma Hunalik* reveal clearly enough the extent to which the functions of the Ottoman government were gathered together under the tight control of the Sultan and his trusted staff, chief among whom was Ghazi 'Uthman Pasha, a field marshal generally known as the hero of Plevna, that being the Bulgarian town that the Ottomans had successfully defended against a Russian siege during the Russian-Turkish conflict of 1877–1878. While al-Muwaylihi's account of the various offices that were now subsumed under this general category may contain a good deal of anecdote about individual personalities and interdepartmental feuds, the sequence of chapters certainly follows the hierarchy of the system—the Sublime Porte, the office of the Shaykh al-Islam and of the Chief Eunuch, the General Staff of the Armed Forces, and the bureaucracy—in much the same way as those historians who have relied on what might be described as "more neutral" sources (and who presumably had no access to al-Muwaylihi's text in any case).[20]

One aspect of 'Abd al-Hamid's Sultanate upon which Ibrahim al-Muwaylihi spends a great deal of time is the spy system. Here again, one needs to observe that the author himself had been a target of the system on more than one occasion during his sojourn in Europe, but the accounts of the Ottoman capital and its bureaucracy during the period are virtually unanimous in recording that his insistence on focusing on this phenomenon, its almost universal prevalence, and its deleterious effects on almost every aspect of public life was by no means unjustified. His account is very successful in capturing the prevailing atmosphere in a society in which it appears that every second person is spying on someone else, and, alongside reports on the ways in which careers were ruined by the system, it also provides details of the absurd lengths to which such procedures could go. To quote Andrew Wheatcroft in this context (one of any number of possible sources),

> The flood of information from the periphery to the centre provided an enlarged sense of power, but also a ramifying impression of subversion and threat. Informers were valued by the plots they uncovered, the incompetence they unearthed, the dangers which their efforts averted. In consequence, they developed skills at reporting the embers of dissent as a raging conflagration. A chance remark at a coffee-house grew into a network of revolutionaries. As the sultan himself believed that his throne was in danger, he was susceptible to very wild suggestions of conspiracy or sedition. And at the hands of his investigators, skilled in all the techniques of torture, his worst fears were confirmed.[21]

The actual pervasiveness of such systems of espionage, as opposed to the creation of the impression of such widespread effectiveness, is, needless to say, one of the byproducts of the investigation of the secret, something that only becomes a known factor through its revelation. Yet again, it would appear that al-Muwaylihi's account of his experiences in `Abd al-Hamid's Istanbul during the 1880s and 1890s seems to contribute valuable extra detail to a general picture whose outlines are already reasonably clear. Of all the aspects of *Ma Hunalik* that may have caused the Ottoman authorities to demand its withdrawal from circulation, it is perhaps this revelation of the intentionally secret that aroused the most anger and concern.

After devoting some attention to the official rituals involving the Sultan (including the above-mentioned procession to Friday prayers), Ibrahim al-Muwaylihi then turns his attention to his other major source of rancor: the group of four shaykhs who served as `Abd al-Hamid's religious counselors: Shaykh Abu al-Huda from Syria; Shaykh Ahmad As`ad from Medina; Shaykh Fadl al-Malibari from Dhofar; and Shaykh Zafir al-Maghribi from Libyan Tripoli. All four are from Arabic-speaking regions and represent different religious groups, most particularly Sufi ones. However, of the four it is Shaykh Abu al-Huda who is widely regarded as the "éminence grise" in that he has been able to make ample use of his astrological talents to cater to the Sultan's highly superstitious nature and his ongoing interest in predictions of what is to come. Although the major role that Ibrahim al-Muwaylihi attributes to Shaykh Abu al-Huda in *Ma Hunalik* is based, as is his wont, on a good deal of anecdotal information, there is other evidence to suggest that the latter did indeed wield a good deal of authority through his close relationship as "spiritual" adviser to the Sultan. It will be recalled from the account of Ibrahim al-Muwaylihi's life that he had worked very closely with Jamal al-din al-Afghani while both men were in London and that, when al-Muwaylihi accepted the Sultan's invitation to come to Istanbul, the two men had remained in contact concerning the former's movements. It would appear that, in 1892, the Sultan and his entourage decided that al-Afghani needed to receive a similar "invitation," all as part of an ongoing policy (already noted) of "gathering in" those political and religious figures (insofar as the two dimensions were separable) whose views were regarded with suspicion. Just to make sure that the invitation was not to be declined, Shaykh Abu al-Huda sent al-Afghani a letter in which he unsubtly points out some of the recent statements of the latter that might be interpreted in ways contrary to the best interests of Islam and its Caliph. The letter seems to have been sufficiently efficacious, in that al-Afghani did indeed travel to Istanbul in 1892 and was to remain there for the remainder of his life, a virtual prisoner.[22] This decision on the part of the Ottoman authorities (and presumably with the full knowledge of the Sultan himself) and the way in which it was implemented cannot fail to have had a deep effect on Ibrahim al-Muwaylihi himself, particularly when he observed the limits that were placed on al-Afghani following his arrival in Istanbul. It was not long afterward that al-Muwaylihi made the decision to follow his son, Muhammad, who had already returned to their native Egypt.

When we bear in mind the fact that al-Muwaylihi's text, *Ma Hunalik*, in book form was banned within days of its publication in Cairo in 1896, it is surely no mere coincidence that, following this highly critical chapter on the four "Arab" shaykhs in Istanbul, he launches into an explanation, indeed a justification, for writing the series of articles.[23] He suggests that, of the two principal goals that he has set himself, he has clearly failed in the first: informing people in authority about the imminence of the disaster that will strike them and take the state with them; but that he believes that he has succeeded in the second: to inform people about the general condition in which people in positions of authority have left the state. It is, no doubt, some combination of this sense of failure, coupled to his awareness of the fate of al-Afghani and his disgust at the reliance of the Caliph of Islam on such a group of shaykhs, that leads him to make the decision to leave the Ottoman capital and return to his homeland. It also goes without saying that his decision, once made, did not remain a secret from the Sultan's spy system. However, his rationale for leaving— a desire to return to his homeland and to see his son again—seems to have persuaded the Sultan, in that he was indeed given permission to depart.

All of which brings us to the final section of the book, in which al-Muwaylihi talks about Sultan `Abd al-Hamid in person. Photographs of the Sultan tend to confirm the accuracy of al-Muwaylihi's depiction of him: "a thin man of medium height or indeed under the average height for men." Lord Kinross's description penetrates more beneath the surface: "Pale, silent, and melancholy, with a 'sinister and scrutinizing' look that belied his polite manners," while Wheatcroft's portrait, he being one of the regime's more sympathetic European observers, reflects a major theme in al-Muwaylihi's account: "a shabby little figure in his fez and stambouline, he embodied both physically and symbolically the decline from the great sultans of the past, with their turbans, furs, and egret feathers."[24]

Beyond his portrayal of such personal features and traits, al-Muwaylihi is perhaps rubbing salt into an open wound by listing as a parting gesture in his text the various circumstances under which previous Ottoman Sultans had been deposed. Since `Abd al-Hamid's accession to the throne and his eventual departure from it (1909) both resulted from that very process, it must be seen as a not terribly subtle final comment on al-Muwaylihi's part; indeed, in view of the series of events that transpired in the Ottoman dominions following his departure from Istanbul, it can be viewed as a harbinger and warning. Here again we detect that ambivalence that al-Muwaylihi seems to feel toward a ruler who has had a direct and often negative impact upon his career but who at the same time is the public figurehead of a community of faith, the Islamic *umma*, in whose interests he—al-Muwaylihi—has been fighting (and intriguing) for decades.

We have already noted above that `Abd al-Hamid's upbringing and his awareness of the fates of his predecessors had engendered a highly suspicious personality, something clearly symbolized by his decision to "retreat" behind the increasingly high walls of the Yildiz Palace.[25] As has been suggested above, the very autocratic regime that `Abd al-Hamid instituted and maintained made it almost inevitable that the personality of the Sultan and the assessment of his conduct of political affairs should become scrambled. Stanford Shaw illustrates how the two came to be seen as one:

> Late in his reign, however, as the terrorist threats and foreign attacks mounted, his fears of personal assassination or dethronement led him to subordinate his concentration on reform to his desire to destroy treason and revolt within the empire.[26]

Lord Kinross also describes the system as being "in effect a police state, a bureaucracy centralized within the palace of Yildiz."[27] And yet he also insists that, politics apart, the Sultan "was no blind reactionary." Wheatcroft takes this discussion about the ambivalent image created by `Abd al-Hamid's autocracy one stage further by placing it into a broader context:

> It is not uncommon for political adversaries to describe an opponent as "evil" or "mad." The enemies of Abdul Hamid, both inside and outside the empire, considered him both mad and bad. His "madness" lay in not following the approved path of Westernization.[28]

Wheatcroft goes on to point out the way in which the Sultan had not only vigorously implemented several aspects of "reform" initiated by his predecessors (as noted above) but had also invoked the notion of pan-Islam as a means of providing his regime with a legitimacy of a different and historically grounded kind. Whence, one might suggest, the direct pleas of Ibrahim al-Muwaylihi in the text of *Ma Hunalik* to the Sultan in person to do something to alter the prevailing atmosphere of suspicion and corruption in the Ottoman capital.

With this account of depositions, abdications, and one case of martyrdom, Ibrahim al-Muwaylihi finishes his survey of Hamidian Istanbul. Bearing in mind the difficult circumstances that the author of *Ma Hunalik* confronted before his journey to the Ottoman capital and during the years that he spent there, it is almost inevitable that his own impressions, along with those of the people with whom he consorted and whom he himself chose to consult, would provide him with a picture of the Sultan's regime that is at best mixed. The above sampling of a potentially much larger repertoire of accounts, historical, diplomatic, and otherwise, concerning the period of his sojourn in Istanbul (approximately the mid-1880s to the mid-1890s) has shown, I believe, that, while al-Muwaylihi did indeed choose to accentuate the negative in his account—based to a substantial extent on anecdotal information culled from a venue and in an era in which anecdote and rumor seem to have become the primary mode of communication, there was in fact a good deal of negative development upon which to comment, whether viewed from within or without.

In conclusion then, *Ma Hunalik*—long since absent from any account of this period—now returns to the public domain, not merely in order to reflect the impressions and attitudes of an inveterate Egyptian political intriguer, opponent of British and European interference in Ottoman (and especially Egyptian) affairs, and proponent of a pan-Islamic vision founded on a strong Ottoman Sultanate, but also to provide further detail to accounts of the inner workings of a government and bureaucracy in its difficult confrontation with the processes of change.

SELECT BIBLIOGRAPHY

The bibliography connected with the history of `Abd al-Hamid's sultanate would potentially be enormous and diverse. The following works include a selection of those that I have found most useful in contextualizing Ibrahim al-Muwaylihi's work.

Roger Allen, "Ibrahim al-Muwaylihi." In *Encyclopedia of Islam* 2nd ed., Leiden: E.J. Brill, 1954–2005.

———, *A Period of Time*. Reading: Garnet Press, 1992.

———, "Writings of Members of the Nazli Circle." *Journal of the American Research Center in Egypt* VIII (1971): 79–84.

Werner Ende, *Europabild und kulturelles Selbstbewusstsein bei den Muslimen am Ende des 19. Jahrhunderts, dargestellt an den Schriften den beiden agyptischen Schriftsteller Ibrahim und Muhammad al-Muwailihi*. PhD diss., Hamburg, 1965.

Carter Findley, *Bureaucratic Reform in the Ottoman Empire: The Sublime Porte 1789–1922*. Princeton: Princeton University Press, 1980.

———, *Ottoman Civic Officialdom: A Social History*. Princeton: Princeton University Press, 1989.

`Abd al-Latif Hamza, *Adab al-Maqala al-Sahafiyya fi Misr*. Vol. 3, *Ibrahim al-Muwaylihi*. Cairo: Dar al-Fikr, 1959.

Nikki R. Keddie, *Sayyid Jamal al-din "al-Afghani": A Political Biography*. Berkeley: University of California Press, 1972.

Bernard Lewis, *The Emergence of Modern Turkey*. London: Oxford University Press, 1961.

Philip Mansel, *Constantinople*. New York: St. Martin's, 1998.

Ali Haydar Midhat Bey, *The Life of Midhat Pasha*. London: John Murray, 1903. Reprint, Arno Press, 1973.

Ibrahim al-Muwaylihi, *Al-Mu'allafat al-Kamila* (Complete Works), ed. Roger Allen, Cairo: Al-Majlis al-A`la li-al-Thaqafa, 2007.

Alan Palmer, *The Decline and Fall of the Ottoman Empire*. New York: M. Evans, 1993.

Sir Edwin Pears, *Life of Abdul Hamid*. London: Constable, 1917. Reprint New York: Arno Press, 1973.

Yusuf Ramitch, *Usrat al-Muwaylihi wa-atharuha fi al-adab al-`Arabi al-hadith*. Cairo: Dar al-Ma`arif, 1980.

Stanford Shaw and Ezel Kural Shaw, *History of the Ottoman Empire and Modern Turkey*. Vol. 2. Cambridge: Cambridge University Press, 1977.

Filib di Tarrazi, *Ta'rikh al-Sihafa al-`Arabiyya*. Cairo: Al-Matba`a al-Amrikiyya, 1913–1933.

Andrew Wheatcroft, *The Ottomans*. London: Viking, 1993.

Gottfried Widmer, "Der Spiegel der Welt." In *Die Welt des Islams* N.S. 3 (1954): 57ff.

NOTES

1. One of the readers of this work in manuscript form suggested that the original Arabic title, *Ma Hunalik*, actually contains an ellipsis of the phrase "*kull ma hunalik*," implying something like "all there is" and thus that Ibrahim al-Muwaylihi is hinting that he has included in his account whatever he could but that there is more that can be said. While that is certainly the case, I am not entirely convinced that the choice of title involves such an ellipsis, but it is certainly an interesting idea.

2. Jamal al-din, renowned as "al-Afghani" (1839–1897), was a major advocate of the ideas of pan-Islamism as being a valid basis for establishing identity in opposition to European imperialism. His radical views did not make him popular with the ruling elites of the Middle East region, and, as Ibrahim al-Muwaylihi's account shows, he finished his life a virtual prisoner in the Ottoman capital (on which, see further below). However, through his teachings and publication activities, he certainly managed to galvanize a number of reformers, most notable among whom was Muhammad `Abduh (1849–1905), the pioneer of Egyptian Islamic modernism, who, having spent years of exile in the company of al-Afghani, returned to his homeland to become its chief *mufti*, to issue a number of controversial verdicts on contemporary issues, and to inspire an entire generation of secular and religious reformers.

3. Carter Findley's detailed study of the Ottoman bureaucracy and its machinations, *Ottoman Civic Officialdom: A Social History* (Princeton: Princeton University Press,

1989), contains a good deal of information about the way in which Ottoman embassies were supposed to "keep track of" dissident opinion (see pp. 222–226).

4. This invitation was also linked to the activities of Jamal al-din al-Afghani and his relationship with the Ottoman Sultan. In London Ibrahim al-Muwaylihi was discussing the wisdom of going to Istanbul with Wilfrid Scawen Blunt. For details on the correspondence involved, see Nikki Keddie, *Jamal al-din "al-Afghani": A Political Biography* (Berkeley: University of California Press, 1972), pp. 246–268.

5. The complete works of Muhammad al-Muwaylihi were published for the first time in Cairo in two volumes in 2002: Muhammad al-Muwaylihi, *Al-Mu`allafat al-kamila*, ed. Roger Allen, (Ruwwad al-qissa al-`Arabiyya series), (Cairo: Al-Majlis al-a`la li-al-thaqafa, 2002).

6. See Muhammad Kurd `Ali, *Memoirs*, trans. Khalil Totah, ACLS Near East Translation Program, no. 6. Washington, DC: American Council of Learned Societies, 1954, p. 89.

7. Bernard Lewis, *The Emergence of Modern Turkey* (London: Oxford University Press, 1961), pp. 22–23.

8. Its impact on Europe can be gauged by the painting of the battle by Louis Garneray, *Le bataille de Navarin*.

9. An illustration of the uniforms of the "new troops" can be found in Andrew Wheatcroft, *The Ottomans* (London: Viking, 1993), no. 17 between pp. 98 and 99.

10. These measures are discussed in detail in Lewis, *Emergence*, pp. 74–128, and Stanford Shaw and Ezel Kural Shaw, *History of the Ottoman Empire and Modern Turkey*, vol. 2 (Cambridge: Cambridge University Press, 1977), pp. 55–171.

11. Shaw and Shaw, *History*, p. 155.

12. Ali Haydar Midhat Bey, *The Life of Midhat Pasha* (London: John Murray, 1903; reprint: Arno Press, 1973), pp. 100–101. The author/compiler of this work is Midhat Pasha's son.

13. An illustration of the opening ceremony can be found in Philip Mansel, *Constantinople* (New York: St. Martin's, 1998), no. 44 between pp. 336 and 337.

14. Midhat Bey, *Life*, p. 127.

15. See Mansel, *Constantinople*, p. 317.

16. See, for example, Shaw and Shaw, *History*, pp. 211–253; Lewis, *Emergence*, p. 178 et seq.; Carter Findley, *Bureaucratic Reform in the Ottoman Empire: The Sublime Porte 1789–1922* (Princeton: Princeton University Press, 1980), pp 227–229; Wheatcroft, *Ottomans*, pp. 200–202; and, for a particularly British view of things, Sir Edwin Pears, *Life of Abdul Hamid* (London: Constable, 1917; reprint New York: Arno Press, 1973), chapter X, pp. 152–204.

17. The complex itself is described by Mansel, *Constantinople*, chap. 13; also Pears, *Life of Abdul Hamid*, 1917, pp. 107–109. For a photograph of Yildiz, see Alan Palmer, *The Decline and Fall of the Ottoman Empire* (New York: Evans, 1993), no. 8 between pp. 146 and 147.

18. Findley, *Bureaucratic Reform*, p. 229.

19. A procession involving Sultan Mahmud II (c. 1810) is depicted in a painting in Wheatcroft, *Ottomans*, no. 28 between pp. 194 and 195.

20. For example, Shaw and Shaw, *History*, pp. 211 et seq.; on page 214 it is noted that at least two holders of the office of Chief Eunuch were given the post of minister, thus placing the person on equal terms with the Grand Wazir and the Shaykh al-Islam.

21. Wheatcroft, *Ottomans*, p. 203; see also Findley, *Bureaucractic Reform*, p. 233: "The reports of these spies, known as "*jurnal*" (from the French *journal*) occupied a great deal of the sultan's attention and, despite the manifest absurdity of many of them, greatly compounded his anxieties." For further estimates of the negative role of these "*jurnals*," see also Pears, *Life of Abdul Hamid*, pp. 336 and 349.

22. For details of these contacts, see Nikki Keddie, *Sayyid Jamal al-Din "al-Afghani"* (Berkeley, California: University of California Press, 1972), pp. 255–264 and 370–371.

23. The relevant article appeared in *Al-Muqattam* no. 2028, 21 November 1895.

24. See Lord Kinross, *The Ottoman Centuries* (New York: Morrow Quill, 1977), p. 534; Wheatcroft, *Ottomans*, p. 206.

25. As Kinross notes (*Ottoman Centuries*, p. 533): "[Yildiz] was likewise a center of fear—the irrational fear of Abdul Hamid himself for his own personal safety, generated through an innate distrust of all men and their motives, and in turn generating a spirit of apprehension in all those around him." See also Findley, *Bureaucratic Reform*, p. 229: "While Abd ul-Hamid was not always as violent as we might infer from some of his statements and actions, he was a strange, complex, and psychologically unsettled man . . . thanks in part to the unwholesome palace environment in which he was reared, and in part also to the circumstances surrounding his accession, he was distinctly paranoid."

26. Shaw and Shaw, *History*, p. 221. For a more negative and personalized assessment, see Pears, *Life*, pp. 332 and 333: "From the first his fear of those about him led him to employ the suspicions of others to defeat the hostile designs he always suspected," and, "As Abdul [sic] grew older his suspicion increased and his temper grew shorter. . . . He would never permit a man near him to attempt to take anything from his own pocket."

27. Kinross, *Ottoman Centuries*, p. 535.

28. Wheatcroft, *Ottomans*, p. 198.

THE TRANSLATION

• 1 •

Concerning the Circumstances
of the Ottoman Sultanate

Al-Muqattam no. 1903, 28 June, 1895

The Sultans of the Ottoman family were not really conquerors, nor [14][1] would they be able to boast of any great achievements which might lend an aura of kudos and pride to their history. Instead they spent their time besporting themselves inside their palaces. They never bothered about affairs of state except when it involved ratifying decrees that their great statesmen submitted to them. During the period of their rule, a stigma came to attach itself to the Ottoman Sultanate because of the wars which robbed them of their territories. And yet even that was not enough to stop them from lolling around like lions ruminating peacefully in the reeds on the banks of the Bosphorus, beasts still feared by those who had conquered them because of that deepseated courage and élan for which the Turks are known. In the East there was a time when the fluttering of the Ottoman Sultanate's flags could rival the moon and stars in splendor, while in the West it was people's hearts that used to flutter in anxiety.

The only reason for the survival of the dynasty's power and prestige [15] in spite of the Sultans' preoccupation with other pursuits was that affairs of state were consigned to statesmen and ministers who, in their resolution and tenacity, numbered among the most illustrious men of their generations. They were always afraid of being asked questions from above; but, if they occasionally made mistakes, there were a host of other occasions when they were right.

The fortunes of the state fluctuated in accordance with such changes. A Sultan possessed of great magnanimity and ambition might come along; as a result, the fortunes of the Sultanate would prosper because of the energy that noble personage would insert into the glorious cause. His goal would be to strengthen the pillars of the state through the hardships of war and conquest.

In that he would be in the company of brilliant and experienced tacticians from among his army commanders. But then there would come another Sultan who preferred to adopt a more laissez-faire attitude and to indulge in his own private pleasures. As a result, matters of state and administration would be left in the hands of competent statesmen and ministers selected by the Sultan in person. Things continued this way until the deposition of the late Sultans `Abd al-`Aziz and Murad.

After this crime-ridden period of upheaval, His Majesty Sultan `Abd al-Hamid the Second succeeded to the throne of the Ottoman dynasty. He soon realized that the only way he could hope to reestablish an atmosphere of calm, preserve order, and safeguard his own power and person was to retain control of all state business, major and minor, for himself. But, unfortunately for the Ottomans, [16] the Hamidian throne is surrounded by a bunch of province-grabbers of various shapes and sizes. Once they had used various forms of cunning and deceit to gain his trust and confidence, they came to realize that there was only one way to get what they wanted, to maintain their own position, and be assured of a continued life of ease: that involved keeping His Majesty busy, thus increasing the general public sense of terror at everything and depriving him of the time necessary to carry out affairs of state. Gradually they got what they wanted (gradation being, after all, a good way of encouraging excess). It has now reached such a stage that you would scarcely believe what people tell you if they did not swear a binding oath. From the Sultan's threshold they have banished every honest and reliable person whose alert mind and initiative make him qualified to serve the state. As a direct result, all the decent people who used to be employed by the state to solve its problems have now been scattered to the four winds. The only people left behind are those who are utterly ignorant (or who pretend to be so) and sheer cowards who want either to keep their jobs, to get a better one, or simply to stay in Istanbul.

On this particular topic one story can serve as an example for many others. A minister had a friend with him. A six-year-old son of the minister came in, stood by his father, and started asking the kind of questions that six-year-olds tend to ask. His father laughed and told his friend that that sly old fox, Kamil Pasha, would sometimes ask the Sultan exactly the same questions the six-year-old boy was asking.

This is the kind of thing that happens to competent statesmen in the government. By now, death, banishment, or sheer terror have removed them all from the scene, so no one worth mentioning is left. For some twenty years an entire group has now grown up in an atmosphere of cowardice; they are so afraid of any display of affection for the homeland that they have removed from their pamphlets and newspapers any reference to the word "*milla*" (religious community).[2] They no longer say: "For service of state and community," but rather, "for service of the royal personage." Their entire thought process is so permeated by the idea of spying that sons think nothing of spying on their fathers, brothers on brothers, and wives on husbands—things unheard of in previous eras.

On this particular subject there are many celebrated stories that could be told. However we'll mention just one and leave the rest till the appropriate point later on. One day, Jamil Pasha lost patience with the kind [18] of news he was conveying to His Majesty the Sultan, so he went to see Namiq Pasha, his father, who in terms of both prestige and age was senior minister. "Dear father," he said, "my brother has been in exile for a long time. His sons cry for him every night. You are on very close terms with the Sultan; he has a very high regard for you. Some people are accusing you of being ineffectual, which has a negative effect on your prestige; other people say you're being callous, which reflects badly on you since you have declined to ask for your son's release for so long. Ask for permission to submit a request to the Sultan asking for my brother's release." The minister declined his son's request on the grounds that circumstances were not right for such a petition for fear of backchat. But his son kept on at him until he started writing the petition. Once the son had perpetrated this piece of trickery on his father, he left. He proceeded to submit a memo to the Sultan suggesting that his father was going senile; he (the son) wished to disassociate himself entirely from the petition his father was about to make asking for pardon for his exiled son.

Can there be any moral depravity lower than this? How can there possibly be any hope of sound rule and prosperity for a state which has fallen into the hands of such people?

Al-Muqattam no. 1904, 29 June, 1895

Once the younger generation realized that salaries and positions could only be obtained through espionage and displays of sheer [19] cowardice, they started competing with one another. Eventually they took things to levels that are enough to repel your very ears and lead your very nature to recoil in disgust. All free Ottoman subjects should weep, or rather maybe they should weep and then laugh. Somebody will be reading a book reprinted many times with government permission in Istanbul; in it they'll come across a sentence, write it down, and use it to build a case involving the imminent destruction of the entire state. Orders will then be given for the book to be collected and burnt. That is precisely what they did with Sayyid `Abd al-Ghani al-Nablusi's work, *Al-Tariqa al-Muhammadiyya*, and thousands of others like it.[3] The reason for the ban was that this fabled reader found in the book the following saying of the Prophet—prayers and blessings upon Him!: "The leaders of the prayer are from the Quraysh." Telegraphs whistled their way through the night to every governor with instructions that the book was to be collected from every nook and cranny, and burned; all traces of it were to be eradicated. Nor does this mark the limits of their cowardice. They even go so far as to be afraid of the Holy Qur'an itself. They will not allow any book with verses on jihad or using the words "those who are unbelievers," or anything remotely resembling that, all this for fear that Europe will use it as a pretext for making war. The work, *Al-'Aqa'id al-Nasafiyya*,[4] stayed in limbo for years, tossed back and forth between the Ministry of Education and the Office of the Shaykh al-Islam. Each office was hoping to be absolved of the responsibility for giving [20] permission for the work to be published by placing the burden on the other's shoulders. However, neither party was able to outwit the other, so they conspired to hold on to the manuscript and refuse permission to publish. All this was because *Al-'Aqa'id* contained some mention of the Imamate and the requisites for the office of Caliph. They also banned another book entitled *Al-Ahkam al-Sultaniyya* (a work on Hanafi jurisprudence[5]) from even entering Ottoman territories because it contained discussion of the same requisites.

The Armenians would never have caused the disturbances they did if it had not been for the cowardice of such people as these on the one hand and the way they kept the Armenians firmly under their thumb on the other, that too being a consequence of their own paranoia. The Armenians are no longer as ignorant as they used to be; in fact, they are now being educated at schools specially created for them by American missionaries in Istanbul and other Ottoman towns. It has now reached the point at which Armenians are ahead of their fellow countrymen in both science and general knowledge, the primary reason being that Ottomans have so little intellectual drive and ambition that they lag behind. There's an amusing story, to the effect that an Armenian scholar wrote a Turkish-Armenian dictionary and submitted it to the government requesting permission for it to be printed. When government officials found the word *sword* in it translated in both Turkish and Armenian, as one would expect in any dictionary, they ordered that it be expunged; no [21] Armenian dictionary was to contain the word *sword*. What can be the effect of such a ridiculous decision on a people who are well aware of the way things are in the world and have excelled in American schools? If readers don't believe all this (and they have every right to be incredulous), they can ask anyone in Istanbul. They'll discover that it's the truth; I have only passed it on here after confirming its veracity.

This then is the way things are with the generation of younger men connected with the Sultanate who have become intermediaries between the people and their ruler. If it so happens that someone who is truly outstanding emerges in their midst, the general atmosphere of terror forces him to devise some fault to match his talent, that being the only way he can protect himself from the intrigues of such people. By now their cowardice has reached such a point that they are censoring words and phrases in newspapers more than in ideas. For example, no newspaper is allowed to mention the phrase *The American Republic*. If it has to be mentioned, the newspaper will say "the American community" instead. This is all because they're afraid the very mention of the word *republic* will bring about the government's downfall. No newspaper may mention "the Russian Crown Prince," the fear being that the phrase *Crown Prince* will cause revolution against the [22] Sultan's authority. Later on, we'll be citing a lot more of these rare delights when we talk about newspapers and the government printing house.

People have now gone to such lengths in distracting His Majesty the Sultan and perverting facts that they submit to him some one hundred and fifty reports every day, every last one of them a tissue of lies and falsehood. Among the more remarkable aspects of this situation is that, when one of these spies is caught lying, he is not punished for it; the thought being that one day he may actually provide some genuine information. One incredible tale relates how there came a night when one of the men of Almabayn[6] requested an audience with His Majesty the Sultan; he was anxious to report to him on an important issue in person. Since he was well-known, the man was given permission to enter. He told his Majesty the Sultan that that very day he had spotted Mahmud Pasha al-Damad in Bey-Oghly[7] (he being someone who had been banished to Al-Ta'if in the Arabian Peninsula where he had since died). He had been disguised as a black slave, the man told the Sultan, and was talking to a foreigner in English. With this piece of information the whole of Almabayn was roused; night turned into day. Police and spies were dispatched to all corners of Istanbul to search for this Pasha daubed in black to look like a slave. Night telegrams were sent [23] to the Hijaz and to the Sharif in Mecca, requesting that this important matter be investigated immediately. The reports were soon sent back with the news that the man was long since dead and buried. Meanwhile the police in Istanbul had been causing a tremendous uproar as a result of their investigations. They returned to the palace with the confirmation that a search of the whole of Istanbul had failed to find any trace of this black-daubed Pasha; not only that, but they had also established that he had never learned English in any case. So that particular liar who had caused so much alarm for an entire night and day in Almabayn, Istanbul, and the Hijaz was not punished or reprimanded in any way. The Sultan's doubts were only removed when Mahmud Pasha al-Damad's head was brought back from al-Ta'if.[8]

We will be describing the current state of the Sultanate in some detail in later chapters. That way, people may be able to understand the reasons for the circumstances in which the Ottoman people and the Sunni Sultanate find themselves during a period that is fraught with problems and difficulties. They may then be able to ask God to so inspire His Majesty the Sultan that he may see fit to banish the people who are taking up so much of his time and distorting facts.

By so doing he can rescue the state (may He be exalted) from its current state of crisis as was done in former times.

I shall next describe Almabayn, its personnel, their status, roles, and relationships with each other; then the Sublime Porte, with its Grand Vizier and other ministers, and so on till the very last of those officials charged with those truths that no one dares to disbelieve. People will then come to realize that what I am [24] recording about the state comes from a free spirit, from someone who is anxious to explain the extent of the corruption in order that it can be replaced with propriety. As the Qur'an states: "I only wish to reform to the extent that I can; my success comes only from God."[9]

NOTES

The first chapter of *Ma Hunalik* is prefaced in the 1896 book publication by the texts of two newspaper articles: one entitled "Al-Din wa-al-Nasihah" [Religion and Counsel], *Al-Muqattam* no. 1960, 3 September, 1895, where it is attributed to "one of the worthiest Imams of Egypt who is extremely knowledgeable about conditions in the Ottoman state"; and a second entitled "Al-Umma al-'Uthmaniyya" [The Ottoman People], *Al-Muqattam* no. 1898, 22 June, 1895.

    1. The numbers in brackets [ ] refer to the page numbers of the original Arabic text of *Ma Hunalik*.

    2. For this and other technical terms retained in this English version of Ibrahim al-Muwaylihi's text, please refer to the glossary.

    3. 'Abd al-ghani al-Nabulusi (d. 1731), a renowned religious figure and Sufi scholar who lived in Damascus and wrote a number of important religious and literary works.

    4. *Al-'Aqa'id al-Nasafiyya*: See GAL S I, 758, II, 408.

    5. A work by the Shafi'i jurist, al-Mawardi (d. 1058); see GAL S I, 668, 686.

    6. Almabayn means literally "the place in between," the area between the private quarters of the palace and the public rooms where state business was conducted; the term was also given to the department charged with palace administration. It is the topic of chapter 2 of *Ma Hunalikno*.

    7. In modern Turkish, Beyoglu, the district on the northern bank of the Golden Horn in Istanbul.

    8. The original newspaper article added the following at this point: "If banalities like this can preoccupy the authorities in Istanbul, how can the real interests and problems of the state be properly addressed?"

    9. Qur'an, Sura 11, v. 88.

• 2 •

Almabayn

Al-Muqattam no. 1908, 4 July, 1895

The term *almabayn* is used in Turkish to refer to a room with two doors, one leading to the harem, the other to the servants' quarters. It then came to mean the Sultan's palace specifically, while the word *palace (saray)* is only used in Istanbul for the Sultan's house. In Egypt it is used differently; country estates and hamlets belonging to ordinary people have *sarays*. If we were to follow current official usage in Istanbul, the word *palace (saray)* would only apply in Egypt to `Abidin [Cairo] and Ra's al-Tin [Alexandria] palaces, but no others.

As is the case at `Abidin and Ra's al-Tin the Istanbul palace has two entrances: a private one for His Majesty the Sultan, kings, foreign ambassadors on official visits, and members of the Sultan's family; and a public one for everybody else, ranging all the way [25] from the Grand Vizier to the most ordinary porter. Two sentries stand by the entrance with their rifles at the ready in order to keep the peace. Before we go in, I will refer to a story to show the reader that, when something reaches the extreme limit of its significance, people pay little attention to it. During the month of Ramadan, a man left the palace at night in the company of one of the secretaries from Almabayn and a senior shaykh. As he was leaving, he happened to turn round and noticed that one section of the gate was closed. He saw that it had been mended with a piece of fresh white wood which stood out clearly against all the old black wood of the gate itself. "Take a look at the gate, Sir," he whispered into the shaykh's ear. The shaykh looked round. "Everything in the palace is patched like that," he replied with a smile. "God help His Majesty, our lord and master, the Sultan!" He then proceeded to recite a line of poetry by Abu al-Tayyib al-Mutanabbi:

> Among the common faults of people, I have seen nothing to match the fail-
> ure of capable men to bring things to fruition.

Eventually they reached the man's house. The person who told me this story
said that the shaykh would chant al-Mutanabbi's verse at a variety of volumes.
Sometimes it would be in a low voice that was scarcely audible; at others, he
would raise his voice or whistle an [26] accompaniment so that the listener got
the impression the man was laying before him all the scenes stored in his ca-
pacious memory. He would unconsciously provide each scene with melodies
that best suited the mood of the verse.

Once across the palace threshold, which, to cite one of their expressions,
is on the level of the firmament itself, the person entering will encounter fifteen doormen in utterly distasteful uniforms. Beyond the entrance is a room
with four windows in which sits one of their Secretaries; he has a notebook
in which he records the names of everyone going in or out that are dictated
to him though the windows. Whenever someone arrives whom they do not
know, they ask him for his name and whom he wishes to see. They keep him
waiting while one of them goes to find out whether the person in question is
willing to see him. If that person agrees, they let him go in, but only after removing any kind of stick or umbrella he may be carrying. They record the
name of both the visitor and the person he is going to see, and at day's end
they run a check on the names of everyone who went in and left. Once that
is done, they hand over the notebook to someone who is supposed to check
it once in a while. If the person checking notices anything untoward, he submits the name of the visitor and the official whom he came to see to His
Majesty the Sultan, who then decides which of the various means at his disposal he will use to [27] discover something about the circumstances of this
person and his connection with the official who admitted him to the palace.
During those frequent periods when the palace is in turmoil, His Majesty the
Sultan will read this notebook for himself.

Within the palace itself there are a number of departments: the department of the Privy Purse (*Ceb-i-Humayun*), that of the Chief Clerk, that of the
Almabaynjiyya, and that of the Chief Aga. There used to be a special department for the Chief of the Secret Police (i.e., the spies) as well, but when spying became endemic, this special office became defunct.

Before discussing the people in the palace, I will quote from a European
scholar of ethics who said: "In all languages of the world there is no single word
that manages to combine so many facets of evil as the word 'courtier,' or, in
other words, the people who make up the entourage and coterie of the ruler."
At another point the same scholar points out that courtiers have three qualities
in common with marble: heaviness, coldness, and smoothness, all of them just

like a gravestone. No king can be without them either in life or death. Someone else has pointed out that courtiers are like coils of flame: when they burn, you cannot get near them; when they go out, they are useless.

The department of the Privy Purse (*Ceb-i-Humayun*) is at the palace [28] gate. It is made up of a Chief and a group of translators. Their primary function is the same as everyone else's, namely spying. Their second is to translate everything His Majesty the Sultan asks to have translated from European newspapers in various languages as well as whatever he, the Caliph of the Prophet Muhammad, orders to be translated from newspapers and other sources in Arabic. These translators do not need to go to their place of work because they have to rely on each other, nor because they need documentation to support the translations they make from newspapers and other sources as a means of maintaining their positions, nor even because spying keeps them busy much of the time. They have the power (and may God grant them a just reward for their labors!) to trump up all sorts of lies against God's people, something that converts their sheer incompetence into a profitable business to which is attached gratitude and beneficence from the Sultan himself. If you were to enter their spacious quarters when most of them have left, you would discover that the few who have stayed behind make it look like a chessboard near the end of a game. His Majesty the Sultan will often go there in person to look for someone to do an essential piece of translation, but will be unable to find him. People will start looking all over the palace for a translator to do the job, but they won't find anyone. One night, they gave up on the search; the only person they could find was a junior clerk in a wing of the palace. They brought the poor young fellow into the Sultan's [29] presence. His Majesty was delighted and invested him as a Mabeyince on the spot. That junior clerk is now `Arif Bey al-Muntafikh, whom Sait Pasha, Kamil Pasha, and the Shaykh al-Islam himself spend much of their time flattering. He is one of al-Sayyid Abu al-Huda's agents.[1] In spite of the large number of people who are charged with this important function, such functionaries are never blamed or reprimanded for their incompetence. The reason for such tolerance involves a degree of group solidarity, even though that factor only involves really crucial interests.

At the Privy Purse office there is a reception hall for foreigners where they come for the honor of witnessing the Sultan's procession to the Friday prayer. On occasion more than fifty foreign ambassadors and princes gather there with their wives and children; they experience such finery and sheer beauty as no human eye has ever seen before, nor ear heard the like, nor mind conceived. Even so, they always regret the experience, and rightly so. The procession only lasts for a short time since the distance from the palace gate to the Hamidi mosque is a mere fifty meters. In that short space of time they get to see Arabian horses carrying Imperial guards arrayed in rows like dolls, a wide variety of people standing around, generals and officers in their gold uniforms [30] with jeweled decorations surrounding the golden carriage that serves to transport its revered load, all serenity, piety, glory, and pomp. To the observer it may even appear that the carriage and its enveloping halo of officers and generals is itself a golden dome studded with jewels. Foreigners leave the occasion, swearing that they have never seen or heard it said that God had given any one king on Earth, not even the King of China, as much finery as he had to the Caliph of the Prophet Muhammad. The Prophet, it will be recalled, used to repair his own shoes. Not only that, but during his prayers he would say (may God bless and preserve him!): "O God, let me live and die in poverty, and gather me together with the poor."

An Englishman once asked Amin Bey, the Almabaynce (who had been detailed by the Sultan to present his greetings to these guests), about this huge troop and all the people who were standing around rather than praying at the precise moment when they were supposed to be praying. "Are the Sultan's prayers sufficient to compensate for theirs?" the Englishman asked. Amin Bey slunk gracefully away without answering his question. That very day, he was promoted to the rank of albala as a reward for his inspired evasiveness.

We will have more to say about this important issue elsewhere in our presentation.

NOTE

1. For much more on al-Sayyid Abu al-Huda, see chapter 13 on the shaykhs.

• 3 •

The Chief Secretary's
Department in Almabayn

Al-Muqattam no. 1911, 8 July, 1895

$\mathcal{T}$he Chief Secretary's Department in Almabayn is one of the most distinguished and important departments in [31] Almabayn. It comprises the Chief Secretary and twenty other secretaries of various ranks, from the second class to that of *bala* (the most senior rank). While on the subject of the *bala* rank, we should point out a mistake that Egyptian newspapers make every single day. They always call people who hold the rank of rumeyli beylerbey or miraman by the honorific title "Utufatlu so-and-so Pasha." Actually the title "Pasha" should only ever be used with "Utufatlu" in the case of two specific titles, *Serasker* (Commander in Chief) and *Damad* (son-in-law) of His Majesty the Sultan. In that case, you have to say Dawlatlu Utufatlu So-and-So Pasha. The holder of such a rank should properly be addressed as Daulatlu Utufatlu Efendi or Bey, according to the way he was addressed before. It constitutes the senior secretarial rank, after which come the various levels of minister. Thus, when someone with the rank of rumeyli beylerbey is promoted to this rank, he officially drops the word "Pasha" from his honorific name and puts Efendi or Bey in its place. Egyptian newspapers should make a point of adhering to the [32] rules of protocol within the Ottoman Empire as long as this particular rank is a part of its administrative structure; then they won't make two mistakes by using one word, combining "Pasha" with "Utufatlu." Whenever people in Istanbul notice this mistake in Egyptian newspapers, they have a good laugh. In Istanbul newspapers not a single letter is out of place when it comes to official matters; there is a special law to punish anyone who infringes such regulations.

The secretaries to whom I have just referred are all young men who have been brought up within the prevalent system of ethics. They all spy on the Chief Secretary, so much so that, to quote the poet:

It seems as though he is ringed with eyes.

But he is just as likely to be spying on them. Disagreements keep them at odds with each other; and so you will find in general that they have utterly different attitudes. It is a palace custom that the Chief Secretary should have a beard to reflect the dignity of his office and the prestige that his position affords him; he is the principal intermediary between His Majesty the Sultan and the government, the Grand Vizier and the Shaykh al-Islam. Another custom stipulates that the Almabaynje should not have a beard.

Regarding the Chief Secretary, this regulation has been followed right up to the present-day, even though others may have been flouted, the one concerning the Almabaynje, for example. In former times, when a man was removed from the post of Chief Secretary to Almabaynje, he had to shave off his beard to conform [33] with custom. Another rule states that the Chief Secretary must come from the Sublime Porte, that he should be well versed in the epistolary arts in both Turkish and Persian (but not Arabic), and that he should be already renowned for his eloquence since that is an essential part of his function as the Sultan's spokesman in both speech and writing. This practice was continued right up to the last Chief Secretary, but he died very suddenly. The current holder of the office, Tahsin Bey, was not a secretary in the Sublime Porte, nor was he in any way renowned in any of the epistolary arts. In fact, those who have to work at his side place him on the level of people who regularly make mistakes when they write letters themselves. He is in his thirties and was *mektubci* in the Ministry of the Navy where he served with Hasan Pasha, the minister whose general reliability and loyalty has meant that he has been able to retain his post in every ministry for the past twelve years. With regard to this particular Chief Secretary, there was one factor that allowed him to go against the normal set of prerequisites for the office and to have himself promoted to such a prestigious post over the heads of other aspirants, namely the complete confidence that the Minister of the Navy had in him when it came to keeping high security matters secret, to which can be coupled the useful fact that he is also the son-in-law of Mahmud Nadim Pasha, the mentor of Lutfi Agha (the Hercules of Almabayn). His elevation to this lofty post to which all men aspire was the direct result of a feeling of confidence in [34] Lutfi Agha's recommendation. Another Chief Secretary, Sait Pasha, was appointed Chief for his eloquence and wide general knowledge, he being the first person to attain a ministerial post in a job that had previously been confined to holders of the *bala* rank.

All official documents from the Sublime Porte, the office of the Shaykh al-Islam, and the other ministries and governmental agencies are referred back to the Chief Secretary. From his office they are issued to the Sublime Porte and all other quarters. He will send a summary of their contents to be placed on the Sultan's desk. From that quarter the Chief Secretary learns of the decrees through the conveyance of the Almabaynjiyya or whoever else it might be in the Imperial retinue that is instructed by His Majesty the Sultan to convey the information. The Chief Secretary sends official decrees under his signature on small stationery to the Chief or to whichever undersecretary or minister it specifically concerns.

Heaven help us all! In olden times one such piece of paper was enough to publish the basic law, to convene the Chamber of Deputies, to parry any danger of foreign interference in state matters, and to bolster Ottoman prestige. But today—more's the pity—dozens of them get published every single day: to search someone's home here, interrogate someone else there; to banish someone here and imprison someone else there.

When the Chief or someone else receives these decrees, he [35] will record on the piece of paper the hour and minute when it was received along with the name of the dispatcher. The Chief Secretary keeps a notebook in which he records the name of the decree's carrier, its general appearance, and the precise minute when it was issued. To these details he will then append his signature. That is actually a new and previously unheard of procedure, made necessary by the fact that some conveyors were actually bringing forged decrees.

Because official decrees seem to be subject to so many changes and alterations, the Chief Secretary is forced to hold on to them until all doubt has been removed as to whether they will be ratified or invalidated. Such a situation results from the atmosphere of jealousy that exists among the Sultan's entourage and the fact that they keep things secret from each other. If one of them ratifies a document, someone else will declare it invalid. Sometimes the mistake will be corrected; the proper courses will be followed in spite of such disagreements among members of the entourage and the fact that they nullify each other's efforts. For example, if one of them requests a decoration or rank for someone else who does not deserve it and the decree to that effect is issued from the office of medals and promotions, somebody else may well come along and inform His Majesty the Sultan that his colleague is involved in a fraud. At that point another decree is published canceling the first. If on the other hand, such a decree is issued relating to an official who is genuinely deserving, someone with a grudge may come along and stir up trouble to make sure the official doesn't get it. In such a case the Sultan's decree gets no further than this [36] troublemaker desires; sometimes it disappears altogether. Some of these officials have gone to colossal lengths in their swindles, throwing the state's prestige overboard in the process.

Decrees were obtained from His Majesty the Sultan for kindness awards to be given to women when court etiquette clearly does not allow for them to have any contact with such things. When the entire situation became clear, the awards had to be reclaimed. They were indeed returned to the state, but only after each woman concerned had been given fifty pounds as compensation.

I will now mention a story that happened recently. His Majesty the Sultan issued an order that Hasan Bey Sayyadi, the son of Shaykh Abu al-Huda (one of the Sultan's closest confidants) was to be given the Majid Medal Third Class. The decree authorizing the award was followed by one postponing it. The young man went to see the Chief Secretary and informed him that the decree referring to his award was not one of the ones that had been delayed or sent back. It was only the ones pertinent to X and Y (referring to the women mentioned above). When the young man left the office, the decoration was in his pocket.

The Chief Secretary is one of the most significant members of the palace spy system. In addition to his senior official status, he reviews secret police papers referring to him. He devotes the greater [37] part of his time and attention to such documents. They don't stay in his possession for longer than it takes him to deal with them, after which they are dispatched to the Imperial presence quicker than a plunging waterfall. From such papers he learns about decrees on the spot, whether it involves an interrogation, an inquiry, a memo, or a reward for the supplier of information. On the other hand, official documents and papers submitted by special petitioners are dealt with in a particular manner, one that never changes. They may be delayed for months, or else a stream of other documents gets ahead of them; in which case, there is absolutely no point in looking for them even if there were a way.

The Chief Secretary will stay at work in the palace till late evening. Even then, he will leave someone else to carry on recording the decrees issued during the night. When people with petitions ask to see him, he welcomes them gladly and answers their requests courteously. How very different that is from the kind of thing we find in Egypt and Ottoman provinces where even the most junior *ma'mur* will receive people with a glower on his face and respond gruffly to requests. And when it comes to senior officials and provincial governors, they will shun you like Jadhimat al-Abrash;[1] if they even do give you the time of day, it is as though they had made you a gift of life itself and given you vast territories.

The Chief Secretary and some other secretaries wear official [38] uniforms in order to attend the Friday evening prayer (in the Salamlik). He will stand with the other people there until His Majesty the Sultan appears with his large retinue.

While on the topic of the Friday prayer,[2] it is worth mentioning that seven thousand soldiers stand round the Hamidi Mosque during the prayer. They themselves do not pray. Indeed, if one of them were to do so, he would be punished by military law, even though he might be holding the Qur'an itself in his hand. Below the Hamidi Mosque in the Beshiktash district, Hasan Pasha, the superintentent, makes the rounds of taverns in back alleys and uses a stick to drive people to the mosque for prayer. "Do you command others to be righteous and forget yourselves?"[3]

NOTES

1. Jadhimat al-Abrash is a proverbial figure allegedly named after a tribal chief who was a leper. See Edward Lane, *Arabic-English Lexicon*, under the root B-R-SH.

2. This final paragraph was part of the original newspaper article, but was omitted from the book version of the text.

3. A quotation from the Qur'an, Sura 2, v. 44.

· 4 ·

The Almabaynjiyya
Department in Almabayn

Al-Muqattam no. 1917, 15 July, 1895

𝒻aced with the task of describing the Almabaynjiyya Department in Almabayn, the author finds himself completely at a loss. After discussing them, he had planned to describe the esteemed shaykhs, those luminaries of the Sultan's palace. But the only way he can find to describe them involves repetition, forcing him to say that the shaykh is the almabaynji and vice versa, except for the fact that in certain cases the shaykh is more common.

Just imagine yourself traveling alone at night through a forest with intertwining tree branches, a place where the darkness is all-embracing, the winds reverberate and howl, lions roar, and adders slither beneath your feet. You will never encounter any path or form of death that could possibly be more terrifying than the kind of people who tread the floors of this particular [39] department. When dealing with ordinary people, they are utterly vile. Whatever good they do is confined to themselves in that they stand at a door which may produce boons or sheer spite, glory or ignominy, freedom or slavery, participation or tyranny, happiness or misery, life or death, all this at the hands of a great Caliph and Sultan:

> From his throne he glances right and left; when he repeats the process, some find reward, others punishment.

They can afford to wait for just the right moment to malign someone in His Majesty the Sultan's presence in order to achieve their purpose. It is quite the opposite for other people who request fulfillment of their needs by submitting them in writing. The submitter of such a petition may well be the Grand Vizier or the Shaykh al-Islam himself, but at the time he can have no

39

idea what the Sultan's personal demeanor may be when he reads the document. This is the main reason why people fail to get their requests granted, whereas these men manage to get their own way. They have complete control over the minds, the property, and the honor of what is left of the Ottoman Empire from Yildiz to Iraq, and they can behave exactly as they please. The only way to find peace of mind is to devise a way of being of service to them, obey all their orders, put up with any injustice they may cause, and perpetrate all manner of fraud for their sake. They are so incredibly shrewd and have been serving [40] the Sultan for so long that there is absolutely nothing in the minds of men that escapes their notice; for them everything is open to scrutiny. They are six in number, and the seventh is their chief, Al-Hajj `Ali Bey. All of them hold high rank, and people in the know estimate that one of them, Raghib Bey, has a fortune of some eight hundred thousand pounds. In the days when he lodged in Munif Pasha's house, he used to be extremely penurious, but that was before the latter brought him into the Sultan's entourage. He is of Greek origin and has another function besides that of being an almabaynji, namely of interrogating *ma'murs* in much the same way as Shaykh Abu al-Huda has the job of interrogating the `ulama' as one of his functions. The two of them share the cloak of glory involved in being party to the Sultan's secrets, although Shaykh Abu al-Huda is more interested in glory than in making money. In that quest he has a colleague in the poet Imru al-Qays:

> Were I aiming at the lowliest of livelihoods, I would be content with little money and would not seek for more.
> But my quest is for a noble glory; the likes of me may well achieve such.[1]

Raghib Bey's renown for interrogation even surpasses the stories of Phaleris's bull,[2] while Shaykh Abu al-Huda's technique is so [41] skillful and deft that it puts people in the equivalent of Ibn al-Zayyat's oven.[3]

It used to be the custom that men of the Almabaynjiyya rarely [42] went home. Now, however, they take it in turns to be at the Sultan's beck and call; whoever is on duty sits by the door of the room that gives on to the audience chamber where the Sultan himself hears petitions and issues decrees in the manner we have just described. Al-Hajj `Ali Bey, the Chief Almabaynji, has a large room of his own to sit in; delegations of all kinds that come to the palace are referred to him. Once he has communicated their arrival to the Sultan and told them everything they need to know, the way he will deal with them will depend on their status and prestige. He has many roles to play; the guises keep changing and being updated, from a spy in disguise to a bogus ascetic or a daunting glutton. If you happen to talk to him outside palace hours, you will discover that he is utterly vulgar and illiterate; he may be able to write one or two letters, but they do not constitute anything meaningful. Sometimes three or four secretaries will have to get together to decipher something he has written, but the only way they can ever glean any meaning from it is by guesswork and conjecture. In his palace work on the [43] other hand, he is in his proper element and keeps things under control. He owns an industrial plant, thus continuing the tradition of his ancestors who owned the Ottoman press, and is a member of the Gilani Order of Sufis. He can never stop talking about Sufi orders and comparing them with each other, so much so that His Majesty the Sultan has wasted valuable time arguing with Shaykh Abu al-Huda and discussing the relative merits of the Rifa'i and Gilani orders. Indeed the Sultan's residence, the source of foreign policy relating to Europe, sometimes sounds more like a Sufi hostel where poor people spend time arguing with each other.

He serves as the right-hand man of al-Sayyid As'ad, the warden of the Prophet's Resting Place in Medina. The latter extolled his virtues to the Sultan to such an extent that the latter made him second class Almabaynji when 'Uthman Bey was in charge. One day he made an agreement with al-Sayyid As'ad to bring about 'Uthman Bey's downfall. On the second day of Ahmad Wafiq's tenure of the Grand Vizierate, al-Sayyid As'ad went to see His Majesty the Sultan. With considerable dismay he reported to His Majesty that at that moment 'Uthman Bey was meeting the Grand Vizier and some other ministers; they were in 'Uthman Bey's office, secretly drawing up a document authorizing the Sultan's deposition on the basis of a *fatwa* issued by 'Iryanizade, the Shaykh al-Islam. His Majesty the Sultan immediately issued orders that 'Uthman Bey was to be brought in under [44] armed guard. When they brought him in, the Sultan gave orders for him to be searched for the document in question, but after a thorough search they came up with nothing. Al-Sayyid As'ad told him to hand it over, just like the miser in Moliere's play who accuses his servant of hiding something he has stolen. 'Uthman Bey was thoroughly searched again, but still nothing was found. Once more he was ordered to hand over the document. Even though nothing was found, the Sultan became very suspicious of 'Uthman Bey; the ministry was dissolved only a day and a night after it had been put together. We will come back to the subject of this *fatwa* and the way it was trumped up at a later point.

Al-Muqattam no. 1921, 19 July, 1895[4]

The Almabaynji reckons that he will gain the most recognition and prestige by pretending to have some connection with a foreign embassy in Istanbul and to have struck up a friendship with some of the key personnel in it. He can then demonstrate to His Majesty the Sultan that he spends night and day charming this friend of his and gleaning crucial secrets for His Majesty, who will in turn encourage the Almabaynji to even greater efforts. Actually the Almabaynji will be relaying to his friend in the embassy everything that goes on in the Sultan's palace, word for word. In return all he gets is bits of information which will only benefit the country in question when conveyed to the Sultan. However, all the Almabaynji is really worried about is making sure His Majesty the Sultan knows that he has a crucial connection with such-and-such an embassy; that very fact serves as a means of protection, something that the Sultan will have to take into consideration whenever he has it in mind to do something unpleasant to him. Nothing ever happens in Almabayn without the embassies getting to hear about it; no embassy can submit a petition without first receiving an undertaking from these Almabayndjiyya that it will be approved; and all this goes on without the Sublime Porte's knowledge.

Having now described the official functions of the Almabaynjiyya and their relationships with the embassies, it remains for us to discuss some special issues.

His Majesty the Sultan will never send anyone to Europe on private business without that person engaging in a special partnership arrangement with an Almabaynji by which they can both misappropriate the Ottoman people's monies. They subdivide the funds that have been collected from poor Ottoman subjects in the form of grain and small coins. When some of these people have died in Europe, they have been worth millions. What is more, some of their associates among the Almabaynjiyya are worth millions too.

Within the family of the Caliph, the descendant of Muhammad the Prophet of God—may God bless and preserve him!—the daughters who remain unmarried are dying in poverty, while their sons also eke out a living in conditions of starvation and poverty. Their cries may be heard from Mecca to Istanbul and should melt the hearts of such callous people. If one of them finds it necessary—would that it were not so!—to grovel, cheek to the floor, at the threshold of some eunuch or underling, all he receives is a paltry piece of bread cast in his direction with a disapproving frown or a look of utter disdain. On the other hand, when the wife of one of the Almabaynjiyya died, he was presented with another one from the palace; a bed was purchased for her that cost three hundred pounds. The previous wife's expensive bed was sold for a mere fifty pounds, solely in order that the new wife would not have to enter such a beautifully furnished home with the first wife's bed still there. Even when its craftsmanship and proportions had been duly admired by the people of the Balistan, it was purchased by a wealthy amir for his daughter who was about to get married. But waste such as this is a mere grain of mustard seed in the desert, a drop in the ocean:

> Yazid's daughters were secluded in palaces, while the Prophet's daughter was out in the desert.

The business associates of these Almabaynjiyya have spread themselves around the capital cities of Europe. Some of them serve as spies and receive incredible salaries, ranging from sixty to a 120 pounds a month. Others serve as emissaries to the European press empires where they manage to keep one newspaper quiet while at the same time firing up five others. Their colleagues among the Almabaynjiyya and their fellow workers send them news that at the time His Majesty the Sultan does not think worth mentioning; after all, things are always happening at the palace that can be discussed one day whereas they were totally banned the day before. If newspapers happen to draw attention to such matters, the telegraph wires start buzzing and money is dispatched so that the emissaries to the various press companies can keep the squadrons and armies of reporters off the topic of the Ottoman Empire.

Here is an embarrassing tale, one that should cause Ottoman swords to shrivel up inside their scabbards and Ottoman pens dry up in their inkwells. Some of these people intervened on behalf of that wretched Egyptian Jew, Abu Nazzara Zarqa',[5] so that he could come to Istanbul like some eminent potentate to see His Majesty the Sultan, the Commander of the Faithful. When he entered the Imperial presence, he said: "Efendi, I have named my son `Abd al-Hamid after Your Majesty. `Abd al-Hamid Junior will thus ever be at the service of `Abd al-Hamid Senior." He then took a photograph of his son out of his pocket. His Majesty was utterly delighted with both the statement and the picture. He gave instructions that the man was to be honored and welcomed as an esteemed guest. As a result, Alyavar Wali Bey, who had previously escorted His Majesty the Emperor of Germany, now found himself escorting Abu Nazzara Zarqa' and walking ahead of him as he paid visits to the Sublime Porte and the other ministries, the treasure house, the room containing the Prophet's relics, and the repositories of the Muslim Caliph. He stayed in Istanbul for several days, receiving accolades wherever he went and being cited in the press, which kept talking about "the Shaykh" (sic). Before he left, His Majesty the Sultan invited him to the Sultan's theater in the palace and seated him in his own box. His Majesty engaged him in conversation, with Munif Pasha, the translator, sitting between them, and showed his usual personal charm. The thing they talked about most was the Egyptian problem. By the time he left Istanbul, he had been honored and feted by His Majesty the Sultan, the Grand Vizier, the Shaykh al-Islam, and the undersecretaries of state. All the while, Egyptians resident in Istanbul watched in utter amazement. "Isn't this so-and-so the Jew," they would ask, "the one who used to sit in the hashish cafés in Egypt playing his flute for cash? Has he managed to conquer some huge swath of territory for the state or to fend off some unspeakable disaster? How else could he be treated with even greater honor than kings and men of major influence?" The protocol officials in the palace could not make up their minds as to whether he should be awarded the Majidi al-Awwal decoration or the Uthmani al-thani. It was only when Shaykh Abu al-Huda started yelling and screaming about the fate of Islam that they finally settled on Al-Thalith al-Uthmani. Sannu` left Istanbul laden with expensive gifts and a jewel encrusted box with a portrait of His Majesty the Sultan on it. He also brought a letter of greeting to his wife from the Sultan. He returned to Egypt in order to work on the Egyptian problem in his famous newspaper[6] and to use his enormous prestige to expel the English from Egypt. Mustafa Kamil, the interpreter, who is even now bellowing away in Paris obviously is cut from the cloth of this very same newspaper:

> We laughed, but that was stupidity on our part. The people in your Egypt should really be weeping.

This wandering Jew was feted and honored throughout his stay in Istanbul and then left enveloped in prestige and good fortune. And we are not talking here about the Amir of Mecca or the Marshal of the Prophet's Descendants on a visit from Baghdad. Can you conceive of a worse parody than this, Egyptians? However, the schemes devised by the Almabaynjiyya and their associates scattered across the length and breadth of Europe in order to make a profit while serving the state go way beyond even this.

A particular group of Ottoman ambassadors to the great powers had become extremely powerful, so these Almabaynjiyya folk preempted them and had orders sent straight to them as being extremely trustworthy. It was only then that instructions were communicated to this set of Ottoman ambassadors whom it was really too difficult to scheme against. Even so, As`ad Pasha, Ottoman ambassador in Paris, died of sheer grief, while Sa`dallah Pasha, Ottoman ambassador to Austria, committed suicide out of sheer contempt and as a way of avoiding the burden of their coercion. Some of these Almabaynjiyya have exploited their associates in order to get a share in such benefits as high status, prestige, and the kind of trust that is not even accorded the state's most loyal servants: to an Ottoman general, for instance, who, with loyal heart and steadfast zeal in the face of cannon and rifle fire, has won victories for the state and people; or to a minister in politics who spends the entire night at work and in the early morning light prays to God to grant him some brief respite from all the things he has to do, erasing and checking documents as part of the complex process of resolving political intrigues, convincing opposing parties, covering up failings, and extolling praiseworthy qualities; or even to a bookless scholar-author who has abandoned this world and all its frippery to other people in order to be of service to the people (the reason why I say "bookless" is that, when you ask permission to print a book, they burn it instead and keep no copies).

Some holders of these special posts used to say flattering things to the Sultan in Almabayn in the hearing of the senior figures there, the sort of fawning nonsense that no Caliph has ever tolerated, except, that is, for `Abd al-Hamid, the patient sage of the Ottoman dynasty and his Arab equivalent, Mu`awiya ibn Abi Sufyan, the Umayyad Caliph. The person that I have in mind at this point compared his position with that of the senior people in Almabayn, assessed his ease of access as compared with theirs, and realized the prestige he had as opposed to their insignificance. With that he decided not to aspire to higher rank or decoration so as not to be placed within the same bracket as them. He was once even heard to say in Al-Hajj `Ali Bey's office that he would not accept ministerial rank because he had no desire to be on a level with so-and-so and so-and-so (naming certain ministers). When he heard that some Egyptians thought it a great honor that His Majesty the Sultan had sent him a condolence telegram, he laughed. "His Majesty the Caliph always addresses me as '*bendeniz*'," he said. That originally meant "your servant." However, frequency of usage has changed its original meaning; now it's come to mean "your host."

No one should regard the things I am reporting here as being too outlandish to be true. In the current situation only the clear and undiluted truth will serve. The state is that of the Ottoman dynasty, one founded upon two principles of leadership: the religious and the political. It is a dynasty distinguished by the bravery of its soldiers, the panache of its generals, and the skill of its politicians, but a dynasty that has never in its history reached the low ebb at which it now finds itself. What can be more mortifying for a free Ottoman subject than to hear that the great powers are demanding that the state carry out reforms in its own territories? All the while, the state responds that it is making every possible effort to implement and expand the reforms throughout its territories and not merely in the Armenian provinces.

This promise to implement reform is the surest and most undeniable proof of the state's weakness. For example, if one of the great powers were to demand of the Greek government that it implement the reforms being demanded of the Ottoman government, it would be enough to cause a war. What can one say about people who invoke God, His prophets, and His Angels (although they are liars to do so) in order to assure everyone that the state is strong, vigorous, highly regarded, just and fair, when all the while the Grand Vizier, buried in the bowels of the Sublime Porte, keeps yelling that he's ready to implement reform in the future not just in Armenia but throughout the Ottoman domains? His Majesty the Sultan himself gives credence to the word *reform*, with its five Arabic graphemes, in both his written decrees and statements, but then the newspapers start croaking idiotic nonsense to deny the official statements of His Majesty the Sultan about his country's backwardness and the need for reformist principles.

Dear reader, if only you could witness the undersecretaries' council and the Grand Vizier with the sweat pouring off his brow, the undersecretaries lost in thought, and the Shaykh al-Islam pulling at his beard, all of them racking their brains to find a satisfactory explanation for the Powers to justify the slow pace of implementing reforms, to come up with some words to delay the demands of the Bulgarian government, to produce something to prevent the Greeks from moving any further, to provide the Powers with an excuse for the murder of their consuls in the Hijaz, to find millions of pounds to cover the annual deficit in the state revenues, and this and that . . . I once actually saw someone standing in front of them; he was reading from a piece of paper to the effect that the Ottoman state was secure and peaceful, splendid and glorious, possessed of great riches, and so on . . . it was hard to know whether to laugh or cry.

Whenever someone reads from a free newspaper over there, one that presents a genuine picture of the situation, people put down their pens, wipe their foreheads, and listen very carefully. They learn more about the state's real situation and discover the previously hidden faults that need to be fixed. As the saying goes: "God have mercy on those who point out our faults to us! The real friend is the one who tells you the truth; the enemy the one who flatters you."

NOTES

1. See Imru al-Qays, *Diwan*, ed. Muhammad Abu al-Fadl Ibrahim, Cairo: Dar al-Ma`arif, 1969, p. 39.

2. Note in the original text: "Phaleris was a tyrant who ruled over the Slavs in about 600 B.C. He was proverbial for his tyranny and cruelty. Cicero even terms him the tyrant of all tyrants. To purge themselves of his evil rule and requite his savagery, his own people stoned him to death. The story goes that a skilled craftsman named Barlas built him a bull out of molten brass. He used to torture people inside it till they died and used to love listening to their screams. The first person on whom he tried out this bull was Barlas, the very person who had built it for him."

3. Note in the original text: "Ibn al-Zayyat was the minister of the Caliph, al-Mu`tasim [833–842]. While he was minister, they say that he made use of an oven with sharp iron nails jutting out like hairs on a beard. He used it to torture bailiffs and heads of diwans who had been asked to raise money. In whichever direction they turned in such searing torture, nails would stick into their flesh; it was excruciatingly painful. No one before him had ever tried out this form of torture. When a victim begged him to take pity, he told him that pity displayed a weakness of temperament. Eventually [the Caliph] al-Mutawakkil had him arrested and put in the same oven; he was bound with no less than seventy-five *ratls* (Egyptian) of iron. He begged the Caliph for mercy, to which they latter gave his own reply, that pity displayed a weakness of temperament. He asked for paper and ink which were brought for him and then wrote: 'It is the way.

From one day to the next it is like a vivid dream while sleeping. Do not panic, rest calm! They are but lowly estates, moved from one people to another.' He had the lines taken to al-Mutawakkil, but he was too busy and only looked at them the next day. After reading them, he ordered Ibn al-Zayyat to be released. But when they got to him, he had already died. This all happened in the year 233 A.H. [847–848 A.D.] He was in the oven for a total of forty days." The original article attributed this footnote to "*Al-Muqattam*," but the attribution was omitted from the book version of the text.

4. At this point, the book version of *Ma Hunalik* omits two episodes of the original text as published in *al-Muqattam* in 1895. The translations that follow are taken from copies of the original articles transcribed by the translator. The fifth chapter of the book resumes with the episode published in no. 1927 of the newspaper, 26 July, 1895.

5. The nickname of Ya`qub Sannu` (1839–1912), the famous pioneer of early Egyptian drama. See M. M. Badawi, *Early Arabic Drama* (Cambridge: Cambridge University Press, 1988), pp. 31–42.

6. For Sannu`'s newspaper *Abu Nazzara Zarqa'* and other journalistic enterprises, see Irene Gendzier, *The Practical Vision of Ya`qub Sannu`*, Harvard Middle Eastern Monographs XV (Cambridge: Harvard University Middle East Center, 1966); also Nikki Keddie, *Sayyid Jamal ad-din "al-Afghani"* (Berkeley: University of California Press, 1972), pp. 184–189.

• 5 •

The Department of the Chief Eunuch in Almabayn

Al-Muqattam no. 1923, 22 July, 1895[1]

*I*n the Sultan's palace the Chief Eunuch is just like the Grand Vizier in the Sublime Porte and the Shaykh al-Islam in that particular office: in a word, no one can rival the enormous influence, prestige, and authority he possesses. In this particular Eden he serves as Rudwan, the gatekeeper to Paradise. At night, once he has followed the long-established procedures and rituals connected with conducting His Majesty the Sultan to the harem, he keeps the key in his hand.

His official honorific title has the same arrangement as that of the Grand Vizier and the Shaykh al-Islam. That of the Grand Vizier is written: Fakhamatlu Dawlatlu Efendim Hadratlu; that of the Shaykh al-Islam as Dawlatlu Samahatlu Efendim Hadratlu; and that of the Chief Eunuch as Dawlatlu Inayatlu Efendim Hadratlu.

In order to describe the Chief Eunuch, I'll make use of a story, even though its topic is somewhat trivial. We will occasionally counterbalance important subjects with lighter ones so that the reader can get some idea of the situation regarding the Ottoman state, it being one that is opposed in Europe by eighteen other states, each of which boasts all the benefits of modern civilization, harbors a grudge against the Ottoman state, and relishes the very thought of seeing it disappear. Meanwhile we carry on regardless and fool around, while our armies and fleets are curtailed in the name of the balance of power in Europe. It is as though we are putting all our trust in the inexorable passage of time and assuming that this magic phrase, "the balance of power," were the fixed pole around which the universe revolves. I am also telling this tale so that people will be aware of the ways in which one gets promoted in our state. In that way no one will be surprised to see senior officials to whom people bow low out of obeisance and respect being appointed to the loftiest

49

positions in a trice, quite regardless of whether or not they are competent; nor will people be able to express annoyance when they find out how useless such people actually are and utterly lacking in decency. People will always tend to look after their own interests first and take the quickest route to get there. For people with no self-respect, the quickest and easiest way is to go around kissing people's feet, tugging on coattails, and groveling at thresholds. A phrase which is now in constant use as a mode of greeting goes like this: "I rub my face in the dust of your feet." These days, no conversation or document is ever without it, whereas no such expression was ever used in the discourse of civilized people or indeed any other phrase that was even several levels of sycophancy below it.

How are ignorant people supposed to steer clear of vice when they come to realize that the only way to achieve anything to their own advantage is to use flattery and hypocrisy, and that the quest for decency involves misery, failure, and a waste of time? And so much the worse for anyone who strives for excellence; he is forced to put on a display of turpitude. With autocratic governments there can never be any hope in the quest for decency; if such a rare person comes along, he will simply spend time as a guest in Socrates' prison cell on his way to the next world.

The late Bahram Agha got a message from His Majesty the Sultan's son-in-law, Mahmud Jalal al-din Pasha, saying that an Egyptian who was a renowned chess player had come to Istanbul. The Agha issued instructions that the Egyptian was to be brought to him. The Sultan's son-in-law apologized to the Egyptian for not taking him over himself, saying that he did not feel well. Instead he told his deputy to accompany him. It was only afterward that the Egyptian realized why the Sultan's son-in-law had pretended to be ill: the Chief Eunuch had treated him in an extremely casual way, and the Sultan's son-in-law had not wanted the Egyptian to get the impression that this was a slight on his status. At any rate, the Amir's deputy accompanied the Egyptian to the Chief Eunuch's department. They found him lying on his back, with people clustered humbly around him as though they were in the very Kaaba itself standing around the black stone. They were all waiting for that word or glance emerging from the sides of his nasal protuberance that would enhance his good fortune and prestige:

> A black, one half of him lip; people tell him: "You are the full moon on a dark night."[2]

The deputy kissed his foot and apologized for his master's indisposition, but the eunuch did not say a word. "The man you ordered to be brought here has arrived," he went on. At that the Chief Eunuch guffawed and gave such a whoop that all the servants and visitors started running. He ordered the chess set to be brought in, and everyone lent a hand. He told the Egyptian he had only been playing the game for six months, but he had made such rapid progress that even in Europe people had heard about it. Recently some famous European chess players had come to play against him, and he had managed to beat them all. He had trounced the vice-president of the Ottoman Bank, and so on. . . . With that, he launched into a string of curses and lewd expressions which emerged in a constant stream, just as a conjuror manages to produce pieces of brass and other things from his mouth that he could not possibly hold in his hands.

The Chief Eunuch now turned to the Egyptian and asked him which pieces he would like him to remove from the board. The Egyptian replied that his host's lofty opinion on such a matter clearly could not be bettered. At that the Chief Eunuch told him he would remove the two rooks and the queen. He then proceeded to play with what was left and put them all out in the wrong positions. Every time the Chief Eunuch moved his hand to the board, his flatterers would start chanting a paean of praiselike movements in a suite of music, while he kept guffawing and clapping his hands. While he was engaged in playing, a general came in, stood by his foot, and kissed it. The Chief Eunuch totally ignored him and paid no attention whatsoever.

With all this going on, the Egyptian was completely confused and befuddled. He had no idea how to get himself safely out of the predicament. When the poorer player won, he started guffawing and hopping all around the room on one foot, clapping his hands and yelling: "I won, I won!" It was now that hypocrisy and flattery emerged in all their raw ugliness, as the "defeated" Egyptian was made fun of and became the butt of their sarcastic remarks. He made his exit, vowing never again to return, even if they gave him a barrel load of promises. Even so he was much envied and was able to use al-Mutanabbi's line about Kafur to describe Bahram:

> What have I encountered in the world? The amazing thing is that I am envied for things that make me weep![3]

This story may serve as a yardstick when it comes to other important events too. Were I not writing for a respectable newspaper, I would discuss the things that go on in his *majlis*.

This is the man who dismisses ministers, conducts court business, and organizes matters for the general public. He is the one who put forward `Abd al-Rahman Pasha and engineered his appointment as Grand Vizier. He also gave a helping hand to al-Rafiq Pasha who was appointed Amir of Mecca, and that after this slave had had the sheer effrontery to stretch out his foot in front of the son of successor of the Prophet (may God bless and preserve him!) for him to kiss it. This is the man who was so eager to get `Abdallah Pasha al-Najdi a high position that he informed his retinue that he was proposing to request the rank of rumeli beylerbey for him since at that point he did not merit the rank of *mirimiran*. This is the man who kept His Majesty the Sultan and the entire cabinet under his control during the recent Bulgarian problems; right in the middle of the cabinet meeting he yelled that there was no alternative but to declare war on Bulgaria. This is the man who interferes in every aspect of state business. Nothing major or minor can be initiated without him getting involved, and his opinion will always win the day in the long run. Through the enormous influence and authority he is able to exert, he manages to defeat all opposition. There is only one exception, and that is Al-Sayyid Abu al-Huda, whose Arab determination and forbidding nature prevent him from succumbing to the whims of a eunuch who is considered neither male nor female. As a result, he has crossed swords with the Chief Eunuch.

Their battles keep changing just like the seasons, with long days and short nights followed by long nights and short days. . . .[4] Indeed, ministers used to go in for an audience, kiss his feet and hands, and emerge with their noses in the air, an eloquent tribute to his own arrogance. They would carry his superciliousness around like a burden and unleash it bit by bit on God's people.

Now all enthusiasm has vanished, all ambition is dead. People no longer think sensibly, and any notion of decency is suppressed. [The remainder is to follow.][5]

Al-Muqattam no. 1927, 26 July, 1895

[44] Here is a message addressed to all Egyptians with a sense of honor, everyone who is fortunate enough to enjoy the soft bed that freedom affords, the considerable wealth and serene sense of well-being that he enjoys, the combined peace and security that he has, and the way that fortune smiles on him. Every Egyptian should feel sorry for his Ottoman brother who is forced to fidget and squirm as he lies on a thorny bed of trial and anguish, cowering between the claws and jagged teeth of injustice. Egyptians should ask God to release their brothers from this situation and to lighten the terrible burden that [45] makes every day seem so long and keeps them awake at night. Egyptians should pray that the Ottoman state will recover its former transcendent splendor, raise its lofty minaret to the sky once again, and banish from its domains people who reveal to its rulers things that they do not keep to themselves, people who praise others to the skies in their presence and then castigate them in private. The situation has become oppressive, and the crisis is getting worse and worse. People are feeling throttled, and the chains are being pulled even

tighter. The Ottoman state's lair is being attacked by a marauding pack of neighboring hyenas, and it is being governed by a group of people who used to be its slaves. It treats them kindly, but they repay it harshly. Alas for a people whose courage and prowess on the battlefield have brought them into the purview of Europe! Now they have started:

> Rewarding the tyranny of tyrants with forgiveness and the offences of evil folk with charity.
> It is as though, for the purpose of instilling fear of Him, your Lord had created only them among all people.
> Would that I had at my disposal a people who would mount an attack against them with cavaliers and escort when they rode out to fight.

Where can one find now those great army commanders who opened up the Mamluk territories with swords as the key and who then used humiliation and contempt as weapons to lock them up? Where are the politicians who managed to control those Mamluks with such cunning sagacity? Death and exile have decimated their numbers, and the people who have taken their place possess none of the gallantry and fortitude that their [46] fathers bequeathed to them. Soldiers are willing to commit their lives to the state until such time as they may be needed, but now they find themselves used in operations where they have no idea of the reason or justification involved. By devoting themselves in this way, they are fully aware of the bloody death that may await them in the service of the state, the rugged life they endure for love of it, and the risks they take in order to safeguard it. But, having dedicated their very souls to the service of the state, how are they supposed to be compensated for the prospect of varieties of promotion, honor, happiness, and luxury, by being allowed the privilege of kissing a eunuch's foot?

Zaki Pasha, the person who European newspapers are claiming today is responsible for the entire Armenian problem, went in to see the late Bahram Agha. The room was crowded with ministers and senior figures. At that particular time, the state wanted to dispatch Zaki Pasha as commander to [Libyan] Tripoli. He stood in front of the Chief Eunuch. "My Lord," he said, "the state has appointed your servant commander of its army in Tripoli. I have a request that I would dearly like your eminence to grant in order to protect me from the doubting hand of fate, to kiss your exalted hand." The eunuch guffawed. "Since when did you achieve such a status," he replied, "that you can graduate from my foot to my hand?"

Can anyone of intelligence possibly imagine that the scar [47] left by such a comment, uttered to an army commander by the Chief Eunuch in such a large gathering of people, will ever heal? Every time they see anything black, they are bound to feel it hurting them.

Let us suppose that Rashid Pasha, the Grand Vizier, and his colleagues, `Ali Pasha and Fu'ad Pasha, were to rise from their graves and ask someone in the street what had happened to the state following their deaths.[6] The answer would read something like this: Rumania has seceded; the Serbs are now independent; the Black Mountain has vanished; Eastern Rumeli has gone; the Bulgarians have broken away; Cyprus has been lost, so has Tunis; Bosnia and Herzegovina have been spirited away; Batum has been snatched from us; Qars and Erdehan have gone; Thessaly has vanished; Zayla` has fallen; Massawa` is lost; Sudan has been abandoned; and our lands in Egypt are now in English hands. This is the part of our former empire that is completely lost and where there is no longer any contention. In the meantime, the French have their eyes fixed on Syria, the Italians are looking at Tripoli, the Bulgarians are pointing their fingers at Macedonia, and the Serbs are keeping a watchful eye on Qusuh. Greece has almost annexed Yania, Crete, Manastir, and Samos, while the Armenian provinces keep demanding independence or reform. This is the segment of our empire over which there is some dispute. And then, the people of Basra and [48] Baghdad are spreading the rumor that the government of Iran and the Yemen are trying to foment rebellion. Muslims live in fear for the safety of the Hijaz itself. Aleppo, Edirne, Izmir, and Bursa are the only places that have remained loyal to His Majesty the Sultan. During the golden century under the tender care of Hasan Pasha with all his deep secrets, the ship of state has been eaten away by rust. Meanwhile, British ships have been at the shores of Ottoman domains, and people have been complaining about the way *ma'murs* have been appropriating their lands and adding them to the royal estates. The Ministry of Finance has no budget, and the Judiciary is in chaos. The Sublime Porte has nothing to do (it is best not even to discuss that); following your deaths, the Council of Ministers included a group of ministers and soldiers who beggared description, not only them but the rags and tatters they wore. Only a photograph could do them adequate justice:

> People are in chaos, with no real champions to lead them; How can there
> be when ignorant fools are in control?

The three dead statesmen would then dissolve into tears and ask: "If all that has been lost, has anything worthwhile been gained?" The reply would be that seventy *takiyyas* have been erected, twenty mosques [49] have been repaired, the Emperor of Germany has made a state visit to Istanbul, the title of Caliph has been revived after remaining unused by previous Ottoman Sultans, and there has been an increase in the number of sacred titles and a doubling of the number of decorations. Faced with such details they would clearly acknowledge that considerable improvements had been made, but that you cannot use a mustard seed as a balance for a rock. The three dead statesmen would rush back to their tombs, reciting these lines of poetry as they did so:

> Woe upon us! Is there no one who can shout out news
> other than that a port is lost or a religion wiped out?

> City after city is being captured,
> one track after another is being eradicated;

> Here we see that Egypt and its people has perished save for a few,
> and the Hijaz stands on the brink.

Can any Muslim listen to facts like these and simply gloss over them? The very act of covering things up has produced this devastation. If the state authorities had allowed investigators and critics to go about their business, things would not have reached this pitch. As it is, they have assigned spies and watchmen to keep an eye on everyone who makes use of their tongue or pen. They draw such people into their net and find ways of keeping them quiet, some aboveboard, others not. The purpose is to make sure that stories about their misdeeds do not reach the ear of the Caliph who is enjoined by God, the Qur'an, Muhammad, and his community of believers to watch over the Islamic domains and to preserve their best [50] interests himself and not to permit others to use it as a means of bolstering their power.

It is man himself who aids the flatterer in carrying out his deceit. What is even more remarkable is that the critic lends a hand in his own deceit. Were he to find someone to eulogize him, flatter his every word, and make him forget his own egocentrism, he would soon realize what a trap he had fallen into; a layer of joy would spread all over his face. That being the case, what can be said about an ignorant fool who only ever hears people extolling him and his every deed, whether he is standing, sitting, or recumbent; he receives nonstop adulation for himself and everything issuing from his office. The result is that he is utterly puffed up with a despotic arrogance, while others see in him things that he cannot see for himself.

For example, the Emperor of Germany sent His Majesty the Sultan through a German prince the Order of the Black Eagle. His Majesty entertained the Prince as his guest in the royal palace. Bahram Agha was informed that it would be polite for him to pay a visit to the Prince. "How can I go to visit him," he commented, "when I am an 'Altesse' and so is he?" Al-Mutanabbi's patron raised the same sort of laugh when he has this to say about him:

> That you should bind up your foot puts me in mind of the time when it
> was deeply scored and you used to walk around naked in a greasy garb.[7]

We have just reached the point of threatening Greece and making this and other similar gestures to the Bulgarians.

Another incredible story about the eunuch tells how he appeared in [51] the public part of the palace at the time when the Russians had reached San Stefano. Panic was at its height. His Majesty the Sultan was preoccupied with the major crisis besetting the Ottoman throne that he had inherited from his illustrious forefathers. The eunuch entered the Sultan's presence. "Mighty Lord," he said, "don't worry. I have ventured out into the public areas of the palace and looked to left and right. Everything that I have surveyed belongs to Your Majesty. There is no call to be angry; that much property is sufficient for us." God curse such a slave! It's as though the entire purpose of the caliphate and sultanate were to provide a living for the Sultan and himself.

Dear reader, I would like you to know how Tunisia came to be lost as part of Ottoman territories. The government wanted to arrest Midhat Pasha, the Governor of Izmir. He took refuge with the French consul. When the Ottoman government demanded that he be handed over, the French stalled. After some correspondence, the matter was settled in the following manner: France agreed to hand over Midhat Pasha with the right hand, while receiving Tunis with the left. Everything was agreed, and the state proceeded to purchase a [52] single man for the price of a dominion. How expensive the state thinks such men are! When the French moved into Tunis, the Bey started yelling and screaming, sending letters and messengers requesting help from the Ottoman government. But nobody listened. He then sent Mustafa ibn Isma`il, the Vizier of Tunis who now lives in Istanbul, to see the late Bahram Agha, all this by way of al-Sadiq Bey, the Governor of Tunis. He asked for help and sent gifts as well. The eunuch graciously accepted the gifts, but had nothing useful to say on the primary purpose of the visit.

> Everything is corrupt. Abandon all declension, for today proper speech is reckoned bad grammar. Wretched is the mother, she is this life on earth; wretched too are we, the sons of that mother.

Al-Muqattam no. 1933, 2 August, 1895

Bahram still maintains his overall supervision of people's fortunes and has absolute authority to make life either pleasant or utterly miserable. Once made, his decisions are irrevocable; there's no going back on his instructions. He is able to exert his overbearing authority on distinguished soldiers, scholars, authors, and secretaries; he makes no distinctions, lording it equally over members of the Prophet's family or the Virgin's children. He thrusts his foot out to be kissed right in the faces of people who are honored by God. Neither faith nor the Qur'an provides any sort of restraint to keep him within the bounds of decency when dealing with the members of a house to whom the Qur'an has been sent down. God Almighty has said: "Say, I ask for no payment for him save that [53] you love his relatives," and also, "God only wishes that the Prophet's family may rid you of abomination and purify you."[8] He feels not the slightest sense of shame about doing such abhorrent things in the Caliph's own residence; everything happens in full view of people of both high and low rank and within earshot of people about whose probity one needs to entertain the gravest doubts. After all, they manage somehow to claim, even after witnessing such behavior, that they love the Prophet—prayers and blessings upon him—and revere the members of his family. On matters of great moment he keeps playing al-Walid's game,[9] toying around like an ignoramus with matters of public concern. Egypt is one of the pieces in the game he plays with the shaykhs; at one point he will take it, then he'll discard it. So the game swings this way and that till it ends up in their hands. Once he has finished, the Agha goes on his way and leaves them to take care of it. When England asked for Ottoman troops to be sent to Egypt, he was the one who recommended that they not be sent, the pretext being that it would require a reduction in the detachment of troops guarding the Yildiz Palace. The Agha apparently failed to realize that the Ottoman Empire has no lack of troops and soldiery. What actually led him to say such a stupid thing—which even a tiny [54] child would not think of doing—was that he wanted to put on a big show of dedication to the protection of His Majesty the Sultan as a way of gaining even more influence with him.

When Bahram Agha died, he was succeeded by Sharaf al-din Agha, who had big plans to step into his predecessor's shoes and wield the same sort of influence as he had. However, internal feuds developed inside the palace, and he allowed himself to trip. When word finally leaked out, it was discovered that he had been dismissed and banished to Jerusalem.

In composing this next paragraph, the pen really needs some extra help. A custom has developed recently whereby criminals, murderers, and people under suspicion are banished to the two sacred cities in Arabia. Once they have incurred someone's wrath, they are exiled by stages, one at a time, from the city of the Sultan to the shrine of the Merciful One. Whoever it was who suggested this policy to His Majesty the Sultan failed to bear in mind that their suggestion was utterly abhorrent to God, the Prophet, and Muslims in general, and that the people they were sending might well include some who were being unjustly treated. Such people were to be sent to a place that was, of all places on the face of this Earth, the one where prayers were most likely to be answered. God Almighty has said: "We entrusted it to Ibrahim and Isma`il to purify my house for those who are circumambulating, for those who wish for seclusion and for prostration."[10] In the name of God's mercy, when will the banishers of such people show some sympathy? It is utterly [55] intolerable for them to turn this pure and blessed spot into a place where people can be banished whose only crime is to have incurred the wrath of someone in Istanbul.

Sharaf al-din's successor in this position is Yavar Agha; he holds it at the moment. He is over ninety years old and does not meddle in political matters. By temperament, he is more inclined to entertainment and frivolity. As a result, employees and servants in Almabayn will try to curry favor with him by making him laugh whenever they enter his quarters. Among such people you will sometimes find Raghib Pasha, a person of considerable wealth, who makes use of his sarcasm to get into the Agha's good graces. The old man is completely lacking in any sort of perspicacity and clearly feels no urge to interfere in matters of policy. He lives in perpetual terror of intrigues that might carry him off to the Prophet's sanctuary in Arabia. He asks every visitor to help him and requests that this person mediate on his behalf by pointing out that, if someone trumps up a false charge against him, he is quite ready to travel. He points out that he needs to make no financial demands on the state; all he requires are the clothes on his back, the rings on his fingers, and the rosaries in his hands which have been valued at thirty thousand pounds.

Among the eunuchs there exists a particular group known as the "companions" (*musahibun*). Like the Almabaynjiyya they transmit the [56] Sultan's decrees. This term *companion* is very like the Arabic word *comrades* (*qurana'*) which is applied to the Almabaynjiyya. In Turkish they sometimes use the Arabic plural for the singular; when they want to make it plural, they use the Turkish suffix. In Almabayn, the Almabaynji has the same sort of function as the companion, but their categories of work are different. The name "companion" may be given to someone who is not a eunuch, as was the case of Lutfi Agha, the second *tutunji* to the Sultan. He had been a servant of Mahmud Nadim Pasha and had been brought up in his domestic quarters where he had picked up some of his master's malice and trickery. The companions have a chief, the so-called Head Companion (*bash-musahib*) whose name is Jawhar Agha; the second is Muzaffar Agha, the third `Abd al-Ghani Agha, and so on. Each of these eunuchs belongs to one of the Sufi orders, such as the Shadhiliyya, the Rifa`iyya, or the Qadiriyya; they follow the counsels of the shaykhs of these orders far more than they do the imams of the four schools of Islamic law.

Jawhar Agha, the Head Companion, has the most important job in the palace, that of supervising the Chiragan Palace. It is at this point that the writer has to stop to try to find some means through which to gain access to this palace, a place that constitutes one of those mysteries that neither guesswork nor surmise can penetrate; nor can its secrets be gleaned through [57] contemplation. All we can do is to record the various things that foreigners and Ottoman subjects have had to say about it.

There is a group of Europeans who are prepared to deny that Sultan Murad is to be found there. They claim he died shortly after his deposition. In their opinion, the intense level of security that is maintained on the palace is merely a ruse to make people believe that he is still there. A group of Ottomans believe he is still there. One friend will often tell another that the deposed Sultan sits there with his head bowed, often musing about the state of the Sultanate; he is said to tug his beard so often that the hair is getting extremely thin. Still a third group, this one made up of a combination of foreigners and Ottomans, is both dubious and confused; they are reluctant to draw any conclusions at all. Sometimes they will say that it is hard to believe that a mentally sick man could survive for twenty years; on that basis, they are inclined to believe that he is indeed dead, justifying his suppression by citing the desire to avoid exercising people's minds over the issue of the Ottoman line of succession. At other times, however, they seem more inclined to claim that he is still alive and in good health. In short, no one really knows for sure.

The function of the Head Companion that everyone knows about is that of keeping an eye on everything Sultan Murad says and does and watching [58] every single movement he makes. Using his network of spies and watchmen who form part of the retinue of servants and women in the household, the Agha makes a list of everything and submits a report to His Majesty the Sultan every single morning.

Hasan Pasha, the Superintendent of Beshiktash, has the job of guarding the palace from the outside and the soldiers, officers, and servants inside. The Chiragan Palace is one of the Sultan's biggest, lying on the Bosphorus between the Beshiktash landing stage and the one for Ortokoy and `Ali al-Jada. Extraordinary measures have been adopted to guard and protect this particular palace, to such a degree that the steamers of the Charitable Company that pass through the straits plot an arc-shaped course at the point where they are opposite the palace so as to keep clear, even at the risk of encountering increased winds and choppy water. Some passengers on these boats have carried flattery and hypocrisy to new heights by averting their eyes when they pass the palace and staring at the other bank. Barges and ships follow the same course when they approach the palace. If choppy water forces them to steer a little closer, guards yell at them to move away; if they fail to obey the order after a [59] second warning, the guards threaten to fire at them. On the seaside, the palace is defended by bayonets and rifles; on the land side, no passerby is allowed even to glance up at the windows or linger in front of the walls or gates. If they try, giant-sized watchmen grab them and haul them off to see the one who wields absolute authority, Al-Hajj Hasan Pasha, the general who

serves as Superintendent of Beshiktash; holder of the Uthmani Murassa`
medal. He devotes himself heart and soul to the business of interrogation, and
that keeps him busy day and night.

One of the more amazing tales that people will recount to you in private
is that a boat stopped right in front of the palace, apparently because the haul-
ing horses got tired or else became obstinate. The stationary vessel was impounded, and the pilot and all the passengers were subject to several grueling
days of investigation. Inquiries were made about the jobs of the passengers,
where they all lived, and who their relatives and neighbors were. Finally, when
not a shadow of suspicion could be found against any of them, they were all
released, but only after the horses had been examined by a veterinary surgeon.
This sort of tale is enough to impress anyone and to make people wonder if
such things can really happen. However, it constitutes the most [60] significant
activity of that select coterie of favorites who call themselves "*bandegan*" or
"*fedekar.*" *Bandegan* is a Persian word meaning "slave," but it has a special application to those people who are honored with the personal patronage of the
Sultan. "*Fidagar*" is someone who is prepared to sacrifice his own life for the
Sultan. These two words are keys that are used by flatterers to open up treas-
ure chests for their own personal interests, two enormous secrets that allow the
person in the know to do whatever he likes without any feeling of guilt or re-
morse, and all because he has dedicated his life for love of the Sultan.

We thus emerge from the Chiragan Palace just as we entered, completely
ignorant of what goes on. In some aspects this story resembles that of the man
in the iron mask who was a favorite of Louis Quatorze, the King of France.
His identity was shrouded in mystery; to this very day no one knows who he
was. Everything reported about him is sheer surmise and brings us no closer
to the truth. This concludes what I have to say about the Department of the
Chief Eunuch.

NOTES

1. This marks the beginning of the second article published in *Al-Muqattam* but not
included in the text of *Ma Hunalik* in book form (see chapter 3 note 2). An illustration of the attire of the Chief Eunuch can be found in Andrew Wheatcroft, *The Ottomans* (London: Viking, 1993), no. 6 between pp. 34 and 35.

2. A line from one of al-Mutanabbi's infamous satires on the Ikhshidid ruler of
Egypt, Kafur (r. 966–968). See A. J. Arberry, *Poems of al-Mutanabbi* (Cambridge: Cambridge University Press, 1967), p. 121.

3. Arberry, *Poems*, p. 113.

4. The copy of *Al-Muqattam* in the Dar al-Kutub newspaper collection is torn at
this point, and a few lines are lost.

5. This marks the end of the excluded passage.

6. As noted in the introduction, these three figures were largely responsible for the implementation of the "*tanzimat*" reforms during the reigns of `Abd al-Hamid's predecessors.

7. From another of al-Mutanabbi's famous hija' (lampoon) poems against the Ikhshidid regent, Kafur. The poem begins "Urika al-rida" and the rhyme is "-yan."

8. Quotations from the Qur'an, Sura 42, v. 23; and Sura 33, v. 33.

9. Presumably a reference to al-Walid ibn Yazid, the Umawi Caliph (d. 744).

10. The original text reads: "The soldiers receive a quarter of a pound."

· 6 ·

The Department of
the Yavaran in Almabayn

Al-Muqattam no. 1939, 9 August, 1895[1]

$\mathcal{T}$he Department of the Yavaran in Almabayn is made up of senior generals and great heroes [61] from the armed forces of the state. Among them one will find, as the poet puts it:

> Heroes of a realm, lions of a caliphate, people for whom the cool shade of sound guidance is a forest, a dense thicket.

However, the commodity that is in most demand within the palace confines has managed to dampen the aspirations of some of them and blunted their courage. As a result, they devote their attention to keeping their personal whims satisfied and pay no attention to the state of the Islamic world, the very glory of which depended on the swords of their fathers and Grand Vizier fathers. Instead of aspiring to the loftiest of deeds they are content to withdraw sheepishly, waiting eagerly for any opportunity to receive a gift just like poets.

They fall into three categories: *yavar*, *yavar Akram*, and *yavar Fakhri*. The Sir-Yavar (Chief Yavar) is Muhammad Pasha; he holds the rank of general and is His Majesty's son-in-law. There are [62] about twenty *yavaran akram*, all of them illustrious field marshals, 120 *yavaran*, and over 130 *yavaran fakhri*. They hold a variety of ranks, all the way from lieutenant up to field marshal. No Sultan or monarch in any country, whether advanced or backward, has a collection of field marshals such as are clustered together under the authority of the Sultan. In this era of ours no state has had the might, no Sultan the power, no empire the glory, no monarchy the potential, to be able to afford ten field marshals among its military commanders. But the Ottoman Empire has the singular privilege of having no less than sixty field marshals among its military leaders. The Arabic word *mushir* is equivalent to field marshal, as, for example with Moltke in Germany, MacMahon in France, and Wolseley in England.

I have just noted that His Majesty has sixty field marshals clustered around him. The British can only appoint six field marshals, one of whom is the Crown Prince and another is the Queen's uncle. The other four have all distinguished themselves in war; Lord Wolseley, for example, did so in Egypt, and Lord Roberts in India. At the time of France's war with Germany the country had four field marshals, and no one replaced them when they died. Napoléon Bonaparte, the renowned French conqueror, was proverbially famous [63] throughout Europe for his vanity, but his army did not even boast of twenty field marshals. So how can we see fit to have no less than sixty of them? The Russians have only one, the famous Jurko, while the Germans have only one left after Moltke and Monteufel. The Italians have no field marshals; the Spaniards only have one, Campos, who supported the present royal family and suppressed the Carlists.

By the way, the use of the Arabic word *mushir* in its other significance, namely anyone who gives advice, is rigorously avoided by the Ottoman government.

I have never heard of a *yavar* (whom the Europeans categorize as an aide-de-camp to the commander on the battlefield) holding the rank of field marshal. But then, the state has absolute authority and can assign whatever titles and ranks it likes to anyone it wishes.

In Almabayn the rank of *yavar akram* stands above all the others. Jawad Pasha, the ex–Grand Vizier, used to make the following rueful comment on the authority structure in the government: "A Grand Vizier may well be Grand Vizier, but a Yavar gets more respect." Even if it were to be acknowledged that the Vizier has some degree of authority, the *yavar* would still come out on top. The Grand Vizier is well aware of the fact that the *yavar akram* is responsible for the execution of all kinds of personal service for His Majesty the Sultan. As a result, it is only to be expected that His Majesty tends to favor the *yavar* at the expense of the broader responsibility for the Caliphate [64] and Sultanate. From this and other evidence, one gets the clear impression that these worthies regard the Sultanate, the state, the Caliphate, the community, Islam, and Muslims in general as being entities that the Almighty—may He be exalted—has fashioned especially to serve to person of the Sultan, and not that His Majesty the Sultan, whom God has elevated to the position of Caliph, is responsible for and entrusted with their preservation and well-being. The faith of His Majesty the Sultan is above paying any attention to the frivolities of such people; the awesome responsibility of the Caliphate is indeed a mighty one.

Among the *yavaran akram* group is Al-Ghazi ʿUthman Pasha, the lion of Plevna and boon of Yildiz. He is the Marshal of Almabayn and supervises the soldiers who guard the Sultan's palace inside and out. His task is to ensure that no squabbles arise among the guards and that no one neglects his duties. He hardly ever leaves the palace. If he has to do so, even for just a few minutes, they summon him at once and he comes rushing back. He maintains a constant watch, a task that is never entrusted to anyone else. At one point His Majesty the Sultan gave orders that `Uthman Pasha was to be appointed Commander in Chief, but he only stayed in that job for a [65] few days; the Sultan had realized that his functions at the palace were utterly indispensable. When it was suggested to the ex-Khedive of Egypt, the late Tawfiq Pasha, that he send `Uthman Pasha a message of congratulations on his new appointment, he responded that he was afraid the man might be dismissed before the message ever got there. And that's exactly what happened! `Uthman Pasha's status in the Sultan's entourage is unrivaled: His Majesty the Sultan married his two daughters to the Pasha's two sons. The latter has a special department in Almabayn which counts as one of the largest. People, members of the armed forces, and others, come to visit and submit their petitions, and he responds to their needs. That is why any mere soldier serving in Almabayn, who is shown all kinds of respect and has his needs taken care of over and above what is actually required, must be considered better off than an officer outside who remains helpless and confused when confronted with the many needs of life.

Everyone in Almabayn respects this Ghazi for his dignity, his great age, and the tremendous gallantry he has shown in the service of his country. However, there exists between him and Sayyid Abu al-Huda the kind of ill feeling and spite that one expects to encounter between rivals for power. Just to give one example, the Sultan complained to the Ghazi one day that he was feeling a bit weak. The Ghazi suggested that the Sultan might take a rest for three or four days and that the feeling of lassitude would go away. His Majesty thanked him and took his advice. His Majesty then informed [66] Al-Sayyid Abu al-Huda about his condition and repeated what the Ghazi `Uthman Pasha had suggested. "Good heavens!" Al-Sayyid Abu al-Huda replied. "That's not the kind of friendly advice that I expect to hear `Uthman Pasha giving Your Majesty. If Your Majesty were to stop officiating over government affairs for even a single day, it would cause all kinds of gossip, panic, and unrest. How could `Uthman Pasha possibly fail to realize such a simple thing?" At this, the Sultan became very annoyed, and dispatched Al-Hajj `Ali Bey, the chief Almabaynji, to reprimand the Ghazi for the poor advice he had given. The Ghazi will often walk past as Al-Sayyid Abu al-Huda is seated; when the Ghazi is exactly in front of him, Al-Sayyid Abu al-Huda will stick his foot out in contempt—a sign of the tremendous influence he has with His Majesty the Sultan.

Among their number there is also Al-Ghazi Mukhtar Pasha who is one of their most outstanding generals. He is a person of noble spirit and prestige. He serves as undersecretary in charge of the Military Inspection Council in the Sultan's palace. At this point I would like to tell a story which will serve to illustrate his self-respect, high moral standards, and his assiduousness in protecting the military's good name. His Majesty the Emperor of Germany sent His Majesty the Sultan the Order of the Black Eagle by way of a German [67] prince who was a member of the nobility and a personage of considerable prestige, all this as a token of respect and honor to the Sultan's exalted status. When the Prince arrived, the Sultan entertained him on a lavish scale. At the conclusion of the Sultan's banquet, His Majesty issued orders that the key members of his entourage should take turns in inviting the Prince. His Majesty instructed `Uthman Bey Kaylarji Bashi to visit each host as his turn came and to ask what they required to put on a proper banquet; whatever was needed would be provided from the Sultan's palace. Some of them went so far as to remove the curtains and chairs from their house and take them somewhere else, just so that they could have their homes furnished to befit the banquet. However, when `Uthman Bey came to visit Al-Ghazi Mukhtar Pasha's home and asked what he needed in order to be fully prepared, the Pasha replied that, through the munificence of the dispenser of all bounty, our Lord the Sultan, he did not need anything at all. When the Prince had departed, a letter was sent from His Majesty the Emperor of Germany to His Majesty the Sultan in which the German ruler commended Al-Ghazi Mukhtar Pasha on the basis of the report that he had received from the German Prince; he had described Al-Ghazi's perfect manners, his noble temperament, and the breadth of his knowledge of military science, and other topics. The Emperor congratulated the Sultan on having a commander such as Al-Ghazi Mukhtar Pasha. His Majesty [68] gave orders that Al-Ghazi be summoned to the palace. When he arrived, His Majesty sent someone to inform him that he had earned the Sultan's exalted pleasure and favorable attention; he was informed that the Sultan was sending him some of his own special food as a salutation and promised to see him in the morning. That night, the Sultan gave five thousand pounds to `Uthman Bey, the second Almabaynji, to give to Al-Ghazi as a token of the Sultan's generosity. However, `Uthman Bey was no fan of Al-Ghazi. When he went to see him, he shouted at him in a loud voice: "I've brought you a generous gift such as you have never seen in your life, nor your father before you." He then handed over the piece of paper with the amount of the gift written on it. "It is one of the very greatest honors a man can receive," replied Al-Ghazi, "to be able to accept a generous gift from His Majesty Our Lord the Sultan, whether the occasions be rare or frequent. However, I will never accept a gift which comes wrapped in the kind of parlance that you have just used with me." With that he declined to accept the paper and left the palace at night to return to his own home. He wrote a letter to the late Rashid Bey, the private secretary of the Sultan, in which he provided full details of what had happened and quoted the very words that had been addressed to him, words that should never have been associated with any gift that came from the Sultan. Next morning, the Sultan ordered Al-Ghazi to come to the palace once again. `Uthman Bey provided his own version of what had taken place, and His Majesty the Sultan became extremely annoyed. At that moment, [69] Rashid Bey entered and presented Al-Ghazi's letter. Summoning `Uthman Bey on the spot, the Sultan issued a severe reprimand and issued orders that a carriage be sent at once to bring Al-Ghazi. When he was ushered into His Majesty's presence, he was presented with the gift from His Majesty's own noble hand and was treated with the greatest cordiality. Al-Ghazi returned home, expressing his profound gratitude for having received a succession of generous gifts at one and the same time.

Another member of this group is Nasrat Pasha. He is a man of great courage and initiative, but his insolence led to his being banished to Baghdad where he now resides. He used to fool around and act like a buffoon with His Majesty the Sultan, so His Majesty sent him to the Shah of Iran with a decoration for him. When the Pasha got to the Ottoman border with Iran, he suddenly received a telegram instructing him to proceed to Baghdad; and that is where he went. Once, when he was in the Sultan's presence, the general order was given for everyone to be seated. The Chief Chamberlain pulled the chair out from under him, and he fell backward to the floor. Everyone roared with laughter. When he left, he summoned the Chamberlain to his rooms, locked the door, and then beat the living daylights out of him. "Don't play tricks like that on soldiers like me any more," he yelled. There are other incidents that could be mentioned, but they would offend the integrity of the royal throne.

Al-Muqattam no. 1943, 14 August, 1895

Another of their number is Darwish Pasha whose son is His Majesty [70] the Sultan's son-in-law. It was he who was dispatched by the Sultan to Egypt along with Al-Sayyid Ahmad As`ad to put down the `Urabi Revolt during the reign of the late Khedive Tawfiq. Al-Sayyid Ahmad As`ad was the one who was sent by His Majesty the Sultan to confer with the British Ambassador in Istanbul on some political problem. He always manages to wheedle his way out of doing things he cannot do very well by pretending to be ill and putting on a fit of coughing. When Darwish Pasha arrived in Egypt with his companion, they were accorded the most lavish welcome by the late Khedive who did everything he could to make their stay and their accommodations as comfortable and of as high a standard as possible. The Khedive obviously thought that the courage of the one and the intelligence of the other would prove sufficient to stamp out the revolt. However, luckily for them, they managed to get out of Egypt safe and sound, abandoning Egypt to its fate and leaving it in even greater chaos and confusion than before their arrival. They put the blame for the failure of their mission on the shoulders of the Egyptians and started blaming and disparaging Egypt. If Egypt had only been given a modicum of good luck, someone else would have come in their place; they would have managed to put down the rebellion from the very outset before it got out of hand. But what is to be done when people such as these wield the Sultan's authority, and the Sultan on his own is unable to do anything about it?

The above-mentioned *yavar akram* is of Albanian origin and belongs to one of the most [71] prestigious families in that country. In the Sultan's eyes he is an appropriate aide and strong bulwark to be used in order to keep Albanian territory under control. The man himself regards his own country as a personal possession where he behaves as if he owned it. To the wretched inhabitants of the country he represents just one more chain of oppression to hang around their necks.

Still another *yavar akram* is Isma`il Pasha, the Kurd, who is second president of the Military Inspection Council. In Kurdistan he commands the same influence as Darwish Pasha does in Albania. As a result, the status he has at the palace is one of great eminence; his influence is considerable, comprising all benefits accruing from Kurdistan itself. Furthermore, His Majesty has adopted him as a son-in-law. On such a foundation, his influence in Kurdistan increases every time his approval rating at the palace improves. Conversely, palace approval increases every time his influence in Kurdistan is amplified. The process goes on and on, bringing heaven knows what kinds of bliss to the person possessed of such influence but utter misery to the poor people and the country as a whole.

Then there is Shakir Pasha, the state's ambassador to Russia. Because of both his experience in politics at the highest level and the equanimity for which he is renowned, his name has [72] often been put forward for the post of Grand Vizier. His Majesty the Sultan has made him a political emissary between himself and the ambassadors of the great powers in Istanbul, and he was recently selected as overseer of the Armenian provinces because the ambassadors of the great powers trust him. When he was sent to Crete to quell the disturbances there, Jawad Pasha, the *yavar akram* and ex–Grand Vizier, was a member of his entourage. Afterward Shakir Pasha returned to Istanbul while Jawad Pasha stayed behind as deputy-governor. Jawad Pasha was awarded the rank of field marshal, then appointed Grand Vizier and summoned to Istanbul. On His Majesty the Sultan's orders Shakir Pasha went down to the boat to welcome the person who had been a member of his entourage, all this so that he could learn that promotion and demotion are at the Sultan's discretion; it is his judgment alone that dictates what will happen. Shakir Pasha performed this task in a most exemplary fashion for a servant responding to his master's command.

It was Shakir Pasha and elderly commanders like him who had to bear the brunt of Jawad Pasha's period as Grand Vizier. Jawad Pasha had submitted forceful reports and forwarded all sorts of information, and it was this that led him to occupy the highest post in government while still in the prime of his youth. In an atmosphere in which such reports were warmly received, he managed to float over the heads of these older [73] politicians, until, that is, the proverbial trolley inspector came along, bumped him out of the class he was in, and made him go to the class where his ticket entitled him to sit.[2] I don't think any of these commanders, who manage to sleep in comfort on plush pillows and gilded beds, would relax quite so easily if they looked back on the course of their own lives, the wars they had experienced, the misfortunes they had suffered, and the promotion they had accepted on the basis of reports submitted only to be followed by the crushing failure of demotion. However, when three of them, Shakir Pasha, Fu'ad Pasha al-Misri, and Darwish Pasha, were subjected to the all-powerful-one's pride, they submitted a petition to His Majesty the Sultan requesting that they be pensioned off. His Majesty was annoyed by their sheer effrontery and censored them, but then his innate wisdom and political instinct led him to conciliate [74] them.

Another *yavar akram* is Fu'ad Pasha al-Misri. Egypt should be proud of him for his sense of honor, his composure, his resolve, and his friendship with His Majesty the Sultan. The only problem is that these very qualities sometimes get him into difficulties, and on such occasions the situation can turn out to be dangerous. There have been occasions when his naïvetée in telling the absolute truth has led to his interrogation, and he has found himself in trouble. But in spite of that, he has always managed to emerge unscathed from such circumstances, loaded down with lavish gifts because of his good intentions. His Majesty the Sultan sent him to convey a decoration to the Emperor of Austria. While in Vienna, he purchased a weapon that caught his attention, with a view to presenting it to the Sultan. Before he arrived for an audience with the Sultan, people told His Majesty that Fu'ad Pasha had purchased a weapon and ammunition, all with some sinister scheme in mind. When he got there, he was taken away for interrogation. Meanwhile, His Majesty left Yildiz for Beshiktash to perform the Friday prayers; this was before the Hamidian mosque deprived the mosques and people of Istanbul of the pleasure of seeing the Sultan's horsemen and His Majesty himself—a sight to gladden people's hearts. Fu'ad Pasha was behind the horse on which His Majesty was riding, and Bahram Agha was at his side. Ministers and field marshals were on foot. As Bahram Agha feasted his eyes on this royal splendor, he placed [75] his hand on the horse's croup. "My God," he exclaimed, "how wonderful!" The horse reared and lashed out with its leg, hitting Field Marshal Fu'ad Pasha's hand; he came very close to being seriously injured. People who are permanently looking for an occasion to flatter His Majesty the Sultan started suggesting that both Fu'ad Pasha and Bahram Agha would need to be interrogated when the Sultan got back to the palace. The Agha managed to exculpate himself with a few words, but even greater suspicion was focused on Fu'ad Pasha because he was already being interrogated about the purchase of the weapon. He was kept in the palace for three days with no food and came close to killing himself. When Sa`id Pasha, the Grand Vizier (who, at that time, was the Sultan's chief secretary), heard about the matter, he brought it to His Majesty the Sultan's attention. An official decree granting Fu'ad Pasha a pardon was issued. This then is life in the palace that so many people hanker after, the object of the most intense rivalries. Fu'ad Pasha's enemies accused him of even worse things. When he could no longer stand the intrigues of those sycophants who cannot endure the thought of having a decent person in their midst, he tore off the chevrons on his uniform and threw them on the floor in front of the Sultan. With that, His Majesty the Sultan made him a gift of [76] a mine which he subsequently sold for eight thousand pounds. Last year, there was still another intrigue, and the attacks against Fu'ad Pasha started again. This time, they claimed he had brought some explosives like dynamite and other things from Europe. A search warrant was issued, and his house was ransacked. All they found were some fireworks that he had brought back to use for the celebration of the Sultan's accession anniversary.

This is the sort of things that trustworthy people have to put up with in an environment made up of traitors. His Majesty the Sultan's time is continually being wasted, time that is desperately needed for the reform of the state. They are all well aware that he alone has control of all state matters, whether great or small, and already has insufficient time to do everything. The way the great powers have started interfering in our affairs is no small matter.

I have now discussed all the *yavaran* who merit separate mention. The majority of them will only be referred to in the next article which deals with spies, or secret police, as they are usually known.

NOTE

1. This marks the beginning of the second article published in *Al-Muqattam* but not included in the text of *Ma Hunalik* in book form.

2. The text has a footnote at this point: An Englishman wrote a treatise on the lives of twenty men who were promoted when they did not deserve it and were soon demoted again. We can draw an analogy between them in their promotion and demotion on the one hand and people who ride in train carriages of a higher class than they are entitled to be in on the other hand. The inspector arrives, looks at their tickets, and tells them to leave the higher-class carriages for the class to which their ticket entitles them. Writers use this analogy very frequently as a moral.

· 7 ·

Spies

Al-Muqattam no. 1947, 19 August, 1895

$\mathcal{I}$n the quest for learning, people are willing to forgo pleasures [77] and give up an easy life. In search of wealth they will travel abroad and gather the earth's resources. Striving for the heights they will take on courageous foes and face terrible danger. When the large part of their life is at an end, they will have earned the title of scholar, rich man, or man of influence. In Istanbul, there is a very economical way of reaching the heights, something that in a single day can bring wealth, high status, and a reputation for learning. All people need to do in order to achieve such a status is to write a false report in which reliable and perfectly innocent folk are accused of doing something. Such an action will cause dinars to start flowing and soon a medal gleaming like the moon will appear on the chest. The state will begin to mention the informant's sterling qualities and good fortune. When others perceive that this is the technique for gaining wealth and influence, they too start crowding in and infiltrating on all sides. Once the plague has spread far enough, it kills off all worthy qualities in people and brings all kinds of vices to life. Enemies laugh while allies weep. Honest people are turned into paupers and hypocrites get rich. The ruler and the ruled are separated by feelings of enmity and hatred. [78] The ruler decides to keep himself secluded, far removed from contact with his subjects; he leaves them to rue his actions. He cannot relax, nor can they. When a father has to live in fear of his own children, life is bitter indeed; the consequences are even more dire and bitter. This explains why the judicious ruler will always burn pieces of paper with bits of false and slanderous information on them without even looking at them. By such prudent actions as these he can counteract any feelings of malice and hatred that people may be nursing. Instead he will be able to instill in their hearts a sense of affection and a recognition of

73

his intelligence and resolve. As a result, such a ruler will live with his people in an atmosphere of trust and security, of affection and good intentions. Sleepless nights and anxious days will be at an end.

On this particular topic, one story tells how Muhammad `Ali Pasha dispatched one of his Mamluks named `Abd al-Latif to Istanbul on an assignment. The government officials there offered him bribes as they usually do to any member of the Egyptian entourage who falls into their clutches. They bestowed on `Abd al-Latif a high-ranking title and got him to agree that, when he got back to Egypt, he would start work on founding a society to oppose Muhammad `Ali. When `Abd al-Latif returned to Egypt, he did exactly what he had been instructed to do. Muhammad Bey Lazoghly[1] got to hear about the [79] formation of this society and had `Abd al-Latif summoned. Lazoghly ordered him to be put to death. "Before you have me killed," `Abd al-Latif told him, "there are some things I would like to tell you." Lazoghly refused however and told them to kill him immediately. One of his colleagues objected and said that he should listen to what `Abd al-Latif wanted to confide to him. Muhammad Bey responded by saying that he was afraid that the people with whom `Abd al-Latif was in league might get suspicious; people would be affected if things went wrong, and he was supposed to be responsible for their welfare.

If a king looks favorably on calumny and slander, gives lies precedence over truth, smiles when confronted with the despicable, and frowns at people of nobility, then people's hearts become corrupted; and with that the troubles start multiplying. If people feel afraid and resentful, then no amount of gifts and largesse will manage to reconcile them; all the courtesy and smiles in the world will be useless. Actually gifts will simply make matters even worse, and smiles will merely increase the agony. The disease does not respond to treatment, and in the end the public interest of the state as a whole becomes subsumed within a single personal concern, namely that of the ruler's interest in self-preservation. At that point the ties that bind authority together are loosened, and alien hands extend to grab them, aided and abetted by the people within whose goal is to take revenge and be rid of the regime. The absolute ruler now finds [80] himself beset by troubles and crises. The people demand that he get rid of foreign control over the country, while his inner self keeps telling him to protect his own flanks against intrigue. The great powers meanwhile place the entire burden of reform on his shoulders. Since he cannot possibly undertake all these things at once, he concentrates all his faculties on self-preservation.

If people with a truly critical eye read what I have just written with due care, they cannot claim that I am exaggerating when I suggest that the current situation in Istanbul has reached such a point; indeed it may even have gone well beyond it.

Yusuf Rida Pasha has told one of his friends that His Majesty the Sultan is now so inured to receiving daily reports from his spies concerning alarming situations that, if a day goes by without him getting fresh alarming information about some new plot or the formation of a new society, he starts to imagine to himself that the thing he's been worried about and hearing reports about has already happened. He is beside himself with fury until the spies manage to cook up some fresh report along these lines for him. He then sets about checking on the report's veracity. Once he discovers that it is as untrue as are all the other reports, he cheers up and feels relaxed again.

When His Majesty informed a member of his entourage that he had heard that a certain group of people were plotting against him, the man started proving to the Sultan that the rumor could not possibly be true, all with the hope of ridding him of his anxieties. However the Sultan now became suspicious of the man's motives and thought he was trying to cover things up because he was involved in the plot himself. There was one day when the Sultan complained to one of his close associates that he had so much work to do; he had received, he said, three separate reports while he was completing his ablutions.

After His Majesty has attended to such details, any time remaining is devoted to matters of state and to attempts to bolster its power, to support the shari`a law, the organization of the armed forces, proper administration of justice, regulation of finances, provision of more educational opportunities, cementing international relations, administering political affairs, building ships, and enhancing public services. That leaves very little time to hear further reports from the shaykhs and to incite some of them to scheme against others. Then Zayd gets to take `Amr's place, and Bakr can grab Khalid's post.[2] If the most brilliant set of professors were asked to come up with a plausible case to present to the Europeans these days, to the effect that Islam is not, as they assert, detached from all ideas of civilization and reform, but rather reflects justice, fairness, wisdom, and enlightened guidance, that would only be supremely appropriate for a group of clerics who need three full lines in order to write down the titles of just one of them, so that the poor reader only gets to read the text after lines of names.

[82] The spies found out that only reports specifically dealing with the Sultan himself were given any attention, and that there was no penalty for lying (according to the dictum among the men of Almabayn which says that "if we punish spies for telling lies, then we sacrifice the truth as well. So it's their prerogative to lie, and it's up to us to assess their information with a critical eye."). With that in mind they have amplified yet further the atmosphere of fear that prevails between ruler and ruled and engineered all manner of intrigue. They have sunk to the very lowest level of espionage. You can find, for

example a *ma'mur*, someone of decorated rank, standing in a corner of the ministry in which he is an appointed official, chatting to one of the black women who sell candies. When you listen in on their conversation, you discover that at his instigation the girl is going to accuse a member of the public, stating that she heard him talking to someone else about a scheme which involves doing harm to His Majesty the Sultan. Thereafter Nazim Pasha, Chief Inspector of Police, has to spend days and nights investigating this complete forgery and sends a continuous stream of documents to the palace.

To anyone with intelligence it is hardly conceivable that people in Istanbul could talk themselves into betraying His Majesty in such a way, something he should regard as worse than betraying his very faith. And yet these spies keep themselves busy instructing people in the art of intrigue and dragging them down to ruin. [83] It is no fault of theirs that the Sultan is angry or displeased about something. It is for this very reason that His Majesty has put an end to the custom followed by his predecessors and ancestors, namely performing Friday prayers in the mosques of Istanbul. On some Fridays he used to pray in the *takiyya*³ that he had built for Shaykh Muhammad Zafir close to the palace. However that made someone jealous—and please, don't be surprised that someone should get jealous about the site of this mighty blessing! As a result a telegram was sent from outer Bulgaria, conveying the dreadful news that some dynamite had been placed under the floor of the *takiyya*. All hell broke loose in Beshiktash. The floor of the *takiyya* was dug up and part of the structure was demolished, but nothing was ever found. By now however, a germ of suspicion had been planted in the Sultan's mind, so he stopped praying there and transferred this enormous privilege to the Hamidi Mosque. But how can any ruler relax when surrounded by such an entourage, continually trying to deceive him? The mouth may smile, but the heart is full of vengeance. They all liken one another to a minaret: on the outside it looks straight, but inside it is actually crooked and twisted.

The spies used to maintain an office inside the palace. In it would sit the Secret Police Chief (i.e., the chief spy); it used to be Ahmad al-Sharkasi. Even he wasn't protected from their intrigues. They thought he wanted to create a Circassian Sultanate [84], so they conducted a cross-examination of him inside his own department. Even though he was completely innocent and loyal to his master, the Sultan, they had him exiled to Aleppo. He was replaced by Qadri Bey, who had previously been his secretary. However, when espionage became so widespread and everyone in the palace was in effect chief spy, the special post was abolished. The use of the term *secret police*, with its connotations of spying, no longer implies any sort of reproach in Istanbul. Actually it has become something akin to a source of pride. A Royal Princess once told an undersecretary of state: "So, Pasha, I gather you're a spy," by which she implied disapproval. In reply he noted that such a designation now brought him honor and pride. "Your Highness," he said, "by now we're all His Majesty's spies."

Spies are divided into two groups: key government figures who are given titles of high rank as an object of pride, and others who simply receive a monthly salary. One of the more incredible stories tells how a legacy came up for sale. A general came along, anxious to buy the things he liked. He admired a collection of chairs, and purchased thirty-five of them. Spies immediately filed a report, to the effect that General So-and-So had come to the sale of So-and-So's legacy and had bought thirty-five chairs. If he weren't planning to form some kind of society, [85] he would never have needed to buy so many chairs. As a result, an order was issued for the General's dismissal.

Al-Muqattam no. 1952, 24 August, 1895

Hasan Fahmi Pasha wrote a book about the rights of states that was widely admired by scholars and everyone else who read it. It was printed and published in every part of the empire; indeed the author of these pages himself has studied it several times with students at the law school. A copy was sent to His Majesty the Sultan for deposition in the Sultan's library. Turkish, European, and Arab newspapers all talked about it, and the Ministry of Education designated it a textbook for use in the law school along with all the other texts that it had selected for study there. At this point a spy in the Ministry of Education started raising a hue and cry against Hasan Fahmi Pasha, accusing him of treason and treachery against the Sultan. The reason given was that there was a sentence in *The Rights of States* which this spy regarded as pernicious, harmful, and malicious; it would undoubtedly lead to serious consequences. The sentence in question provided the Sultan with a pretext for allowing foreign interference in domestic affairs that are supposed to be the exclusive concern of the nation state in question. The burden of the sentence was that, if the internal affairs of any state became totally unstable, then the neighboring state has the right to demand reform. This particular spy wrote a report [86] and sent it to the Sultan. He was summoned to the palace and accorded a warm welcome. An official decree was immediately issued, requiring that the book in question be collected and burned; there was to be no further mention of it at the law school. It was further ordered that Hasan Fahmi Pasha be sent a reprimand for the things he had written, and that the spy be given the reward of First Order, First Class, along with 150 pounds. On leaving Almabayn, the spy commented to a friend that, if he produced another report like this one, he'd be made a minister.

What a corruption of learning, what an enormous market for ignorance! Truth has hit hard times, and lies prosper; the honest man falls and the hypocrite thrives; the trustworthy man weeps and the traitor laughs. The seat of the Ottoman Sultan, something that used to be a lion's lair, has now turned into a hornet's nest, with spies buzzing around in its cells. Through the malign influence of ignorant fools, scholars have now started to discredit the very principles of learning that they are supposed to incorporate in their writings. Meanwhile, the spy treats scholars unjustly, yet still struts arrogantly all over the place. How can anyone feel at ease in a country where spies spread around news of huge rewards such as these, thus corrupting every decent quality and [87] infecting them with this spying disease. This is why, whether you're walking, sitting, or riding, it's impossible to turn round without seeing a spy writing things down, folding up a report, or getting into a carriage to go to Almabayn. Young people in cafés have started offering people a brazier and inkwell as soon as they come in; the spies make use of the first to burn tobacco, and the second to burn men.

Spies send their reports to Almabayn. Some of them use their own seal and send reports to one of the chamberlains with no address on the outside. These are dispatched to the Sultan immediately. This method is only used by key state officials and confidential spies. Other spies present their reports in open form to friends in Almabayn. The latter put them in envelopes, seal them with no address, and then hand them over to the chamberlains to be delivered to His Majesty the Sultan. If a spy is too slow in forwarding information to his friend in Almabayn, he is often blamed for his slackness and accused of choosing someone else as contact for his reports. In order to avoid the first and prove himself innocent of the second, he therefore proceeds to inflict misery on innocent people. Then woe betide any of his friends [88] whom he bumps into on the street. His name will form the rhyme word for his next line of poetry.

There's a remarkable story told by a man who used to visit the Minister of Police, Nazim Pasha, in his own home. A spy came to see him and told him that X (he named the person involved) was holding a wedding banquet that evening—as though such banquets were some kind of offense! Hardly had the spy finished speaking before two young men entered, their appearance showed all the manifestations of a life of luxury. Nazim Pasha greeted them both with a smile. After the two young men had had some coffee, one of them asked: "So what's the number of people `Efendina' has in mind to keep his children happy?" "Six," the Minister replied. The visitor was not paying any attention to this incredible scene, something that no one of the face of the earth had ever heard or witnessed before. It almost looked as though the young man were requesting a certain number of police in order to put on a show of status and pomp. The first young man now said the number was not enough, whereupon the Minister increased the figure to eight. The second young man now stood up and stood in front of him, looking even more submissive than the author when he was asking the Ministry of Education for permission to print his book. "Dispenser of bounty," he said, "our family is more numerous than that." When the visitor heard this last sentence, he suddenly realized what this remarkable scenario was all about; now he was all ears. The Minister raised the figure to ten. He instructed the police to go along with the two young men [89] and not to admit to the banquet any more than that number. The young men left. Funeral ceremonies might have been more appropriate than the joy of a wedding banquet. The visitor now turned to the Minister, his eyes speaking as loudly as his mouth. The Minister replied with a laugh that he was only trying to help the young men. He was the one who had made this regulation, and it was being applied throughout Istanbul. No one was allowed to give a banquet without first getting permission from the Police Department, stating how many people would be present. The purpose, he stated, was to make his task and theirs that much easier. It would be more difficult for spies to find such extensive scope for inventing lies and false rumors. He could then restrict his time to the responsibilities he already had, and people could relax without the ongoing threat of torture, cross-examination, imprisonment, and eventual release. He started complaining about the unbearable trials and tribulations he had to endure as part of his position; he noted that, during the few hours in which he could snatch some sleep, he would still be woken up six or seven times to receive official decrees about His Majesty the Sultan's private affairs. That was how spies managed to keep the Sultan on edge. Al-Shihab al-Khafaji[4] was able to survey the entire scene from behind the veil of absence and had this to say: "Istanbul is a silver tray loaded with vipers and scorpions."

Another strange tale [90] tells how a man from Salonika named `Abdallah Efendi was sitting in a café; he was extolling the piety and learning of a member of the `ulama'. As he left the café, he found the police waiting for him. They took him away to Yildiz. When he entered, he found an interrogator waiting for him. This man started asking him questions about the learned man he had been praising. He replied that he was a neighbor of theirs, and that his father had known the man for a long time. In these interrogation chambers there are places from which His Majesty the Sultan can survey the proceedings without ever being seen and thus personally direct the course of the investigation. For that reason the official in charge of the interrogation kept leaving the room for a while, then coming back and asking types of question that were quite beyond the scope of the man's knowledge. Did he, for example, know of any liaisons between the Grand Vizier and the Shaykh al-Islam? To that question he responded in the negative. He was completely at a loss, having no idea of how to reply to such questions. They then took him down into a dark subterranean vault where the poor devil was subjected to all kinds of torture and agony. Eight days later he was sent to the Police Department and brought into the offices of an investigative committee [91] that looks into private matters connected with the palace. After sitting him down, they asked for his name. With that, they proceeded to issue the following unbelievable verdict: In that `Abdallah Efendi from Salonika has committed a very grave crime, it is unanimously decreed that he shall be imprisoned for an unspecified period of time and permitted access to no one. The president of the committee and the other members signed it, and he was sent to prison. The prison where he was sent was tiny, and they made arrangements for the warden there to give him some bread and water at irregular intervals. One day, he tried to buy a type of food that the prison grocer did not have in his shop. The warden informed him that nothing could be brought in from the outside because the grocer had purchased the shop from the Police Department for 280 pounds per year and thus held the monopoly on prison purchases. Four months later, the officer ordered his release from prison, and the poor wretch emerged looking like a caveman, unkempt and filthy. No one recognized him. Some time later, he discovered that the learned man whom he had been praising was related to Imam Rashad al-din Efendi, the Crown Prince. Heaven knows what the spy in question had written and what elaborate stories he managed to concoct on that basis.

Spies [92] have been harassing the Armenian community in Istanbul, thereby reducing them to the kind of level that we can all see and hear for ourselves. The restriction and supervision of their activities were so awful as to beggar description. If a spy discovered a drawing on a cigarette carton or box of matches that looked like a sail, oar, rudder, or any other part of a ship, he would immediately take the item away. He would then write a report in which the Armenians would be accused of demanding independence. After all, they were employed in that type of trade, and the drawing in question portrayed a ship, which is a symbol of authority in their culture. Anything with a picture on it would be thrown on the fire. The Minister of Police would set to work, investigating, cross-examining, and searching diligently for the society created with the purpose of demanding independence. Spies used to spread out far and wide to uncover members of this "society." Some were put in prison, others were exiled, all via official decrees that were referred to his attention. The government imposed travel restrictions on Armenians which blocked their escape routes. Every ship leaving Istanbul is watched by no less than ten spies until the moment of departure.

When any government is so dominated by cowardice and fear, [93] when its affairs are run by despicable fools, when its entire body is infected by the spy disease, it is time to give its rulers the glad tidings that the whole edifice is on the point of collapse and ruin.

Al-Muqattam no. 1955, 28 August, 1895

One of the genuine scandals of this era of ours is the way in which public security in Istanbul, seat of the Sultan, capital of the empire, and residence of the Imamate, has been so adversely affected by allowing these spies to roam loose like a pack of wolves. The people they are attacking are the sheep asleep in the very paddock of the Caliph of Islam. The spies pilfer, steal, rifle, and falsify. They disgrace people, carry arms in public, and fire on the Sultan's weak and helpless flock. The various levels of court then proceed to issue verdicts against such spies. It is at this point, just when all that remains is to execute the sentence, that they are pardoned with a smile and their criminal record is trampled underfoot. Spies thus manage to avoid the penalty for whatever it is they are doing. That is exactly what happened to Hasan Fahmi Pasha, the spy mentioned above. He shot his son-in-law in his own house. In accordance with normal practice, he was brought before the courts. Newspapers gave full details of the sordid tale. The court sentenced him according to usual guidelines for the crime he had committed, but he was pardoned before the sentence could be executed. He got drunk [94] and started picking fights with people all over again. People should be weeping for justice, if they are able to do so; others should simply laugh at us Ottomans.

Much the same sort of things happened with Muhammad Mahri, another confidential spy and member of the town council (*shahre amanat*). He was in debt to a man whom he employed in his shop as a secretary in the period before he gained prestige and achieved the exalted status of spy. When the other man died, he forged a check and used it to claim one thousand pounds, a sum that he demanded be paid from the legacy. The case went to court. From the outset it was clear that he had forged the check. As a precaution, the court ordered that he be imprisoned, and he remained there for several months. Thereafter, every court, including the Court of Cassation, sentenced him to three years in prison and ordered him to repay the full amount he owed to the orphan heirs of the other man. But, just as the police were on the point of implementing the sentence, his pardon came flying on the wings of providence. For a long time afterward, this man was able to laugh at the courts and the law. It did not take long for him to be tyrannizing the weak and poor again.

Tell me, dear reader, which pregnant woman in this most honest and upright of cities does not exhaust honorable scribes with requests for written prayers and supplications, night and day, morning and evening, and all so that she can give birth to a spy? Which father is there who does not want to have a son [95] who will enter this profession, provided, of course, that he himself can be guaranteed immunity from the ravages that spies can cause. In Istanbul now many sons are now implicating their own fathers. Were it not for fear of boring the reader with too much detail, I would supply some names.

Every day one hears stories of crimes being pardoned and trumped up charges leading to prosecution and sentence. Charges brought against one spy were referred to the Appeal Court. The members of the bench could not agree on the length of sentence to impose, but the President calmed them all down and resolved the issue by pointing out that they should not waste time on cases in which the accused would be pardoned in any case.

Another curious fact is that the more astute shaykhs and other people who are fully in the know about the way things really work and the mystical secrets involved regularly resort to very arcane methods and a kind of sheer cunning in order to persuade spies to submit reports about them. All this happens in a situation when such shaykhs are already under suspicion for truly appalling offenses and have been accused of the most dreadful crimes. When such reports are submitted to His Majesty and he issues orders for them to be interrogated, they manage to get off by using precisely the avenues that they have managed to open up through the submission of these other reports. As a result, they emerge from the proceedings like a shot from a bow. That is the way they manage to ingratiate themselves and achieve the boon of being "proved innocent."

All these reports that His Majesty the Sultan keeps receiving inevitably leave their mark in his mind. [96] He is well aware of such people's real capacity to foment evil and corruption and of the fanatical way they use their influence to cause mayhem. As a result, some of them have managed to reach the ultimate levels of advancement and proximity to the Sultan himself. They have used such status to erect mansions to their own glory and employed such illusions to render themselves safe and secure. They then proceed to scare people and sit cross-legged on their seats of honor, not bothering about any report that may be written or letter that is printed. And, if His Majesty does get to hear any true reports about them, they start yelling and screaming, using previous reports that have since proved to be false as evidence of their innocence of any charges against them. What is truly remarkable is that some of them even present their misdeeds and crimes in a guise that cannot be recognized by the Devil himself or comprehended by normal human beings. With such amazing feats of cunning, they manage to extract good from bad and produce sweet honey from bitter colocynth. Often they succeed in hitting many targets with a single shot. To give an example: one night Yusuf Rida Pasha was having a drink with a spy whom he really detested. He wanted to take revenge, and so he started criticizing certain aspects of His Majesty the Sultan's policies. He cunningly persuaded the spy not to divulge a word of what he had said. The next morning, Rida Pasha went to the palace and begged the Sultan's forgiveness. [97] Without thinking of what I was doing, he said, I said certain things in the presence of X—please accept my humblest apologies; and with that he mentioned the name of the man in whose presence he had uttered the criticism. The Sultan was pleased to forgive him because of his display of loyalty and the fact that he had admitted his guilt without any need to involve an informer. Yusuf Rida Pasha also got his wish regarding his enemy, because the Sultan was furious that this spy had not passed on the criticisms he had heard. All this delighted the Sultan, since his own wisdom and discretion clearly have placed him firmly in control of affairs, kept people's tongues within proper bounds, and injected a sense of fear in their hearts. They have all been watched by a system of spies, to the degree that by now anyone who has committed a crime will rush to admit their offense before informers can report it. In that way the penalty will be that much less.

O God, all people can do is to stretch out their hands to beg for mercy and beseech You to drive these evil men far away from His Majesty the Sultan, the possessor of such power for good or evil. If just ten of them were jointly involved in the most well-organized state in the world, they would have it in ruins in a few days.

There's a group of spies whose task it is to stick like a shadow to the person they have been told to watch. Four such people watch the Shaykh al-Islam; the only time when they leave him is when he enters the women's quarters. When he is in there, [98] female spies take over the job. Thus, even though he is still fairly young and in the prime of his youth, you will notice how pale and thin he is. He's so weak that he can barely stand against a slight breeze. It's the same situation with the Grand Vizier; he can't move a single inch or say a word without it being noted down by the spies who are watching him.

Other spies accompany the carriages of members of the Sultan's family (*Al-Shah-zadat*). One of them rides a horse and stays fifty paces behind the carriage in question. They used to hang on to the carriages and jostle the retainers who rode behind, but then the Sultan's own son hit one of them for charging forward and behaving too brazenly. Thereafter they were told to stay at a distance. It's the job of an army general, Isma'il Pasha (and it was this job that recently got him the rank) to sneak behind trees and hide behind walls on the route taken by the Crown Prince, Rashad al-din Efendi. Every night he has to submit a report to Al-Hajj Mahmud Efendi, the Director of Humayuni protocol. In this report he records, for example, that the Crown Prince was in the park today; he kept scowling and frowning, and, when he got to such and such a place, he turned round and stared for some time. [99] When he passed such and such a spot, he put his head out of the carriage. There were two men on the street whom he has seen twice in consecutive days at the very same spot. With that, heaven and earth are turned upside down to locate those two men.

Many innocent people are taken into custody and accused of wrongdoing while the search goes on for these two imaginary men. If, for example, the General describes them by saying that one has a brown complexion and the other joined eyebrows, narrow eyes, or a red face, so much the worse for anyone with those particular features who just happens to be walking along the street. Different versions of events emerge from the interrogations because the people being questioned are scared to death and totally bewildered. Anyone who is being interrogated will automatically assume they are under suspicion and worry in case they are declared incompetent or insane if they do not confess to something. As a result, many people choose instead to keep their heads down and stay out of trouble.

One day during the festival season, Shaykh Muhammad Zafir encountered the Crown Prince's carriage on a narrow street. The Prince greeted him, but even so his blood froze and he felt shattered. Once he came to himself again, he went straight to the palace to see His Majesty the Sultan and tell him what had happened. He discovered that the spy had beaten him to it, [100] and the Sultan already knew the story. Later, when Hasan Agha, who had been appointed from Almabayn as the person in charge of service at Shaykh Zafir's *takiyya*, was accused of having some sort of connection with the Crown Prince, Shaykh Zafir himself was not free of suspicion, and all because of the greeting the Prince had given him, even though it was years earlier.

If the Crown Prince himself is beset and restricted like this, subject to all kinds of suspicion and fear so that people are kept away and not allowed to see him, what possible kind of relationship is he supposed to have with the people and they with him? All they get to see of him is a retiring person who is full of resentment because everyone hates him. Considering the restrictions placed on him and the contempt he has to endure, he has every reason to have such feelings.

This then is the great misfortune that people have to endure. Incredibly enough, people don't bother to think about the gravity of the situation. Their own misery or future felicity are both dependent on this situation, since human beings do not live for ever. If an Ottoman subject observes the kings of Europe and watches the way in which their crown princes are treated—the complete freedom that they have, the training they receive, the way they can travel abroad and mingle with political figures, they will weep [101] over the situation of the Ottoman Crown Prince. They will also come to realize that in this country authority has a different significance from that of other lands. Here it implies that the Sultanate is an inheritance that enables the Sultan to live a life of pleasure and luxury while his own people suffer through a regime of misery and hell:

Oh kings of the land, you have been given long life; and yet throughout it your practice has been oppression.

The goal of the people is pleasure; they feel no sympathy for the tears of women, fancy or otherwise.

NOTES

1. Muhammad Lazoghly was a major adviser and retainer to Muhammad `Ali as ruler of Egypt, beginning in 1805.

2. These Arab names are habitually used in grammatical examples in language textbooks.

3. A *takiyya* is a small shrine or mosque, often associated with one of the Sufi sects.

4. Shihab al-din al-Khafaji (d. 1695) was a prominent Egyptian litterateur and biographer who served for many years as a legal official during the Ottoman period.

• 8 •

Anniversary of the Sultan's Accession

Al-Muqattam no. 1958, 31 August, 1895

*O*n this august occasion in the year 1876, His Majesty Sultan Al-Ghazi `Abd al-Hamid Khan the Second acceded to the Sultan's throne and the Caliphs' chair through canonical inheritance from his fathers and forefathers—the succor of peoples and great provider. [102] May God grant happiness, prosperity, power, and glory to the Ottoman people and to him as this splendid anniversary comes round again! On this particular day, Istanbul, the Ottoman capital city and seat of the Caliphate, is decked out overall. The darkness of night is transformed into bright daylight, as the city's inhabitants show their delight and pleasure in view of the legitimate Sunni government. Ottoman newspapers publish poetry and incredibly hyperbolic descriptions that their owners have been planning and keeping in reserve all year, describing exactly how wonderful everything is and how pleasant life can be for the inhabitants of the capital city. The goal is to charm everyone and make the Sultan feel happy. For example, they will say that, on this most holy of nights, 250 million Muslims on the face of this earth all lift up their hands to the heavens in order to pray that His Majesty the Sultan may remain on the throne for all time. Were these upraised hands to be placed one on top the other, they would cover thousands of miles and reach to the very moon itself. With that the symbol of the crescent moon would indeed belong to the Sunni Ottoman Sultanate.

I have decided to describe here some of the real facts about the Ottoman Sultanate from `Abd al-Hamid's accession till now, [103] but without all the distortions that hyperbole brings with it. People will then come to realize that half the Ottoman dominions and the greater part of its international influence have been lost as a result of the treachery of traitors and swindlers, and in full view of the Europeans. The Sultan may then be able—and may God grant him support!—to take the necessary steps to correct things in what remains of his dominions, an area that already displays signs of the very disintegration that so marked the loss of the former territories. Everyone will then realize that the territories that the empire acquired through the blood of their fathers and grandfathers has been cheaply disposed of at the whim of some shaykh or other or else through the sheer ignorance of a eunuch. Then perhaps people will show their sense of loyalty by joining the Sultan in ridding the state of its enormous dilemma; overlooking past mistakes they can hope for better things to come.

When His Majesty ascended the throne, the Ottoman Empire was one of the most prestigious, powerful, and renowned in the entire world. Its fleet, which will now be passed over in silence for sheer embarrassment and shame, was second only to France. According to a census conducted by an Ottoman military newspaper, the empire consisted of 42 million inhabitants: 10 million in Europe, 14.5 million in Asia, 11.5 million in Africa, and 6 million in Romania and Serbia. [104] In Europe, Bulgaria, Bosnia, Herzegovina, Montenegro, and Thessaly were all lost, with 4 million inhabitants. Then came Romania and Serbia, with 6 million. In Africa Tunisia was lost and also Egypt and its dependencies, with 10.5 million. Only Tripoli remains, with a million inhabitants. In Asia, Cyprus, Kars, Batum, and Ardehan were all lost, with 1 million inhabitants. The portion that has been lost is bigger than the one that remains.

The first item on the page of miseries to which fate has granted victory was the Bulgarian rebellion and the slaughter it caused, exactly the same kind of thing as we now see happening in Armenia. The great powers started demanding that the Ottoman government implement reforms, specifying them by category just as they are now doing with Armenia. The Ottoman government resisted those reforms (as it is doing today), declaring instead its intention of implementing reforms throughout the empire. His Majesty the Sultan hurriedly issued a decree ordering the creation of a Chamber of Deputies and promulgation of the Basic Law. He discovered however—God give him support!—that some members of his entourage were bent on blocking the implementation of these measures. [105] So Midhat Pasha called together an assembly of Istanbul's notables in the Sublime Porte and asked them for their assistance by providing a definitive response that could be presented by the state to the great powers. This assembly agreed unanimously to reject the great powers' demands and instead to implement more widespread reforms immediately. In accordance with the published decree they moved ahead to publish the Basic Law and organize the Chamber of Deputies. With this decision Midhat Pasha was aiming to put an end to all procrastination by implementing the text of the decree and closing the door in the face of people who kept trying to delay things. However, His Majesty the Sultan strongly disliked Midhat Pasha because the latter was very popular and enjoyed the backing of the great powers in carrying out these measures. He therefore ordered Midhat Pasha's exile to Europe before the chamber even had the chance to meet or the decree itself was formally published. Had the Sultan waited until such time as both measures were enacted, he would certainly have not been able to exile Midhat Pasha. This action made it clear to the powers that things were not quite the way they seemed on the surface; with the expulsion of the one man who was striving for reform, their suspicions that the Ottoman government was not serious were confirmed. As a result, the powers intensified their demands for reform in Bulgaria, and the confusion in Istanbul became even worse. Now everyone was very nervous, and rumors abounded. His Majesty the Sultan decided that, by acknowledging Russia's declaration of war, he would be able to divert people's attention from what was happening inside his own dominions. Once the declaration of war had been acknowledged, [106] the government came to realize that it was completely unprepared for such a terrible conflict. His Majesty the Sultan therefore issued an order convening the Chamber of Deputies specifically so that the government could transfer responsibility for the war on to its shoulders. In fact the Chamber of Deputies itself acknowledged the war declaration. Once the government had obtained exactly what it needed, the chamber was immediately dissolved.

The government was now eager to imitate the actions of the German government during its war with France. Germany had placed responsibility for all war organization and military strategy in the hands of Marshal [Helmuth von] Moltke. In a similar way all orders for maneuvers on the battlefield were issued to commanders of the Ottoman army from Yildiz with the collaboration of Mahmud Pasha al-Damad. The palace managed to overlook the significant facts that the maps of France that Moltke had in front of him were far more accurate than the ones the French army itself had, that the Ottoman government's own maps had been purchased on the open market, and that Mahmud Pasha al-Damad was no von Moltke. Several times, the palace ordered an advance, but the only result was a setback; on the other hand, on several occasions when a delay was ordered, that was the wrong decision too. Following Al-Ghazi `Uthman Pasha's return from Russia [107], he was questioned in the Council of State Secretaries as to why he had allowed himself to be boxed in at Polivna and had not broken his way out while he could. From his pocket he produced several telegrams which instructed him to stay put. One of the secretaries was bold enough to reprimand him for his conduct, telling him that he should have informed his superiors that the person on the spot can make judgments which others many miles away cannot. The Ghazi replied that a soldier is bound to obey his Supreme Commander without question. Many of these maneuvers are said to have been based on decisions arrived at via astrology, geomancy, and even dreams. Some shaykhs are even believed to have informed His Majesty the Sultan that the Russian Emperor had been taken prisoner. Some loyal friends of His Majesty counseled him to follow the precedent set by his fathers and forefathers in times of war and by the Russians too by traveling to Edirne. However, even though His Majesty had previously gone out to raise the morale of his troops in the course of bringing victory to the Ottoman state, this time he refused and sent Mahmud Pasha al-Damad in his place. But then fate makes decisions that neither counsel nor resolution can alter.

The sufferings of the Ottoman army in this conflict are enough to make your heart melt. [108] War preparations were totally inadequate: shortages of food and clothing, poor medical treatment, and no burial for the dead. The Red Crescent Society was created to collect contributions from people of charity. General Husayn Pasha went from Tunisia to the battlefront, bringing with him money that had been collected by himself and the people of Tunisia once he had drawn their attention to the problem. When he returned from the front to Istanbul, His Majesty the Sultan instructed Sa`id Pasha (the present Grand Vizier who at the time was Chief Clerk to the Sultan) to invite Husayn Pasha to one of the Sultan's banquets. He sat beside Sa`id Pasha and started telling him some of the things he had witnessed and the terrible straits in which the Ottoman army found itself (lack of clothing in the freezing cold weather, hunger, and injuries). As he spoke, tears were streaming down his face, since he was a man who had given his total devotion to the Ottoman state. When he got up to wash his hands, he discovered that the basin he was offered was made of pure gold, as were all the other vessels. He refused to use it to wash his hands. He said that, now that he had witnessed the plight of Muslim soldiers, defenders of Islam and the Ottoman state in time of war, he could not possibly use such a basin to wash his hands in the Caliph's own residence. When His Majesty heard his comment, [109] he issued orders for his immediate exile from Istanbul. He left and was never able to return to Istanbul for the rest of his life, and all because he spoke the truth.

As the situation worsened and defeat loomed on the horizon, the palace decided that it needed to transfer responsibility for negotiating a peace onto the chamber's shoulders once again. Orders were therefore issued for the chamber to reconvene. However, when the members met, they were not as obliging as on the first occasion. They demanded an investigation of the reasons for the defeat; the Army Commander was requested to attend the meeting for questioning. When His Majesty's entourage got wind of this demand, they informed His Majesty that this would be merely the first stage in the process whereby the Chamber of Deputies would annul all his sacred powers. If members had their way this time, they told him, they would summon the

Grand Vizier next; before long, they would even be so bold as to request that Sultan's attendance. His Majesty the Sultan now issued a decree dismissing the chamber's members and exiling some of its more famous figures.

As the situation turned into a total debacle and the Russians came ever closer to Istanbul itself, the Ottomans asked the great powers to intervene. Only England answered the call, immediately dispatching its fleet to the Dardanelles. [110] Meanwhile, the Russian Grand Duke reached San Stefano. When he learned that the British fleet had been dispatched, he agreed to start negotiations for peace. The Treaty of San Stefano was signed [3 March, 1878], with all its serious consequences for the Ottoman state. When England heard about the clauses in the treaty that were detrimental to the Ottoman Empire, it forced the great powers to convene a conference. All states agreed except France, which stipulated that there should be no discussion of Egypt, Syria, or Jerusalem—all of which made it clear to the British that they should get to Egypt first.

When the conference convened in Berlin [June–July, 1878], the powers all sent their top officials and foreign ministers. The Ottoman government chose as its representative Iskandar Qarra Tivaduri Pasha, a man of Greek origin who is now Governor of Crete, along with a field marshal. He was of considerably lower rank than the other participants at the conference and participated less in the discussions because he was neither an important figure in the Ottoman government nor even a State Secretary. By not sending its most important minister to a conference which had been convened specifically for its own benefit, the Ottoman government obviously made a huge mistake. It behaved in exactly the same way when it sent `Ali Pasha as its representative to the Paris Conference; and what a representative he turned out to be!

[111] It is really peculiar that Greece was given Thessaly and Ibir at this conference, although the Greek government had no representative there and was not involved in the war itself. Some statesmen have suggested that Qarra Tivaduri Pasha was sent to represent the Ottoman government and Greece, and successfully represented both governments. The conference handed over to Montenegro a port called Dolshino. After the conference the Ottoman government was slow about surrendering it, so the great powers sent a fleet in to see that it was handed over; the Ottoman government eventually did so. This and other instances clearly show that the Ottoman government's word carries little weight with the great powers.

It was the British government that played the largest part in preventing the Russians from entering Istanbul, the Caliphal seat, also in buttressing the Ottoman throne. His Majesty the Sultan had in fact already decided to leave Istanbul and go back to Bursa, the old seat of the Ottoman dynasty; actually he had already transferred the royal treasures to the boat. It also played a decisive role in getting the Treaty of San Stefano annulled; otherwise it would have been the death knell for the Ottoman government. [112] Britain also played a major role in convening the conference that guaranteed the protection of Ottoman territories. Only someone eager to delude himself can gainsay the truth of these statements.

The conference concluded by granting independence to the dominions under the rule of the Ottoman government, removing their territories from the empire and placing them instead under the protection of the great powers. Before the Paris Conference [1880] Prince Maeternick, the Austrian minister and a famous politician, advised the Ottoman government to put its affairs in good order so that there would be no need for protection from the great powers. As he pointed out, the "protector" has the right to interfere in internal affairs, and one day that would prove detrimental to Ottoman interests. That is precisely what has happened with the Ottoman government today. Half a century later, Maeternick's prediction has become a reality.

Then the conference broke up. Meanwhile, countries had been demolished, many men killed, money wasted, and Russia had almost reached the very gates of Istanbul. The Ottoman government had been forced to ask the great powers for help. When Britain was the only one to answer the call, they had to put up with Britain's "kindness." The Ottoman government's representative returned to Istanbul with only half its former empire. All these events happened as the result of an attempt to implement reforms in one Ottoman province, and the same thing is happening now. That is the reason why it cannot get independence not merely for itself but also arrange it for other provinces as well. Now it is up to the Ottoman government to compare present with past [113] and implement the necessary reforms quickly before the same thing happens to the second half of the empire as did to the first. Only then can it make sure that another conference is not held which will abolish the entire empire.

Once the conference had concluded and the empire endured such severe losses, His Majesty the Sultan was apprehensive about appointing any Ottoman citizen as Vizier, in case the obvious mistakes that the government had made were revealed. So he decided to bring in a Vizier from abroad, namely Khayr al-Din Pasha. He summoned him from Tunis, where the Bey had already dismissed him in anger and forbidden him to communicate with anyone. Khayr al-Din left Tunisia and came to Istanbul. He was duly appointed Grand Vizier. His Majesty the Sultan made Khayr al-Din swear on the Qur'an and the *Sahih* of Al-Bukhari[1] that he would not involve himself in any conspiracies against the Sultan's person, while the Sultan in turn promised not to fire him. The first thing that Khayr al-Din wanted to do was to take revenge on Al-Sadiq Bey, the Governor of Tunisia. He therefore offered his assistance in the deposition of Isma`il Pasha, the Khedive of Egypt, and sent his former master a letter, threatening to inflict the very same consequences on him too and in the near future. Al-Sadiq Bey rushed to seek the protection of the French government as a way of warding off his former servant's evil designs; truly the servant had now become a ruler. This of course gave France [114] the opportunity to keep the Ottoman government quiet by handing over Midhat Pasha when he sought asylum in the French consulate in Izmir. The Ottoman government now set about trying Midhat Pasha and his colleagues, while France set about making Tunisia a protectorate. Both parties thus achieved their objectives: France got Tunisia, and His Majesty the Sultan was able to exile Midhat Pasha, Nuri Pasha, Rushdi Pasha, Shaykh al-Islam Khayrallah Efendi, and Mahmud Pasha al-Damad.

Mahmud al-Damad was the one who had been jealous of Al-Sayyid Abu al-Huda because the latter was on such familiar terms with His Majesty the Sultan. This all went so far that he intimated to His Majesty that it was not in accord with the glory of the Sultan to allow "one of those Arabs" to play any role in important affairs of state. As a reward for this insult directed at a people among whom numbered the Prophet himself, God inspired the Sultan to exile him to the Arabian Peninsula where he found himself humiliated and eventually died. The major figures in Istanbul often use the term *Arab* as an insult; by "Arab," they imply "Negro" or "Black dog." As an example, one of the Sultan's own doctors with the rank of general, named `Arif Pasha, was present in a very crowded company. He was having an argument with someone, [115] and things became so heated that threats were exchanged. "If I don't do such and such to you," he said in a fury, "then I'm an Arab." No one should be allowed to utter such things in the seat of the Caliph of the Arab Prophet. However this is just another thing to add to the list of terrible things we have been mentioning already.

Once Tunisia had been lost, the `Urabi Revolt occurred in Egypt [in 1882]. Once again the politics of greed managed to reduce the situation to its current disastrous state. The Ottoman government was convinced it had found a way to use political intrigue as a means of retrieving some of the concessions that Sultan Mahmud had made to Egypt in the form of capitulations. There was correspondence between the shaykhs and Ahmad `Urabi, and Al-Sayyid As`ad even went to Egypt from the Hijaz and met `Urabi himself. When he returned to Istanbul, he gave His Majesty the Sultan a glowing report on `Urabi; it would be in the Ottoman government's interests, he said, for `Urabi to be in Egypt. The Ottoman government refused to send any troops to Egypt because of objections from the shaykhs that the Caliph's prestige would be damaged if he sent any troops to fight against fellow Muslims; this would be particularly the case among Muslims in India who, with a thought to the future, were being wooed by the Ottoman government through the shaykhs' mediation. His Majesty the Sultan therefore sent [116] the late Darwish Pasha to see the ex-Khedive and As`ad Pasha to see `Urabi. Both men kept up a private correspondence with His Majesty the Sultan, although Al-Sayyid As`ad did not encounter the same level of hospitality with `Urabi as he did on his first visit, because of the latter's reliance on Shaykh Zafir. As a result, he wrote a report which was forwarded from the Grand Vizier's office to Almabayn in which he requested the issuing of a decree declaring `Urabi's movement to be a revolt. Among `Urabi's offenses was that he belittled the members of the Prophet's family and showed no interest in them.

The upshot of all this was that the Egyptian question was handed over to the shaykhs and Bahram Agha. The Sublime Porte only got to hear about it from official correspondence, all in accordance with current practice. When His Majesty the Sultan summoned a group of government officials to a meeting in Almabayn under the chairmanship of the Grand Vizier, Sa`id Pasha, one of the officials asked the Grand Vizier how they could possibly discuss a problem about which they knew nothing. The government had instructed newspapers not to print a single word about it, and any foreign newspaper that included information about Egypt had been banned. [117] To which the Grand Vizier replied that he knew no more than the official who had asked the question.

Is England supposed to quit Egypt when it hears that France has demanded that it not be mentioned at the Berlin conference? Will they give it up when they know full well that France bought the Ottoman government's silence about Tunisia by handing over Midhat Pasha? What confidence can they have about Egypt when they see its affairs handed over to the shaykhs? Will they be happy to leave when they were the ones who rescued the Ottomans from the clutches of Russia?

As current events show all too clearly, the second half of the Ottoman Sultanate is turning into a carbon copy of the first; our previous articles have clearly shown that to be the case. We will not prolong matters by repeating the information. Who can tell what the future will bring?

> Abandon all encomia and congratulations;
>   More appropriate to our situation are elegies of condolence.

We ask God to grant His Majesty the Sultan all success in supporting the people and government and in distancing from his illustrious person all traitors and manipulators of his own virtue. Amen!

NOTE

1. Al-Bukhari (d. 870), compiler of one of the two authoritative collections of "*hadith*," accounts of the Prophet Muhammad's sayings and actions during his lifetime, that constitute, after the Qur'an itself, a major source of Islamic law and conduct. The other collection is by Muslim ibn al-Hajjaj (d. 875).

· 9 ·

Spies (II)

Al-Muqattam no. 1964, 7 September, 1895

There's an incredible story about a man from Tripoli, Lebanon, named `Abd al-Hamid, who came to Istanbul to take a job in the Justice Department. Munif Pasha knew him already and came to offer his respects (in accordance with the normal practice of people in Istanbul). The Pasha inquired as to when he had arrived and where he was staying. The man replied that he had arrived that very day and was staying in Yildiz. The Pasha, thinking by "Yildiz" the man meant the Sultan's own palace, asked how that could possibly be the case. To which the man responded that he was staying in a hotel near Al-Sarkaji called Yildiz (which means "star"). Munif Pasha stood up at once. He told the man to move out of the hotel as quickly as possible and find another one. The man stood up too, feeling absolutely astonished; he could not understand why he had been given such curt instructions. "Have you forgotten that your name is `Abd al-Hamid," the Pasha told him, "and that the hotel is called 'Yildiz'? What kind of disaster are you trying to bring down on your own head and mine too?" When the man realized the coincidence that he had not taken into consideration, [119] he almost passed out. He left at once, cursing his father and mother as he went. When he reached the hotel, he found a group of policemen already waiting for him. Now if only this level of alertness and speed could be applied in the public interest, we would be ahead of everyone else! They took the man away for interrogation. When he emerged from the terrifying ordeal, his mind had gone and so had his money. For a while he stayed in Istanbul with this coincidence as a kind of "blessing," but he was not able to find either a job or any assistance.

It should not come as a surprise to readers to see Munif Pasha, Minister of Education and a wise and brilliant figure, worrying about this matter even more than it deserves. On one occasion he too had been struck like a thunderbolt by the word *Yildiz*. In his case he had written a book in which he happened to mention the glowworm, an insect with a tail that glows like a star at night. He described it as a "Yildiz animal" (using Yildiz in the sense of "star"). Spies raced to the palace and submitted reports to the effect that Munif Pasha was attacking His Majesty the Sultan by using the double-entendre glowworms to mean "Yildiz animals." Munif Pasha was immediately dismissed [120] and was dogged by bad luck for five years, and all because he had aroused His Majesty the Sultan's wrath by using a single word in its literal meaning. However, the spies managed to pull back the drapes and open the Sultan's eyes with all these trumped up stories. If only they had to face some kind of penalty, they would think twice about launching these assaults on the Sultan's throne and burdening it with these phony interpretations. It is incredible to see how they manage to distort the facts, so that the guilty person is made innocent and vice versa. All this is achieved through largesse, methods of persuasion, the powers of magic and hypnotism, and still other means that remain unknown to us.

Another story relates how a spy wrote a report to the Minister of Police, stating that Mustafa Rushdi Efendi, a member of the Education Council, had in his possession some papers that were prejudicial to the Sultanate and the Sultan in person. The Minister sent the police to raid his home, and they took away piles of books and papers. They immediately brought in a translator from the Sublime Porte so he could translate for them. He discovered that they were replete with crimes and offenses. He ordered Mustafa Rushdi imprisoned. That made Al-Sayyid As`ad very angry because Mustafa Rushdi was a protégé and favorite of his. Al-Sayyid As`ad now complained to His Majesty the Sultan about the Minister of Police's actions, [121] accusing the latter of undue haste. Meanwhile, the Minister of Police had been sending copies of the translations of the papers to His Majesty the Sultan hour by hour. Al-Sayyid As`ad had no idea of their contents. They actually contained the kind of attacks on the Caliphate and His Majesty the Sultan that no Shiite would have ever produced to discredit the Umayyad Caliph Al-Walid ibn Yazid [d. 744]. They contained secret information, details of atrocities in the Hijaz, and other activities of the Sharif which would cause anyone to complain, be he Muslim or otherwise. Every time the Minister of Police read another translation of these documents, he made the terms of imprisonment yet more severe. When Al-Sayyid As`ad learned of the contents of these documents, he felt very uneasy. He was terrified because he had come to the defense of this personage in the Sultan's own presence. At this point, "the lion of the squadron caught up with him amid the throng," in that Al-Sayyid Abu al-Huda enters the picture. Actually one of the man's friends had already asked Abu al-Huda how to get out this fix. Abu al-Huda replied that they should not worry; they would put the entire problem on the shoulders of Kamil Pasha, the Grand Vizier, who was acknowledged as being a great expert on such matters and someone who did not flinch under fire. Before the Minister of Police was even aware of what was going on, an official decree was published setting Mustafa Rushdi free, making him a gift of fifty pounds, and giving him his job back. Everyone was astonished, and justifiably so. [122] What is peculiar is that the Minister of Police was holding the decree in one hand and the translation of the two famous lines denouncing the Caliph Musa al-Hadi [d. 786] in the other (the ones that start: He fornicates with refuse, etc. . . .). Rushdi composed many similar lines in order to show what conditions were really like at the moment; he also did a good deal of talking about decrees which had by now lost much of their value and significance because there were simply too many of them. One example is: "Decrees are now as common and plentiful as locusts' eggs." If anyone else had spoken this type of drivel without the backing of someone really important, he would have been given some exemplary punishment. It was this man, Mustafa Rushdi, who was used as a pretext for removing Kamil Pasha from his ministerial post. The two Al-Sayyids, managed to get a decree from His Majesty the Sultan so that Munif Pasha, the Minister of Education, could appoint Mustafa Rushdi to a post in his ministry. They were both fully aware of the fact that Munif Pasha would refuse to accept him because he was well aware of Rushdi's stupidity and irresponsible attitude. The decree was sent back, stating that no post in the Ministry of Education was vacant at that time. A report was immediately forwarded, stating that, when Munif Pasha had met Mustafa Rushdi, he had told him that his little piece of paper (using the diminutive)—meaning the official decree—had arrived but that there was no place for him in the ministry. This report confirmed a direction that people were working on at the time, namely that Kamil Pasha and all his ministers kept on belittling decrees issued by the Sultan. [123] For this reason the Ministry that had been in charge of administering the Sultan's affairs for six years was dismissed:

> O you lovers of reform in an era when Reform itself has become an object of hate!

So how can what remains of the empire be saved? How can it be liberated from the clutches of spies, people whose mouths are split at the edge because they consume so much in bribes, whose very intestines are a version of the purest hell through having to digest so much ill-gotten gain? They extend their hands to garner a harvest of sin, and simply smile at the calamities brought on by tyranny. Reluctant to do charitable acts, blind to the concept of justice, they turn aside when truth is uttered and devote themselves instead to all varieties of evil. To besmirch someone's honor they will crane their necks; to the fount of all falsehood they run hotfoot. They are renowned for their opposition to justice, and masters in the concealment of their own deceit.

> If Al-Dajjal[1] himself were to watch them in action,
>   He would be shedding tears from his only eye.

What can I say; what can anyone say? What can I or anyone else write down to describe a group of people who maintain a distance from all kinds of resistance, argument, disagreement, or discussion? Their only weapon is an oath on God's name on some occasions, and a threatened divorce of their wife on others.

> Abu al-Muthanna is being as deceitful as can be
>   When he swears an oath to divorce his wife.

[124] What can I say about people who would sell the Virgin's own dowry (peace be upon her!) if it were to come into their hands, and all in order to buy pickaxes with which to destroy the Kaaba itself if one of their schemes made such a thing necessary? They have employed the Caliph's title as a kind of noose with which to rob the state of all benefit and instead to cause severe damage. They have managed to achieve all this through cooperation and lending each other support.

In His Majesty's own dreams they are the ones who snore the loudest when they are asleep. They imagine fate to be sleeping with them. It only requires a single gesture from the Caliph, one small decision, to finish them off; and then no magic or magician will be of any help.

A worthy State Secretary has said that the Sultanate has lost all its authority as a result of Zayd's oath, `Amr's rosary, and Bakr's toothpick.[2] Someone told him that there was one decree that could put it all right, namely freedom to publish. This has happened, thank God! Even though that right may not exist in Istanbul, it is certainly there in Egypt.

[125] Here we all are, yelling, writing, publishing, and sending things in every direction by all means, and all with the goal of conveying to His Majesty the Sultan the reality of the demise of the Ottoman Empire at the hands of these men, with all their trickery, swindling, and deceit. It would be possible to send a recording machine to the Holy Kaaba itself and the noble enclosure and then to remit statements of people in misery whose very laps are soaked with tears in the holiest of places. His Majesty would then be able to hear the information for himself and could spare people who live close to God's own house from the clutches of a group of men who regard the Hijaz as their own private province and consider it permissible to shed the blood of pilgrims inside the Holy Mosque itself. It is surely conceivable that just once the Sultan

might choose not to believe their solemn oaths and instead come to realize that they are not only telling lies but also hatching their own schemes. With his own pure hand he would be able to lift the state out of the abyss of decline and save its people from the aftermath of despair. People who have suffered wrongs will no longer have to complain so loudly where nominative and genitive cases have been used so long.

So far have these spies gone in their modes of deceit that not even the Qur'an serves as a deterrent. Certainly no Sultan can restrain them. They have shattered all bounds of conduct and ripped away the veils of prestige and pavilions of splendor. From His Majesty the Sultan they have conveyed to the populace things that have for ever eradicated the awe and respect that they used to have for him, while in the opposite direction they have made known to the Sultan the kind of opinions and expressions that no Ottoman who really loved his country and its Sultan would ever consider using. You will discover that everyone who arrives in Istanbul feels hopeful, content, and cheerful; they pray that His Majesty the Sultan may be successful and victorious. They are prepared to discount information in the free press, if it comes from Egypt, firmly believing that it is false. But, once anyone has been there for twenty days or so, he changes his mind. Now he starts to believe the things that recently he found implausible and keeps his tongue active in prayers of entreaty to God and in statements of sheer despair. If such a person were to meet any of the people whom I have been describing here for just a single day, he would leave Istanbul utterly despairing of any change for the good or any likelihood of reform. Instead he would despise the very things he once admired, discount everything he first thought impressive, and regard everything he once considered of value as cheap and useless. In the end he would hate everything he once loved. To God alone belongs the power and might!

NOTES

1. Al-Dajjal is one of the dire figures who, according to the texts of Islamic eschatology, is to appear at the Day of Judgment.

2. Once again, these names are regularly used in order to illustrate grammatical principles in Arabic textbooks.

· 10 ·

Splendor of the Caliphate
and Magnificence of the Sultanate

Al-Muqattam no. 1970, 14 September, 1895

$\mathcal{S}$tates differ greatly in the way they choose to enhance their own glory. [127] Some choose iron for this purpose, thereby following what God Almighty states in the Qur'an: "We sent down iron which has tremendous strength and will benefit people." [Qur'an, Sura 57, v. 25] The state therefore uses it as the basis of its glory. It manufactures fleets, weapons, guns, defenses, forts, steam devices, railroads, and various other types of energy that can be produced from it. As a result the enemies of such a state beyond its frontiers come to fear it. If such a state makes a definitive statement, then it is final; if it makes a political gesture, then that is law. This assemblage of power in so many aspects has one principal goal, to convince foreign powers of the state's greatness in order to force them to recognize the deterrent force it possesses. People living in such a state will work to their utmost potential and ability to achieve this goal, and the prince of the realm will be no less diligent in his pursuit of the goal than the hired hands.

The Caliph `Umar—God be pleased with him!—often descended to the people's level with this particular idea in mind.[1] [128] When, for example, he heard that Rustum had come down as far as Qadisiyya, he used to go out every day and ask the messengers for news; this went on from sunrise till noon. After that he would return to his family. Finally, when the good news of victory at the Battle of Qadisiyya was brought by a messenger, `Umar was there as usual to meet him.[2] "Give me your news, `Abdallah," the Caliph asked. The messenger said that the enemy had been defeated, whereupon `Umar asked more questions. The Caliph was on foot, while the messenger was still mounted on his camel. When the messenger entered the city of Al-Madina, everyone greeted `Umar as the Commander of the Faithful and started offering their congratulations. The man immediately dismounted. "Commander of

103

the Faithful," he asked, "why didn't you tell me—may God have mercy on you!" "My dear man," said `Umar, "I do not hold anything against you."

Other states prefer gold, regarding it as a more succinct method of attaining their goals. In such a case the ruling family's aims will differ from those of the populace. People holding the reins of power will endeavor to persuade the populace how important the state and its rulers are. Their only concern is that the state's splendor and glory be acknowledged within the country itself. They dazzle people by making something as incredibly important as gold seem almost cheap and despicable. They achieve that by using it to flaunt all kinds of display and decoration [129] which manages to dumbfound all those who get to look at it. In that way they convince the populace that the state is achieving its goal of importance and prestige and that foreign powers view it in the same way. That is why you can find people listening in delight as someone tells them about the contents of the state's treasure-house: how the throne of Sultan Al-Ghuri[3] is encrusted with pearls and rubies, and the stirrups—a gift to Sultan Mahmud from Muhammad `Ali—are made of emeralds. They can go on and on talking about these fabulous jewels. But in England, for example, nobody talks about the London Arsenal. Just to illustrate this point, there will be readers of this very chapter who will spend time preferring to inquire about this stirrup made of emeralds, rather than bothering with the story about the Maghribi at the end of it.

Since the Ottoman Sultanate outstrips every European power in its pomp and splendor by acquiring all these elaborate ceremonial ornaments, I have decided to describe the pomp in its different aspects, covering the festival celebrations and stately processions one by one. The first that I will describe is the procession to the Friday prayers, something people travel from Europe to witness.[4] [130] Caesar in his triumphal victory procession, Alexander on his day of glory—I beg God's indulgence—Sa`d returning from Qadisiyyah, Mu`tasim from Amoreum,[5] none of these mighty historical figures could fill people's hearts with a great sense of awe or offer them such a splendid spectacle as that of the Sultan's procession on Friday. He becomes the cynosure of the populace, the delight of their hearts, true embellishment of the Sultanate and ornament of the state—may the firmament of Yildiz Palace continue to be his rising place and the heart of the populace his setting place for many, many years and generations to come!

Two hours before noon on Fridays soldiers and horsemen are dispatched from various parts of Istanbul to Beshiktash. They number more than ten thousand and are stationed in the streets leading to the Sultan's palace until such time as the official decree is published fixing the actual mosque he will attend. This ritual is continued today even though the Hamidian mosque is now the only one used for His Majesty's prayers. Once the decree is published, soldiers assemble in the mosque square in front of the palace gate and form up in two rows, one behind the other. Meanwhile the carriages of field marshals, ministers, shaykhs, foreign ambassadors, and others are all fighting each other for space. Ambassadors and other senior legates in Istanbul sit in the hall of the Humayuni Purse overlooking the square. Here there is no voice or neighing to be heard, just the rattle of swords and [131] the gasps of awe and reverence from onlookers, waiting in anticipation for the light of the Sultan's presence to grace the scene. When the time for prayer arrives, the Sultan's gold carriage emerges from the palace just like the rising sun. Inside is the Imam, the deputy of the Prophet of God—prayers and blessings upon Him!—with Al-Ghazi `Uthman Pasha sitting in front of him. Field marshals and senior officials from Almabayn are evenly spaced around the carriage and walk with eyes lowered, overcome as they are by the magnificence of the Imam's glory. On other occasions, these same men are the Chosroes's of their time, veritable Caesars in their power and influence. They too are swimming in a sea of gold clothing, all of them wearing medals on their chests that dazzle the eye and stir the heart. The spectator can hardly avoid repeating the phrase "Praise be to God!" time and time again as he considers the sheer number of loyal and devoted men in service to state and people whom He has bestowed on the Ottoman state. That at least might be the impression to be gathered from the words uttered over these decorations, were it not for the fact that the same spectator would be entitled to have severe doubts about their merits. The decoration serves as a title which the state creates and puts on the chest of its bearer as a token to the populace of the twin virtues of zeal and enthusiasm concealed behind it. Thus, when whatever is written on the decoration differs significantly from the things hidden behind it, [132] then the situation becomes similar to that of a salesman putting a label saying "rose water" on a bottle of vinegar.

With all due pomp and splendor the carriage proceeds—with all felicity and good fortune, envied by the very stars and protected by retinues of troops—till it reaches the Sultan's stairway into the mosque. His Majesty enters through the shaykhs' row. First among them is the Shaykh al-Islam, then Sayyid Fadl Pasha al-`Alawi, then Al-Sayyid As`ad, then Al-Sayyid Abu al-Huda, then Al-Sayyid Jamal al-Din al-Afghani, then the supervisor of religious endowments, along with certain ministers and field marshals who form part of the entourage.[6] The Sultan greets them with a gesture of his noble hand; sometimes he will even address a word or two to the Shaykh al-Islam out of respect for his position and single out some of the people standing there for a smile. Then he goes to a special place where he performs his prayers by himself. The ranks of Ottoman soldiers stand in the square, waiting until His Majesty honors the palace with his return following completion of his prayers.

Words cannot describe the level of surveillance and protection under which the mosque is guarded on all of its six sides. You can easily spot hulking guards preventing anyone, however important he may be, from looking out through windows. The mosque roof is covered by loads of spies and detectives. No one can enter the mosque for prayer without being searched like a thief who has made off with the center stone from a ring. Once inside the mosque, he finds a spy sitting on his left and another on his right, and two more behind ready to pounce. Should the poor devil try to yell out that he has been wronged, these bodyguards rush to cover his mouth before he can utter a single word. Four of them then bundle him away like some scroll being folded up for secretaries; he is then taken away to the interrogation prison. Once there the wretches proceed to tie his ribs together, whereupon the interrogator extracts his spinal cord. As a direct result of this, very few people come to the mosque from outside to pray, and the spies and bodyguards are essentially left on their own. In his sermon the preacher has to be careful to avoid any verse or *hadith* that contains any exhortation to act justly, eschew tyranny, or even hint at any encouragement of the notion of avoidance of what is forbidden and promoting what is right. Only one *hadith* is used in the Friday sermon, and it was chosen because it is almost impossible to interpret: "God is beautiful and loves beauty." [134] At the Greater Bayram festival, they substitute another *hadith*: "Fatten your animal sacrifices." The same situation applies to all mosques in Istanbul; only these two *hadith*s can be used.

Once the prayer is over, His Majesty the Sultan leaves the same way as he entered. All the waiting soldiers now yell out shouts of praise and joy and prayers. The crowd disperses, and the soldiers all return to their posts.

Here I'll mention a story. One of the `ulama' from the far West happened to be passing through Istanbul. He still had the basic roughness of desert life in him. When he saw the Sultan's procession and the thousands of soldiers standing around and not praying at the proper prayer time, he asked one of the shaykhs of the Sultan's entourage a question, displaying thereby an arrogance hardly appropriate for someone addressing a Qadi Askar Rumeli: "Tell me, Shaykh of Istanbul, does the *shari`a* law allow tens of thousands of people to stand around the mosque when they have all heard the call to prayer themselves and watch other people praying? None of them, it seems, dares to pray because their actions are controlled by some law or other. Praise be to God! Shaykh of Istanbul, has a servant's ruling overridden God's own command? God Almighty proclaims: [135] 'You who believe, when the call to prayer is given on Friday, hurry to remember God and leave your selling. This is the best thing for you, if you but knew it. When the prayer is finished, then disperse into the land and seek God's bounty. Remember God often so that you may prosper.'[7] The officer tells the soldier to stand there but not to pray. As a result the soldier is obeying the servant, but both are disobeying their Lord. After such behavior do you still seek victory from your Lord. He it is who says: 'If you help God, He will help you and steady your feet.'[8] Our failure is clear evidence of our own disobedience. God does not permit Muslims to abandon prayer under any circumstances. He has even taught us how to pray in times of peril. In His address to the Prophet, God Almighty says: 'When you go out into the land, it will not be a sin for you to cut short the prayer if you are afraid that the unbelievers may surprise you; the unbelievers are your manifest enemies. When you are among them and arrange their prayers for them, then let a group of them pray with you and take their arms away. Then, when they have prostrated themselves, let them move back and let another group who have not prayed come forward and pray with you; then let them take care and bring their weapons with them, for the unbelievers would dearly love you to neglect your weapons and property. Then they will attack you in one move. [136] It is no sin for you to lay down your arms if the rain will do you harm or if you are ill. But take care! The Lord has prepared a shameful punishment for the unbelievers. And, when you are safe, perform the prayer. When you have finished praying, mention God standing, sitting, and reclining. And when you are safe, perform the prayer. For prayer is a prescribed duty for believers.'[9] In every age the imams are representatives of the Prophet of God—prayers and blessings upon him! They should perform the same functions as he did. Every imam who is present within the community during times of peril is given the power of speech. He should lead them just as the Prophet of God—prayers and blessings upon him!—did with the communities when he was with them. Shaykh of Istanbul, during times of great risk for the early Muslim community, blood was flowing, people were confused and panic-stricken, and the enemy was just waiting to take advantage of one heedless moment while the Prophet was bolstering the religion. At that time God commanded the Prophet to divide Muslims into two groups, with one guarding while the other prayed. However, Shaykh of Istanbul, I see no signs here of a fearful situation that makes it necessary to divide Muslims up into two groups. How can it be possible for you to stop Muslims praying all together when the prayer is being performed before their very eyes?"

The Shaykh from Istanbul replied that it was all a matter of politics. The idea was to strike terror into the enemy. "Didn't you notice," he asked the Maghribi Shaykh, "the way the foreigners' faces flushed when they saw the Sultan's procession?" The Maghribi Shaykh said that he knew a fair amount of the *shari`a*, and it was supposed to be above politics. "If you have some canonical pretext that allows you to do this, then publish it in printed form so that Muslims may feel confident about their religion, something that they have entrusted to you. If you have no such pretext, then are you concealing God's own ordinance from the Sultan and doing something that will change the belief that Muslims have in his piety? If you choose to remain silent on both accounts, the fault is yours and not the Sultan's." With that, the Istanbul Shaykh became annoyed and told his Maghribi colleague that, if he remained in Istanbul till the next day, he would be eaten by the fishes for his meddling. As the Maghribi Shaykh turned to leave, he kept telling himself that the only reason they were being so lax about this crucially important matter—something that split apart the very core of the faith, and not telling the Sultan about it— was so that they could keep it in reserve and use it later to discredit the Sultan when they turned against him. When the Istanbul Shaykh heard him mouthing these comments, he duly reported them. With that the poor Maghribi found himself surrounded by spies and their intrigues. He set about looking for a means of escape from the seat of the Caliphate and left under a dark cloud.

Al-Muqattam no. 1976, 21 September, 1895

MID-RAMADAN

[138] Every year, on the fifteenth day in the blessed month of Ramadan, the glorious Imam descends from the firmament of Yildiz Palace in an aura of glory and mercy to the old palace which the Ottoman Sultans used to grace with their presence in days of old. This palace faces Al-Bughaz on one side, is connected to the Hagia Sophia Mosque on another, and to the Sublime Porte on still another. It contains the Prophet's relics that have been consigned to the Caliph and Sultan. The Ottoman Sultans have preserved these relics as something spiritual and have kept them close by their own persons in order to make an exaggerated display of the care they are taking to preserve and honor them on the one hand, and on the other as a source of blessing on themselves. They still maintain control over them as long as day follows night.

Before I talk about this splendid procession and the august celebrations that accompany it, I will first discuss the kind of precautions that the government takes and the various means used to keep people alert so that no untoward activities spoil the tranquility of the occasion—at least, according to their own claims. God knows that the Ottomans dearly love their Sultan and care more for his life than their own, but every day spies devise some new way of keeping the Sultan [139] far removed from his own people and vice versa.

A month or so before the occasion itself, the Minister of Police, the Customs Department, the Department of the Military, the Municipal Department, the Ottoman embassies in Europe, the shaykhs in Istanbul, and the spies both inside and outside the country, are all busy preparing for this illustrious day.

The Police Department's function is to organize male and female spies to enter occupied housing on both sides of the road. This they do on the flimsiest of pretexts, all so that they can keep an eye on the people who live there and the visitors they receive on this particular day. They also remove the keys of empty houses on the route to make sure that no one with a sinister motive can hide there. Prisons are filled with God's servants who arouse the spies' suspicions; the majority of them already have cause for complaint or else are submitting some kind of plea, so they are all rounded up on false pretexts to make sure they don't raise a fuss on the day itself—or so they claim.

The Customs Department involves itself in keeping a close watch on all imports coming in to Istanbul in case some dynamite happens to sneak through. Goods are often retained till after the day itself is over [140] and only then handed over to their owners.

The Municipal Department covers the streets with sand and pebbles, something that actually disguises a close search of the ground in case some dynamite has already been planted underneath the surface. This is a totally stupid idea, of course, but then spies are in the business of training people to be duplicitous and to commit all manner of crimes.

The Military Department is charged with safeguarding bridges. On the night before the day itself, officers and soldiers spend the night in boxes under the bridge, while the military bureau spreads out on the top side of the bridge. No one can cross without having his every glance and gesture scrutinized from all sides. Once it happened that a man crossing the bridge was carrying some object or other. Something happened which made it necessary for him to bend down to attend to it. Whereupon spies and bodyguards pounced on him and took him into custody, the powerful overwhelming the weak. That is why people generally don't cross this bridge on that particular night.

The Ottoman embassies in Europe spend their time trying to find out if any anarchists have ideas pertaining to the East or if any of them have actually set out to go there.

[141] The shaykhs concern themselves with reading portions of the Qur'an, litanies, and prayers to God, that on this blessed night the Caliph of Islam may be under God's own protection. If only the shaykhs would confine their activities to such things.

Spies supervise everyone who is supervising the things we have just described. The day never goes by without everyone involved in the planning and execution feeling completely exhausted by the difficulties they have had to face. Up till today, the Ottoman populace has never shown any signs of rebelliousness to make such difficulties necessary. However, decorations, titles, and rewards are all bound up in this farcical system. As a result they cannot get rid of the root cause without being deprived of the other things as well.

Some people with pressing needs have found a rapid way of getting them answered. A day or two before the Day of Celebration of the Prophet's Mantle (*khirqa*), they start sending alarming telegrams to His Majesty the Sultan from Makrikoy in the Istanbul suburbs with accounts of how desperate and frustrated they are. Fairly soon they find themselves invited to the palace to break the fast and to be given a warm welcome. Through the blessing of that great day, their needs are answered.

On the morning of the day itself, Ottoman soldiers line the route all the way from Yildiz Palace to the old palace; it is like a unified and compact structure, [142] two rows on either side of the street. The distance between the two palaces takes more than an hour to cover. The populace of Istanbul comes out in droves—men, women, and children—to be blessed with a sight of the Imam who preserves the covenants of the Prophet of God—may God bless and preserve him! They have to stand behind the rows of soldiers and all the spies who have been sent out to mingle with them. Everyone stands there, waiting for the Sultan's procession to pass by. Right in the middle is the gold carriage carrying the Sultan himself. It is completely surrounded by *yavaran*, just like people parched with thirst cluster around a well filled with sweet water. No crack or hole is left open so the Ottoman people can actually see their Sultan and Imam. All they get to see is a flash of gold, gleaming jewels, and the *yavaran* with their prancing steeds all around the carriage:

> The flash of lightning was too splendid
>   As it passed by on its wings, mere thoughts.

People return to their homes, regret and frustration writ large on their faces because they have not seen the Imam. I have asked several people in Istanbul [143] what His Majesty looked like. They all shook their heads in shame. How can they describe something they have never seen? His Majesty the Sultan has also deprived them of the privilege of even seeing his picture in photographs. Any photographs purportedly of His Majesty that people may have are not good likenesses.

So this is the situation that spies have managed to create through their efforts. The wife of an Austrian ambassador told His Majesty that she could see that the Ottoman people loved him and were eager to get a glimpse of him. If His Majesty would be so good as to come out sometimes so they could see him, they would consider such a gesture the most wonderful and generous gift he could give them. His Majesty the Sultan thanked her for her comments, but spies swore that she was saying such things with some ulterior motive or with sinister purpose.

While we are on the subject of the love that people have for His Majesty (as this noble lady remarked to His Majesty the Sultan), I will mention here something that happened to the late Sultan `Abd al-Majid. One day he went out to pray in an Istanbul mosque. Contrary to usual practice, he found a large number of soldiers in attendance, so he asked the Army Commander why they were there. The Commander told him [144] that they had heard information about some fools creating a public affray by gathering and making a huge din in the street. The Caliph told him to send the soldiers back to their normal posts at once. He then looked round at the men who were standing there with him, but there was no need for any words of reprimand; his eyes conveyed it all. "If the Muslim people did not want me as their ruler," he said, "why would I accept them as my subjects?" When he had finished his prayers, he ordered just one *yavar* to follow him and toured all the Istanbul streets himself. People came up to him and kissed the stirrup of his horse. No one has ever witnessed a day when so many hearts were won over and so many people thrilled by the experience. Such a command can only be issued by a ruler of great determination, one in a whole chain of ancestors—thirty Sultans who filled the earth with their mighty and awesome presence. If spies would only allow His Majesty the Sultan a little breather from all their intrigues, then he might be heard requiring much the same kind of behavior or even better.

Once the Sultan's carriage arrives at the old palace steps, His Majesty gets out and goes up the steps, while the Grand Vizier, the Shaykh al-Islam, the state secretaries, field marshals, and key `ulama' stand there humbly in their official uniforms and decorations. His Majesty the Sultan enters the lounge and relaxes for a while. [145] He then goes into that place that is held high above all others, in that it contains the relics of the Prophet. In His Majesty's presence guards now open up a silver box and bring out the relics. His Majesty kisses them and then puts them on a table. They consist of: the cloak which the Prophet gave Ka`b ibn Zuhayr;[10] one of the Prophet's own teeth—prayers and blessings upon him!—some of his noble hair; his sandals; the remains of his personal standard; two iron vessels belonging to our lord, Ibrahim the Beloved of God; the coat of Imam Abu Hanifah; and the armor of our Lord Yahya. His Majesty stands facing these relics, with Al-Ghazi `Uthman Pasha standing alongside them. The latter holds in his hand a white handkerchief on which are written some blessed verses from the Qur'an in colored silk. Visitors now enter, and `Uthman hands the handkerchief to each one of them after rubbing the relics with it. The person who takes the handkerchief kisses it, then leaves; he is followed by the next person in line until the visit comes to an end.

This visit to the holy relics is limited to people of the first rank, first grade, and above; to those holding the rank of general and above; to the Beys of Al-Haramayn [146] and Rumeli Beylerbey and above. His Majesty the Sultan is standing there as they enter. When the men's turn is over, the women enter in accordance with their rank. Once their visit is over, the relics are returned to their box, and it is locked in the Sultan's presence. During the course of this visit, spies continue to present their never-ending string of reports to His Majesty the Sultan, and he reads them on the spot. On one such occasion, a spy submitted a report to the effect that the bridge had been rigged with dynamite. The entire palace went into chaos at this dreadful news, and everyone became totally panicked. His Majesty dispatched his most trusty associates to search the bridge, but nothing was found. Furthermore, the spy who had managed to throw the palace into chaos and to disrupt proceedings was not punished, just in case at some point in the future he might just once actually tell the truth. Spies live like this for twenty years, submitting reports and consuming the Sultan's valuable time, but I have never heard of a single one of them uncovering a plot or showing a group to be bent on some kind of crime. One lie and falsehood follows another; that is how they manage to break the bonds of trust and loyalty that are usually to be found in the hearts of loyal folk. Part of the spies' good fortune [147] is never to be punished, since it is assumed that at least once in their lifetime they may actually tell the truth.

Most years His Majesty the Sultan will break his fast in this old palace. Servants bring gold vessels and silver tables from the Yildiz Palace, along with all the other bits of finery and decoration which no other ruler on Earth has—and all this as part of the breaking of His Majesty's fast. For this purpose they fill up a huge boat. The year before last, His Majesty broke his fast in the repository of the Prophet's relics itself, they being precious, sacred objects that for thirteen centuries had been a veil for the lips of kings and sultans. They are neither gold nor precious stones, but simply the crude, woolen garment worn by the Seal of the Prophets. Tables were spread, with all the splendor appropriate to the Sultan's majesty. However fate decreed that the occasion was not to be an entirely happy one; that night the ship taking all the vessels and finery back to Yildiz Palace sank, taking with it fifty waiters from the Sultan's private service. Newspapers were instructed not to write a single word about this mishap.

Sometimes His Majesty returns to Yildiz by a different route from the one he used going to the old palace. [148] Once he is back in Yildiz, people relax again and breathe easier; the ship is safely returned to port:

> Fear is whatever makes men scared;
> Safety is what they regard as secure.

Al-Muqattam no. 1982, 28 September, 1895

READING OF THE NOBLE QUR'AN COMMENTARY

One of the most exalted ceremonies and excellent practices of the Caliph and Sultan is the reading of the noble commentary on the Qur'an; this is done in the Sultan's palace in the presence of His Majesty the Sultan during the glorious month of Ramadan. The practice was started by His Majesty's forebears 150 years ago. By this point, the study has reached the end of the Sura of Booty [*Al-Anfal*, Sura 8]. Each year ten lessons are read during the blessed month.

The palace chooses ten `*ulama*' well known to the palace for the qualities needed to participate in this ceremony. Each one picks ten of his students with impeccable manners to attend the ceremony on the day when their master is reading the lesson. They ask him questions on the passage which he has been commenting on, and he answers their questions. The Sultan already knows the answers to the questions, [149] the purpose of that being to avoid any misgivings and to curtail any idle thoughts that might otherwise slip off the tongue. The days when the commentary is to be studied during this month are fixed by the publication of the official decree to that effect. On the day in question, the teacher of the day arrives at Almabayn with his ten students after the noon prayer and enters the room set aside for the lesson to take place. The shaykhs and other people from Almabayn who have been selected by His Majesty the Sultan for the distinct honor of attending the lesson now arrive; for the rest of the session everyone sits in the praying position in a crescent formation. The focal point of this crescent is the chair where His Majesty the Sultan sits. The teacher starts to read, and the students ask their questions (already known); so it goes till the lesson ends just before the afternoon prayer. Sometimes the Sultan sits and listens; at other times, he reads papers so crucially important that they cannot be postponed for later attention. When this noble religious ceremony is over, teacher and students are given their rewards from the Sultan's own largesse. After reciting the Fatiha of the Qur'an [Sura 1], they leave with prayers and words of gratitude. This noble practice is carried on in this exalted house as long as the crescent moon arrives to announce this holy month to Muslims.

DISH KARASI (PENSIONERS' PAYMENT)

[150] This is an old custom practiced by the Sultan's family during the month of Ramadan. It consists of giving people who break the fast with the Sultan, the Grand Vizier, and the Shaykh al-Islam, along with other ordinary folk who have the good fortune to be present on this august occasion, a purse of money equivalent in value to their prestige. The sums handed out range from a thousand pounds to a quarter of a pound; estimates of the total cost of this custom dur-

ing each Ramadan are put at between six and seven thousand pounds. In recent years most of it has been confined to spies who show up at the palace in droves before sunset. They enter the offices of the people in Almabayn who forward their reports to the Sultan. Once they have broken the fast, the duty officer records the names of the spies who have broken fast with him and sends it to His Majesty the Sultan. His Majesty either knows them personally already or else uses the pieces of paper to get to know them. He then gives each one of them an amount of money in accordance with what his service demands; from twenty to a hundred pounds each. If the Sultan happens to overlook anyone, that person writes a paper and forwards it [151] to the Sultan's noble hand, with a request that he receive his due as an obligation. In the process he will make use of the forms of flattery that spies have learned to use with the Sultan.

During the course of this blessed month (which is supposed to involve good deeds and charity), spies pour into their workbooks every single kind of lie and calumny that they can dream up; this happens even though the books are already chock-full of pernicious information and have no space for any more jottings. They thus manage to spoil people's tranquility at the very time when they are fasting, exchanging visits, and worshiping—all so that the spies' outstanding service to the Sultan can be rewarded. Their purses bulge, but their consciences wear very thin. The spies' methods of intrigue work very well at this particular time because, during this exalted month, people have to assemble in mosques and places of worship like the Hagia Sophia Mosque, the Bayazid Mosque, and the Fatih Mosque. People go to these places to pray the afternoon prayer and listen to sermons, words that have survived from the very earliest times. During this blessed month not a day passes without some preacher being dragged away from his preaching chair to the depths of the interrogation dungeons. People spread out around the preacher like a rosary or necklace, but the system betrays him when a spy records that the preacher alluded to the practice of doing good and discouraging evil. In the wake of such a spectacle people leave the mosque [152] with pale faces, visible even in the midst of a pallor caused by so much fasting. When someone stares at himself in the mirror, he finds it difficult to recognize himself.

At the end of the month, officers and soldiers in the palace break the fast, and the officer receives his allowance in accordance with his monthly salary. The same thing happens with the soldiers.[11]

Soldiers outside Istanbul spend the entire time fasting but hungry.[12] Their entire lives pass by in a state of deprivation because the state neither clothes nor feeds them, but merely expects them to die for love of their homeland.

During Ramadan a fair is held in the Bayazid market called *As-sergi* (the exhibition). It includes goods and expensive luxuries along with all sorts of food and sweets. State secretaries, ministers, and senior officials all flock to it and sit in taverns passing time at the end of each day. All they talk about are official visits, the cold and hot weather, snow and rain. That is because they are afraid of all the merchants, peddlers, waiters, and people just standing around, since most of them are spies. The people in Istanbul always look forward to this fair, even more than the Paris Exhibition itself,[13] [153] and like it very much. All year round important people wait for its arrival as away of relieving their anxieties for at least one hour a day. When they arrive, they barge their way through the populace and salesmen using their shoulders, behaving exactly like prisoners who have just been released from prison and decide to visit the Ezbekiyya Gardens in Cairo on a moonlit night.[14] However, these folk are deprived of that particular freedom, that mother of kindness and mercy who has spread her wings over that Egyptian paradise. God knows that every person of influence who resides in Istanbul, no matter how important they may be, will never know whether the sun coming through the window each morning is shining in his own home or a prison. The person who knocks on his door may be the conveyer of good or evil. Had this curse of spies suddenly descended on the people in Istanbul, they would never have tolerated it, but the gradual approach has the natural effect of inuring people to the suffering it causes.

THE NIGHT OF POWER

This is one of the nights known as "Nights of the Lamp," because on these particular nights lamps are lit on mosque minarets in various parts of Istanbul. They are: the Night of Power; the Night of the Prophet's birthday—prayers and blessings upon him!—the Night of the first Friday in Rajab [154] (called "the Night of Desires"), when the Prophet's mother gave birth; the Night of the Night Journey (*Mi`raj*); and the Night in mid-Sha`ban, which is called the Night of Absolution (*Laylat Barat [bara'a]*). These nights are celebrated by His Majesty the Sultan in the Hamidi Mosque. In the morning senior government officials come to Almabayn to see him and congratulate him on the occasion. On these blessed nights everyone congratulates each other.

On the twenty-seventh night of Ramadan—that being the Night of Power—senior officials, princes, and other key figures go to the Hamidi Mosque after dinner. There they await the appearance of the Imam's gleaming light from the horizon that is Yildiz Palace. Eventually His Majesty emerges amidst the crowd of invited guests in a dazzling array of candles, but the light emitted by the Sultan himself outshines them all. When the Sultan has sat down on his special chair, the Prophet's birth is read out to him, litanies are intoned, the Qur'an is recited, and voices are raised in prayer. Then in these splendid and majestic surroundings the Sultan returns once again to the seat of his Hamidian throne.

BREAKING THE RAMADAN FAST

His Majesty the Sultan emerges from the palace in his splendid procession [155] to perform the festival prayers. He looks resplendent, handsome, and glorious. From Yildiz Palace he goes to the mosque in Beshiktash. Having performed the prayer he mounts a horse and, with Al-Ghazi 'Uthman Pasha right by his stirrup and other key figures, state secretaries and ministers, walking alongside his horse, he moves forward. His Majesty is dressed in the uniform of a lieutenant in the army, with the Ottoman decoration on it. The procession continues till it arrives at the Dolmabahce Palace which is one of the world's most famous and beautiful buildings. During the reign of Sultan 'Abd al-Majid 4 million pounds were spent in building it. The door alone cost eighty thousand pounds; it is made of marble inlaid with gold. There is no building like it in the world.

It remains empty. This was the first debt that the state incurred and required that it start borrowing money. The reception hall is totally unique; Sultan Al-Ghuri's inlaid throne sits in the middle. On this festival day, His Majesty sits on this throne. The first person to see him is the Marshal of the Prophet's descendants (*Naqib al-Ashraf*) who stands before His Majesty (who is himself standing). The Marshal prays that the Sultan may live long and be well supported. Following the Marshal, the Grand Vizier enters, kisses the hem of His Majesty's garment; the Shaykh al-Islam does the same.

The state secretaries now enter and kiss His Majesty's leg, [156] after which they arrange themselves in rows while His Majesty sits down. *Ma'murs* of the first grade of the second class now enter, then the *miraman* from the civilian ranks, the *mirliwa* from the military, and the *Makkabeyisi* from the scholarly, along with any people in ranks above these. They all kiss a piece of edging popularly known as "the sausage" which 'Uthman Pasha holds to the right of the Sultan's throne. Once the ceremonies are over, His Majesty the Sultan returns in procession to Yildiz, and the dragomen from the embassies arrive on behalf of their ambassadors to congratulate him on the occasion of the festival.

Congratulatory telegrams start arriving from kings, emperors, His Noble Excellency the Khedive of Egypt, and the Sharif of Mecca. These are all answered with an official decree. There is no need here to describe the precautions taken beforehand to provide His Majesty with protection on this day. They have already been discussed earlier in this chapter.

GREATER BAYRAM (TENTH DHU AL-HIJJAH)

The only way this differs from the feast at the end of Ramadan is that thirty rams are sacrificed on His Majesty's behalf by a special official called the Chief

Sacrificer. Another difference is that the text of the sermon is changed. Instead of "God is beautiful and loves beauty," they use "Fatten your sacrifices."

NEW YEAR'S DAY

[157] On this day it is customary in the Sultan's family to hand out coins with the date of the new year to people who come to the Sultan's palace in order to greet him on the occasion of the new year, from members of his own family right down to the lowliest of *ma'murs*. On such occasions sums ranging from thousands of pounds down to one pound are distributed. When the senior officials who receive these coins get home, they give them to their children and dependents as a good omen and blessing. In olden times the Grand Vizier used to give coins like these to his *ma'murs* on his return to the Sublime Porte, but the practice fell into disuse when the *ma'murs* took to favoring the Sultan more with their reports. Now they can receive the coins directly from the Sultan in person, just as the Grand Vizier himself and the Shaykh al-Islam do.

THE NIGHT OF THE PROPHET'S BIRTHDAY

This is also one of the "Nights of the Lamp" which have already been mentioned. They all involve the same types of celebration. Mosque minarets as a whole are illuminated, and His Majesty the Sultan goes to the Hamidi Mosque to celebrate the occasion with readings of the Qur'an and prayers.

THE SULTAN'S BIRTHDAY

[158] This occurs on the sixteenth of Sha`ban, the exalted month. Celebrations are the same as for the festival to commemorate the accession, which I have described earlier.

NOTES

1. `Umar ibn al-Khattab (d. 644) was the second Caliph of Islam after Abu Bakr.
2. The Battle of Qadisiyya occurred in 637 when the Muslim armies defeated the forces of the Sasanian Empire.

3. Sultan al-Ghuri was the ruler of Egypt when Cairo was seized by the Ottoman armies under Sultan Selim in 1516.

4. For an illustration of this procession (dating from about 1810), see Andrew Wheatcroft, *The Ottomans* (London: Viking, 1993), no. 28 between pp. 194 and 195; and Philip Mansel, *Constantinople* (New York: St. Martin's, 1998), no. 34 between pp. 144 and 145.

5. Al-Mu`tasim (d. 842) was one of the Caliphs of the `Abbasi dynasty, during whose reign the Muslim armies recaptured from the Byzantines an Anatolian city named Amoreum, an event celebrated in a famous ode by Abu Tammam.

6. Jamal al-din al-Afghani's status had quickly deteriorated following his arrival in Istanbul at the Sultan's "invitation," and by 1895 he had been placed under virtual house arrest. At the time he is quoted as saying: "But what can I do against those intriguers and slanderers who have access to every heart and mind?" See Nikki Keddie, *Jamal al-din "al-Afghani": A Political Biography* (Berkeley: University of California Press, 1972), pp. 383–384.

7. Qur'an Sura 62, v. 9.

8. Qur'an Sura 47, v. 7.

9. Qur'an Sura 4, vv. 101 and 102.

10. Ka`b ibn Zuhayr (seventh century) was a renowned poet (and son of the famous pre-Islamic poet, Zuhayr ibn Abi Sulma) who, having initially refused to join the new Muslim community, eventually decided to do so. He came to the Prophet Muhammad with a poem, which begins "Su`ad is far away" (*Banat Su`ad*). When he finished reciting the poem, Muhammad wrapped the poet in his own cloak (*burda*). Since that time the poem has been renowned as the "Burda" poem.

11. The original text reads: The soldiers receive a quarter of a pound.

12. The original text does not include the sentence beginning "Soldiers outside Istanbul . . ."

13. Muhammad al-Muwaylihi, Ibrahim's son, was sent to London and then Paris in 1900. While in Paris, he visited the Great Exhibition there and sent back episodes under the title "Paris" for publication in the family newspaper, *Misbah al-Sharq*. The episodes were eventually added to the text of Muhammad al-Muwaylihi's famous work, *Hadith `Isa ibn Hisham*, in the 4th edition of 1927, under the title "*al-Rihlat al-thaniya.*"

14. The Ezbekiyya Gardens in Cairo were refurbished during the 1890s and became a favorite meeting spot. They are vividly described in Muhammad al-Muwaylihi's *Hadith `Isa ibn Hisham*, chapter 24. For an English translation of the chapter, see Roger Allen, *A Period of Time* (Oxford and Reading: Ithaca Press, 1992), pp. 289–297.

• 11 •

Appointment to Ottoman Offices

Al-Muqattam no. 1987, 4 October, 1895

Before I came to Istanbul and found out the way things really are, I was talking one day to a noble Ottoman subject. He told me that at some place within the Ottoman dominions I would probably meet or hear about some tyrant or rogue who would plunder, loot, murder, destroy, and lie; a callous personage who would be cruel to God's folk entrusted to his charge, reckless in his use of both gold and blood—right hand dyed with blood, the left with gold; someone who abolishes the practice of the Prophet (*sunna*) and in its place substitutes heresy, who makes what is legal illegal and vice versa, who remains aloof from everyone and habitually utters curses. [159] Whenever I came across such a person, he told me, I should realize that this person had left Istanbul specifically so that he could commit these types of outrage, all as a way of compensating himself for everything he had endured and the oppressive weight of arrogance he had been carrying on his own shoulders when he left the Ottoman capital. This is not even to mention the money he had to pay out just in order to get in, the information he had learned about the situation there, the disastrous state of affairs and the chaotic atmosphere among the populace.

At the time I had assumed this person was exaggerating; I still believed that was the case until I came to Istanbul and found out for myself how bad things really were. It was then that I realized that he was only passing on to me what everyone else who stays in Istanbul for any length of time comes to realize.

*Ma'mur*s of various ranks come to Istanbul in groups or as individuals after they have been dismissed. In the case of one such it will be because he has been in service for a considerable length of time; in another, because he has lost his patronage; and so on. They all arrive, their purses full of money and their hearts of hope. They go from one house to another—senior officials, ministers, state secretaries, and chamberlains, presenting gifts to ministers, state secretaries, chamberlains, boon companions, and friends. They undertake to greet people morning and evening and range themselves in rows in front of the doors of ministry buildings, just like people at prayer. At a gesture or glance [160] they prostrate themselves before any senior official who happens to pass by. They may spend years like this; secretaries keep making promises to them, and chamberlains raise their hopes. These aspirations become like a rope tied round their heart; it is long enough to feel like a kind of coil. Every time they seem to be rid of one twist in it, another one comes along to take its place. Their displays of hardship and poverty—threadbare shoes and weeping eyes—are of no use. People are far too clever to be taken in. Spies and detectives keep an eye on them, and they are well aware that they have lots of money and estates in their own countries; they know exactly how much they have already sold and what is still left. Once they have spent everything they own and shed all their funds like a snake shedding its own skin, they give the *ma'mur*s their job back so they can have another turn at collecting money for them.

When these people leave Istanbul, they are already well aware of the overall purpose of all these things: the Sultanate, the government, the Caliphate, the Imamate, the army, the fortresses and castles, the ranks and decorations. The Grand Vizier's purpose is to protect our Lord the Sultan—God protect him and keep him alive!—and to make community and government alike an object of sacrifice to him. As these *ma'mur*s cling to their jobs, they have no interest whatsoever in either justice or fair play. Since they are permanently scared of being dismissed, they have absolutely no compunction about using violence and tyrannical methods. [161] They have already spent long years in this "school," getting involved in the game and seeing what the faces of the principal players are really like. They find out all about Zayd's fears, `Amr's impotence, Bakr's lies, and Khalid's intrigues. The huge dome that they used to observe from afar has now turned into a mere berry close-up. Thereafter people come to regard them as rapacious tigers, ripping at the flesh of people's limbs; as lions that pull people's corpses apart; constricting snakes; and lethal scorpions. As far as they are concerned, people are simply lambs for the slaughter, with absolutely no means of protecting themselves.

What can you possibly say about a people who are well aware that the government has forbidden any printing press to put any two letters together in a newspaper that will report on unjust conduct or people's complaints? They know full well that there is no punishment for bribery, that cruel treatment is not regarded as wrong, that liars and traitors are never indicted, and that hypocrites suffer no disgrace.

An honest and pious colleague once confided to a close friend of his: "As you know, I was dismissed without just cause. So I've come here and spent three whole years spreading money around and kissing sleeves. [162] Now I have no money or self-respect left. I laugh when they laugh; when they're annoyed, I am too; when they're sad, so am I. All I have from them is a promise which rings in my ear like thunder; the rain which comes with it consists of my own tears, while the lightning comes from their smiling visages. In my own country my father is now dead, my son is sick, my wife has just given birth, and my furniture has been sold off. I have stayed here for so long that I cannot go back without getting something; but I can't stay here destitute either. They appointed me to a position, but, before I even had the chance to leave, they gave it to someone else instead because he had stronger connections and was very influential. Now they're promising me a job in Tripoli, Africa; I'm still waiting to get it, like a sick man looking for a cure. At the moment my own hope is to be one of those people they're consigning to Italy or France."

Such then is the situation with *ma'mur*s; these are their intentions and aspirations. With all this in mind, can the situation be put right? Can the cracks be sealed? Will they ever feel secure again? Most certainly not.

Governors too are often dismissed and transferred from governorships because they have committed the heinous crime of earning the affection of the people they are governing. This is precisely what happened to `Uthman Pasha, [163] the ex-governor of the Hijaz. He was dismissed from his post because people were said to be fond of him and prayed to God in the Sacred Enclosure in Mecca that he be allowed to stay there. This was the main reason for his dismissal, so he left. Many people are appointed governor so that they can be sent away from Istanbul; it's a form of banishment. One such is Ahmad Efendi Qadri, the owner of the newspaper, *Al-I`tidal* (Moderation), which was closed down by Kamil Pasha. For a long time after his newspaper was closed down, he remained in Istanbul confronting the hardships involved. His friends helped keep him alive for a long time because they were anxious to avoid the revelation of any details he might have about their covert activities. When things became too bad, he went to the Ministry of Education. In everyone's hearing he made the following announcement: "I have submitted many petitions to the Chief Clerk, Thurayya Pasha, asking to be of service to His Majesty the Sultan, but I have received no response to any of them. I have therefore borrowed a pistol and loaded it with bullets. It is my intention to shoot Thurayya Pasha in the Hamidi Mosque when his Majesty the Sultan next goes there to pray." News of this immediately flew its way to Almabayn where an official decree was issued to the Minister of Police, ordering first that the pistol be taken away from him and then that he be appointed Chief Clerk in the Mutasarrafiyya [164] of his home town of Tripoli, Syria, along with a gift of one thousand five hundred piasters. It was further decreed that he should remain in the custody of the Ministry of Police till his boat left for those parts. Qadri Efendi was a clever man. He only dared undertake such a perilous course of action, one which would normally have led to prosecution, because he was certain that it would bring him eventual benefit and success. He was a player in the game. With all this in mind, who would this *ma'mur* ever be afraid of? Who could protect God's people from his cruelty and aid them against such a person? On hearing about this and other stories like it, Nafi` Efendi, a first-rate governor who was also dismissed, told Munif Pasha: "I've been out of a job for some time. I too am thinking up some coarse language that I can use in the hearing of some spy or other. Then perhaps I too can be banished to some other position abroad."

Governors, province heads, and `ulama' have all started pretending to have negative traits and evil intentions, the aim being to make sure they keep their positions and stay in their home towns and birthplaces. I'll give just one example. A judge who was both pious and honest was appointed to Istanbul where he had a close friend. A case that involved a friend of this close friend was brought before the court, and he noticed that the judge involved was distorting the facts. As he left, [165] one of the chamberlains asked him how much he was prepared to pay to settle the case. He gave no answer, but went straight to his friend and told him what had happened. This friend of the judge didn't believe the story and went to see the judge. He asked him to make sure that the truth prevailed in the case, and the judge promised as much. When the friend involved in the case came before the judge again, he encountered exactly the same situation as he had the first time. When he left the court, the chamberlain told him that the terms for settling the case were the same as before. The man went to see his friend again and swore that the same set of events had occurred again. At that the judge's friend became angry and went to see the judge once again. He was planning to reprimand him for his conduct now that he had been appointed as a judge. After a prolonged argument and discussion between the two of them, the judge said: "Do you want me to get a reputation for going against the way everyone else does things? People will be resentful and angry; they'll start thinking the worst about me. Then I'll become one of their targets." The man left the judge's house, cursing the pretext that the judge had given him and telling himself that no community could possibly prosper when its judges pretend to take bribes.

All I can say is that, if the judge was sincere when he offered such an excuse, it seems a terrible disaster for the community where bribery has become a matter of pretense, even if it is false. "Carried on the sure foundation of justice in the state," [166] as the poet, Abu al-Hasan al-Jazzar, once said. One day, his friends invited him to go with them on an excursion outside the city. On the way they stopped at a butcher's shop to buy meat; they asked him to choose a piece from the prime cuts. When he selected a poor piece, they protested. He begged them to forgive him. Once behind the butcher's block, he said, the evil ways of butchers got the better of him.

No one in the know about the way things really are can have any doubt in their mind that Istanbul has an incredible record when it comes to handing out appointments to people who are totally unqualified. This is not restricted to administrative, secretarial, and political posts alone, but to civil positions and questions of army and navy ranks too. Incredibly enough, a man was once on a walk when he spotted a naval officer wearing a uniform and sword coming toward him laughing. As they drew close to each other, he greeted the officer, but failed to recognize him. The officer said that he was *X*. "What is this then, *X*," the man said. "You've never been given a post and have never served in the armed forces all your life. Go home and take off that uniform. Surely you realize there's a severe penalty for this type of behavior. I can see you being dragged away by the police if you don't go home by the back-streets and avoid the disaster [167] that your youthful impetuousness has led you into." "Quiet, my good man" the officer replied. "I'm no mere army officer as your comments suggest. I'm an officer in the navy and, by virtue of an official decree, I am also a member of the naval council." "You must be mad," the man said. "May God give us all a favorable recompense for your actions!" With that he said good-bye and sped away, making sure that no one had seen him talking to this man. Two days later however, he discovered that the information that he had gone to such lengths to disbelieve was in fact true. He left Istanbul and never came back.

As another example, there are two holders of the *yavaran* rank, Muhammad Pasha and Muhyi al-Din Pasha, who are sons of Amir `Abd al-Qadir al-Jaza'iri. They were first given the rank of al-haramayn al-`aliyyah, then transferred to the civilian rank of rumeli beylerbey in Damascus. When they came to Istanbul however, they were appointed generals with sword and chevrons. Neither one knows anything at all about military training. When one officer heard this particular news, he wanted to break his sword in two, saying that he could tolerate anything but that.

Al-Muqattam no. 1994, 12 October, 1895

The Sublime Porte used to be the agency responsible for ministries, governorates, embassies, and foreign policy. It was the place from which dismissals, transfers, [168] assignments of ranks, and decoration were issued to people who merited such executive action.[1] The Grand Vizier was responsible to His Majesty the Sultan for all matters, big or small, without the general purview of the government, and pertaining to relations with foreign powers. Together with his state secretary colleagues in the council, he attended to all matters to the best of his abilities—public policy and the appointment of officials. No State Secretary or Minister could speak to His Majesty the Sultan about anything or go to Almabayn without the explicit permission of the Grand Vizier who was responsible for the issuing of firmans from his own office.

Now however all this has changed; the system has broken down. The Grand Vizier does not hear about Zayd's appointment or ʿAmr's dismissal till days after it has actually happened. The Sublime Porte has now been converted into a *diwan* for bookkeeping and maintaining records. All affairs of state are in the hands of the people at Almabayn. As a direct result, positions get confused and are assigned to people other than those who really deserve them. Thus shaykhs are made ambassadors, intended to convey the government's policies to the English—people such as Al-Sayyid Ahmad Asʿad; a tea cook such as ʿIzzat Efendi is made Governor; an Almabayn theater actor like ʿArif Bey is sent to the ambassadors in Istanbul. And so it goes on [169] till positions have become like different colored pearls which someone puts into a tube, shakes up as hard as he can, and then opens up again. All the young men in Almabayn pounce on them and divide up whatever they can grab among their friends. The result of all this is the state of the Ottoman government today, trying to govern the second part of the empire now that the first has been lost.

The last Grand Vizier to retain all the rights and privileges of his position was Khayr al-Din Pasha. One day Bahram Agha was allowed in to see him (Bahram at the time holding the post of *bashmusahib*). When Bahram entered, he presented the Vizier with a long list of names, containing people to be given positions and others to be given raises in salary. "You page," Khayr al-Din told him, "what exactly do you think you're doing here. Go back where you belong at the entrance to the harem. Stop poking your nose into other people's business!" As Bahram Agha left, he asked what the word *page* meant. When he discovered that in Tunisia it implied a minor servant, he was furious and from then on loathed the Grand Vizier. At a later stage Al-Sayyid Ahmad Asʿad came in with a similar list. The Grand Vizier asked him what his position was, and he replied that he was Keeper of the Noble Chamber. With that the Grand Vizier told him that his function was to pray for his Majesty the Sultan. He too left the Vizier's presence gritting his teeth [170] and vowing revenge. Once Khayr al-Din came to realize that he could no longer withstand the pressure from the people in Almabayn, he resigned his position. Kamil Pasha, the Vizier before the present one, tried to restore some of the Grand Vizierate's former prestige, but he met resistance from the two shaykhs, Asʿad and Abu al-Huda. They were joined by others in contriving various intrigues and spreading slanderous gossip. Eventually they managed to convince the Sultan that every Grand Vizier was out to restore the position to its former level of importance. In fact there was no need to keep such a person in office for a single day, as the well-known case of Midhat Pasha clearly showed. So His Majesty the Sultan dismissed him, and the Sublime Porte—formerly the place where the Vizier and ambassadors of the foreign powers had engaged in important deliberations and discussions— now became an arena for fistfights and cursing involving the Grand Vizier and the state secretaries. That is what happened recently between Jawad Pasha, the ex–Grand Vizier, and Husayn Rida Pasha, the Minister of Justice. If ministers had not joined in the fray and the Shaykh al-Islam had not begged them to stop, the blood of state secretaries would have been flowing across the floor even before the blood of Armenians did.

Things are still left under the control of the people in Almabayn, who have their own special mode of conduct. If they get to hear of any worthy person, they exile him or else make every effort to keep people out of contact with him by accusing him of some particular vice. This is what happened to Munif Pasha, someone renowned for his wisdom and virtue. The owner of the newspaper, *Al-Mizan* (the Scales), a *ma'mur* involved in ministry administration, started writing a frank article describing how Munif Pasha's behavior ran contrary to the kind of integrity needed of a minister responsible for the girls' schools under his direction. The Minister remained silent and said nothing in his own defense. He knew that, if the Department of Publications—the one that regularly erased from newspaper copy all reference to freedom, community, people, sermons, swords, power, weapons, republics, representative councils, religious community councils, people's councils, the Crown Prince, societies, meetings, assemblies, and all words linked to them—had read such a slanderous account of a minister's conduct, but had not immediately ordered it erased with a warning to both author and publisher that they would be punished, then it had to have happened with the collusion of people in the Sultan's palace. One of the Minister's friends saw how worried he looked and told him that he himself would have been absolutely delighted to be the subject of such attention; if he went to the palace on that very day, he would be sure of a warm reception. The very fact that people have started disliking you because of this effort to destroy your reputation will definitely put you in good favor with His Majesty the Sultan. The Minister duly followed his friend's advice and went to the palace; there he was greeted with all due attention and hospitality, more than he had ever encountered before.

AMBASSADORS

[172] The Ambassadorship[2] is the post that has the most prestige, since ambassadors represent the ruler and people and are sent to another country and people.

It is the Ambassador's function to improve the image of his own people from the one side, and to learn about the secrets of his own government policy and those of the country to which he has been posted from the other side. For that very reason, ambassadors need to be clever people who are also honest, experienced, and well versed in the ways of political life. However, with the Ottoman regime it is exactly the opposite. If that rare person is found who has both experience and skill, he will be like the late As`ad Pasha, the former Ottoman Ambassador in Paris. Even though he had all the necessary qualities, his knowledge turned out to be more damaging to the state because he began to despair and made greater efforts to make other people as despondent as he was. Once, when As`ad Pasha noticed a diligent man tirelessly trying to give good advice to the state and to rouse it from its slumber by composing letters and speeches, he told him: "My dear hard-working man, how can you possibly expect to revive this state, now that God has ordained that it should die?"

Can an ambassador say such things? The law knows of no penalty for such a statement [173]. These are supposed to be men who carry in their hands the state's spirit in the European context. They represent the ruler and people with their rulers and peoples. What a waste of effort, what a loss for the people, and what a disaster for the state as a whole! But then, what does the Humayuni Palace need when ambassadors are kept busy sending telegrams night and day with reports on what the newspapers have to say about the Sultan? People say that the money spent on those telegrams doesn't cost one-tenth of the entire cost of the political administration of the state. It is indeed remarkable that these ambassadors get to see rulers, talk to them, and associate with them, yet they cannot see the revered Ottoman Sultan who is the one who sends them on their mission. Ottoman subjects should feel sorry when they see this country making use of all kinds of flattery with the great powers, something that has made it a laughing stock among Europeans. Formerly it was the custom for the Ottoman government to give ambassadors from the great powers of the first rank the title of Al-`Uthmani al-Awwal and from the second rank that of Al-Majidi al-Awwal. In return the great powers would give Ottoman ambassadors similar honors. Now the Ottoman government gives ambassadors from the great powers the title of Al-`Uthmani al-Murassa`, but Ottoman ambassadors do not get anything in return. [174] What a decline in prestige! What contemptuous gesture could be any worse?

As I have just suggested, those ambassadors who cannot be singled out from the rest of the mob of stupid idiots and fools do just as much harm with their special brand of idiocy as the rare examples of competence do with all their expertise. I will provide one example as illustration. One day, an Ottoman ambassador in Rome (he is now back in Istanbul) went to a shop belonging to the staff of the newspaper, the *Italian*, where bills of exchange arriving from various countries and regions were sold. An Egyptian happened to be sitting in the shop. The ambassador asked the shop employee why they had there a portrait of the English general, Gordon Pasha of Khartoum, wearing his official uniform and a tarboosh on his head. The man replied that the Ambassador had made a mistake: firstly by sending such a person to this office rather than to the Foreign Ministry; secondly because he was calling the Englishman "Pasha" and overlooking the fact that he was wearing an Ottoman tarboosh. That made the Ambassador very angry. When he started yelling at the employee, the latter lost his temper too and things rapidly reached the level of personal abuse. [175] When the Egyptian saw that the situation was getting out of hand, he intervened and smoothed things over. Firstly he told the employee that the person he was addressing was the actual Ambassador in person. That made the employee laugh and the Ambassador frown, but the entire political incident was thus brought to a close. Monsieur Julien, who serves as Ottoman consul in Rome, reports that one day he was in the process of decoding a palace telegram from the Foreign Ministry with the Ambassador. At one point the Ambassador looked out the window and spotted an attractive woman walking down the street. He rushed outside to chat and flirt with her, leaving the consul standing there with the telegram in his hand. Eventually he came back and gave the consul a cursory apology.

It cannot be too difficult for any country that has an Ottoman ambassador such as this one to get control of Musawwa` [Eritria] and other territories. This particular ambassador spent many years in Rome, decoding telegrams by the window. The majority of Ottoman ambassadors are just as devious.

We pray to God to lighten the burden on a state which has men such as this as viziers, ministers, ambassadors, governors, and judges; to have mercy on it and to fulfill the aspirations of its people.

NOTES

1. For an illustration of one of the rooms in the Sublime Porte, see Philip Mansel, *Constantinople* (New York: St. Martin's, 1998), no. 32 between pp. 336 and 337.

2. There is an excellent summary of the varying roles of Ottoman ambassadors during `Abd al-Hamid's reign as Sultan (including many details that corroborate this account of al-Muwaylihi) in Carter Findley, *Ottoman Civic Officialdom: A Social History* (Princeton: Princeton University Press, 1989), esp. pp. 221–231.

· 12 ·

Court Proceedings in Istanbul

Al-Muqattam no. 1997, 16 October, 1895

$\mathcal{A}$ blind man from the `Abs tribe with a smashed face once came to see the [Umayyad] Caliph Al-Walid. [176] The latter asked what had happened, and the man replied that he had spent the night in a valley. No one on Earth, he said, had ever heard of an `Absi man with as much money as he had. There had been a sudden flood, and he had lost his entire family, property, and children, everything except one son and a camel. The camel had run away, but the son was still with him. So he had left the boy and gone off to look for the camel. However, he had only gone a little way before a wolf arrived and started tearing the little boy to pieces. He had left the boy again and gone to look for the camel once again. When he caught it, it had kicked him in the face; that was why he was now blind and his face was so smashed up. Now, as he told Al-Walid, he had neither money, children, nor sight. Al-Walid told him to go and talk to `Urwa ibn al-Zubayr (who had suffered a whole series of tragedies); he would discover that some people were even worse off than he was.

Anyone wishing to discuss court proceedings in Istanbul is much worse off than either of these two men. In the prayers that mothers and fathers say with their children they should include a wish that they never have to raise [177] any court proceedings in Istanbul. The situation is disastrous: judgments are slow, and settlements are either neglected or, even worse, stayed. Sons often inherit cases from their fathers and grandfathers.

Once someone entered the office of the Police Superintendent; the latter was entertaining a friend. The Superintendent asked his friend if he knew this person, and the latter replied that he did not. However his friend was able to tell him that this man was a Syrian who had come to Istanbul in order to bring a court case. He had purchased a return ticket for the boat, assuming that he would only need to spend a few days. Thus far, he had been there seven years. As the Superintendent could observe from the man's shabby clothes, he had been reduced to total poverty. The case was not yet concluded, and he was still living in tremendous hardship. When people mention "a case in Istanbul" in the provinces now, they mean it as a severe threat. Problematic cases are decided by governors, judges, and *mutasarrifs* (a word for "governor" in current Turkish). Anyone who has been done wrong is usually quite content to remain in that condition rather than be banished to Istanbul where he will only succeed in bringing down on his own head not merely the wrongs he has already suffered but also exile, poverty, and death as well.

One day the late ʿAbdallah Pasha Fikri was walking through the Istanbul markets.[1] [178] In a tavern he found a man selling kerchiefs. He stopped to buy one; during the course of the conversation, he detected that this vendor was a person of good breeding. He inquired where the man was from, and was told that he was from Baghdad and had been of high social status in his homeland. Fate however had propelled him to this capital city in the form of a court case involving a group of men in Baghdad and himself. "I came to Istanbul," he said, "seeking justice from the government, but I've spent twenty-three years here. The case is still unresolved; neither in my opponents' favor, in which case I could seek comfort in despair, nor in mine so that I might gain my due. By now I have sold everything I own, and find myself forced to live as you can see (may God never ordain that you have a court case in Istanbul!)."

The worst calamity of all comes when the word *dorsun* (a stay) is pronounced on a case. We have never heard of any government in Islam (at least, one that adheres to the tenets of the Qur'an) using the imposition of a stay in a case brought by people who have suffered injury as some kind of official canonical procedure sent down from its own political heaven. This stay process can be seen as conforming to natural law. Every case in Istanbul is subject to twin forces: one of attraction, the other of repulsion. If one of the two wins, then the verdict favors the victor; [179] if they come out equal, the whole process grinds to a halt. In local parlance, this is known as a "stay." It is certainly preferable to lose a case rather than have a stay put on it.

There are still other calamities that can occur in court cases in Istanbul. For example, there is an incredible story about a man from Aleppo who brought a case concerning a religious endowment (*waqf*) to Istanbul. He was acting on behalf of a group of widows and orphans numbering about seventy. He stayed for three years in the capital, plying his way between the Ministry of Religious Endowments and the Grand Vizier's office; the case was almost coming to closure. All he needed to do was to go to the office of the Shaykh al-Islam to have the documents verified. He went and submitted the documents to a clerk who promised to give them to the counselor to authorize the required verification. When the counselor arrived and the clerk showed him the documents, he flew into a rage and started cursing the person who had brought the case; the kind of language he used would not even be in the lexicon of total idiots. The clerk ordered the man to be brought in at once. When he arrived and came in with the clerk (neither of whom had any idea why the counselor should be so annoyed), [180] the counselor started swearing at him all over again and almost struck him. When the counselor had calmed down somewhat, he asked the man why he was called "Sultan." The man replied that it was his father who had given him that name; in any case, the name was widely used and many people were called by it. He had spent three years in Istanbul, he said, and had gone backward and forward between the Ministry of Religious Endowments and the office of the Shaykh al-Islam. His name had appeared on documents and records, and in all that time no one had ever challenged him on it. The counselor inquired as to whether the man proposed to issue a complaint against him, and then issued a stay. He then ordered the man ejected from the office of the Shaykh al-Islam, with further instructions that he not be readmitted. The man departed teary eyed; he had lost not merely the case itself but also forfeited the rights of all the poor unfortunates whose interests he was representing; and all because his name happened to be Sultan. He went to visit the homes of various amirs. However, when they saw him, all they could do was chuckle at the bizarre things that had happened to him; not one of them showed any willingness to raise the entire matter with His Majesty the Sultan. When Abu al-Huda saw him, he was very sympathetic and used his well-known eloquence to repeat the story to his own coterie. That renowned smile that has managed to captivate the hearts of so many [181] did nothing to help this particular man. But then only a qualified appraiser can appreciate the true value of a jewel. This man used to complain about this treatment from Abu al-Huda, because both men came from the same country and they had known each other beforehand.

> When generous people become rich, they still recall
>   Those people whom they knew in poorer times.

This then is what happens to people who bring their cases to Istanbul, the residence of the Caliph and Sultan, where heaven-inspired justice and God-given inspiration are to be found, and sword and book unite in their profession of allegiance. When they return home, they feel frustrated and badly done by. They themselves weep, and they make others weep with them. They die of grief and cause others to do so too. Something that further saddens Muslims of East and West is that they can watch European nations where justice has a smile on its face while injustice is left to weep. For Muslims it is heartbreaking to hear the way the great powers keep enjoining the Ottoman government to treat its subjects justly. It would normally be more appropriate for the Ottoman government to have the role of enjoining the European powers to do exactly that. After all, was it not supposed to be the function of the Islamic Caliphate to eradicate all those injustices that people were suffering in different parts of the world? Was any other principle at work in the conquest of other countries?

NOTE

1. `Abdallah Pasha Fikri (d. 1890) was a prominent Egyptian writer and critic, who became Minister of Education in Egypt immediately before the Urabi Revolt of 1882.

• 13 •

Shaykhs

Al-Muqattam no. 2002, 22 October, 1895

$\int$haykhs are "the bearers of the Caliph's throne" [182]. There are four of them: Shaykh Al-Sayyid Abu al-Huda al-Khanshaykhuni al-Halabi, Shaykh Al-Sayyid Ahmad As'ad al-Qaysarli al-Madani, Shaykh Al-Sayyid Fadl Pasha al-Malibari al-Makki, and Shaykh Muhammad Zafir al-Madani al-Maghribi. People have varied opinions about these four men; a number of these differences involve the reasons for their close relationship with His Majesty the Sultan. All four are Arabs. Since the foundation of the Ottoman Sultanate, no Arab has ever been able to place his forehead any closer to where these four men now walk or even to glance in the directions where they can now place their hands. Never before has any Arab been involved in discussions with the Sultan, or with the ways in which Grand Viziers can be appointed, dismissed, exiled, or brought in for advice.

There are those who claim that the reason for this proximity and flattering treatment is the Sultan's predilection for consulting their opinions regarding the occult, [183] an area in which they claim great expertise. Others suggest that the reason reflects their submission of reports in which they claim to be able to keep the Arab people's moods under control, be they quiescent or restless. At their very whim, they claim, they can stir things up or calm things down.

There's a group of older Turks who claim that, when the Ottomans lost the land they did in the Crimean War, the Arabs became the largest racial entity controlled by the Ottoman government. At that time a decision was made to restore lost prestige by reviving the name of the Caliph which up till then had only been used occasionally as one of the Sultan's titles, since it involved the imposition of certain restrictions and stipulations on the holder of the office, and, in any case, the Sultanate had possessed widespread power and authority. The Arab

133

people told themselves that the Caliphate belonged to descendants of the Quraysh by virtue of texts of tradition; they were being governed only by virtue of Ottoman secular power. The Ottoman government thus deemed it advisable to humble the Arabs and rob them of any ability of undertake large-scale initiatives. They selected these shaykhs as leaders [184] and gave them wide scope for slandering each other. The shaykhs duly started the process of leveling all kinds of abuse and slander in published form, accusing each other of varieties of iniquity and apostasy enough to cause the downfall of the entire group of them. This only served to enhance their positions, which became that much more permanent. If just a tenth of what they had been mouthing were to have been said about anyone else, it would have been utterly inconceivable for ruler and Sultan either to keep them as associates or even to let their names be linked to his. Anyone who reads the kind of things they say about each other will inevitably come to the conclusion that there must be some other reason (besides their expertise in the occult and their alleged ability to control the Arabs) as to why the Sultan keeps these men so close to him. After all there are others around who could perfectly well do their job. At any rate, this is the view of the older Turkish generation.

I have decided to describe the way they came to be associated with His Majesty the Sultan from the very beginning. I'll start with Shaykh Abu al-Huda, and then discuss both what they have to say about each other and what their adversaries and friends have to say about them. Then I will detail some of the noble and extraordinary actions that they attribute to themselves and their ancestors.

AL-SAYYID ABU AL-HUDA

Al-Sayyid Abu al-Huda came to Istanbul at the end of the reign of the late Sultan `Abd al-`Aziz; at that time he was known just as "Shaykh." He came in Sufi guise and joined the mystical circle at one of the local houses [185] where he would beat on drums as they do in the Rifa`i order to which he belongs. Also in accordance with the order's practices he had long hair at that time. He has a nice voice and speaks well; he has an open face and is generally good-hearted. He thus attracted the attention of certain amirs in Istanbul who were also Sufis. He is still not averse to participating in Sufi ceremonials and only refrains when he is ill. Thereafter he returned to Aleppo for a while as Marshal of the Prophet's descendants (*naqib al-ashraf*) for the city. Two months after His Majesty the Sultan had ascended the throne, Abu al-Huda returned to Istanbul and was welcomed by all his friends with great honor and respect.

At this precise moment the Sultan happened to have a dream that he related to Halat Pasha. He was a friend of the Shaykh and told the Sultan that he knew a shaykh of broad learning who was in close communication with his Lord. He informed the Sultan that, if he ordered this dream to be related to the Shaykh, he would soon discover that the Shaykh would be able to offer an interpretation linked to reality. His Majesty ordered the Shaykh to be brought in. When the dream's content was conveyed, the Shaykh offered an interpretation that the Sultan liked very much. A few days later, the Shaykh went to Almabayn and said [186] that the previous night he himself had seen the Prophet of God—prayers and blessings upon him!—in a dream. He had instructed the Shaykh to inform His Majesty the Sultan something but to do it with no intermediary. The Sultan's palace was shaken by this news and looked forward with enormous interest to hearing the content of the revelation; at this point the Ottoman government was prepared for the announcement of the Crimean War. The connection with the Prophet himself gave the Sultan additional prestige. Since this period was so filled with complex political issues, the Sultan viewed this particular piece of news as a convenient outlet for his concerns and a useful means of preserving his own status. The Sultan was therefore delighted and ordered through an intermediary that the Shaykh should reveal what the Prophet of God—prayers and blessings upon him!—had said. The Shaykh refused, pointing out that he had been instructed to convey the message to the Sultan directly and with no intermediaries. He was told that his Majesty did not speak Arabic, and he himself did not speak Turkish; so how, he was asked, would he communicate directly with the Sultan. The Shaykh insisted and left the palace. Everyone was dying to know what the Prophet of God—prayers and blessings upon him!—had said. The Sultan now ordered Bahram Agha to act as translator. Once again the Shaykh refused and said that he would only do what the Prophet of God—prayers and blessings upon him!—had told him to do. Everyone was at a loss. Two days later the Shaykh appeared at the palace, his face beaming. He told people that he had come to communicate his message directly to His Majesty the Sultan. He told them he had now learned Turkish, and indeed spoke to them in eloquent Turkish. They asked him how he had managed to do such a thing, and he replied that the Prophet of God—prayers and blessings upon him!—had come to him in another dream and spat in his mouth. He had immediately started speaking Turkish, as they could all witness. The problem was thus solved. When His Majesty the Sultan got to hear about this, he ordered them to conduct an investigation as to whether the Shaykh had known any Turkish before. They produced witnesses, including Hafiz Pasha from the Police Department and others, to testify that before that day the Shaykh had not known a single word of Turkish. The Shaykh now went in to see the Sultan and gave him the Prophet's own message. No one knows what it was.

From that moment on, he has enjoyed an unparalleled position of favor with His Majesty the Sultan. Even ministers and other important men (such as Jawad Pasha, the historian, who died for opposing him) have taken to kissing the Shaykh's hand. This prestige and status lasted until an official decree was issued ordering his exile to Aleppo. To this day no one knows why. [188] As he left, he said he would be back within a few months; the Sultan would publish a decree ordering his return. He was actually correct in that the Sultan's issued the summons to return by telegraph. His friends believe that this was all part of the Sultan's generosity, but his enemies suggest that Shaykh Ahmad As'ad and Hajj 'Ali Bey al-Bashimbanji asked the Sultan to pardon him, and he did so. Once back in Istanbul he abandoned his Sufi practices and entered the realm of politics.

Al-Muqattam no. 2006, 26 October, 1895

SHAYKH AL-SAYYID AHMAD AS'AD AL-QAYSARLI AL-MADANI

Shaykh Al-Sayyid Ahmad As'ad al-Qaysarli al-Madani is of Turkish origin and comes from Caesarea. One of his forebears emigrated to Medina and settled there; they had become Arabs. He was one of the people who made visits to amirs on behalf of people involved in tending the Prophet's Mosque in Medina and who also served as an attendant in the mosque itself. Important men from every region share this important task; each one is in charge of a small area and deputizes someone else to perform all the necessary functions inside the mosque—lighting candles, sweeping rugs, and such things, all of which are reckoned a tremendous privilege. [189] Al-Sayyid Ahmad As'ad came to Istanbul on several occasions and often saw His Majesty during the reign of Sultan 'Abd al-'Aziz when he was authorized to undertake His Majesty's share of the tasks in the Medina Mosque. His Majesty held the Shaykh in high regard, since crown princes will always look to those people who can guarantee the things they most need, namely the performance of prayers and liturgies in the Holy Places in Arabia.

When His Majesty ascended the throne, Al-Sayyid As'ad became his loyal servant and stayed in Istanbul, lurking in His Majesty's shadow and relishing the life of luxury and ease. His devotion and quiet nature endeared him to the Sultan, and he was eventually given a special department in Almabayn. He is one of the few people who can enter the Sultan's presence without having to ask permission. In the palace when they talk about "Sayyid Efendi," they mean Al-Sayyid Ahmad As'ad. His Majesty the Sultan trusts him implicitly. When a slave girl in the Sultan's palace is sick, the Sultan gives instruction that she is to be taken to Al-Sayyid's own house. If she recovers, she is taken back to the palace; if not, she is taken away from his house. The men in Almabayn have enormous respect for him because of his genealogy which allegedly links him to the Prophet of God—prayers and blessings upon him!—and his close relationship [190] with the Sultan.

He is a complete plebeian, with no interest in scholarship or learning. He manages to give himself an austere appearance by remaining silent most of the time. Were he to state that he was illiterate and unable to read or write, it would do him a lot more credit than to claim he can half write. On one occasion a friend of his could not understand what the Shaykh had written to him in a note. He sent his servant round to have the note interpreted. The whole thing was settled when Al-Sayyid put it about among his friends that one of his children was playing by his side while he was writing and had scrawled all over the page. He had actually made a mistake and put the boy's page into the letter instead of his own.

His enemies have also had reason to criticize his alleged connection to the Prophet of God—prayers and blessings upon him! This causes the Shaykh great distress. He has been completely at a loss as to how to respond. Al-Sayyid Abu al-Huda took things in hand and extracted him from the abyss into which his enemies had hurled him. He gave him a Rifa`i name and used it to make him his uncle. This rescue plan also had the effect of eradicating the long-standing feud between the two shaykhs. Al-Sayyid Ahmad As`ad acknowledged to his new nephew that this maneuver had saved his prestige among the men in Almabayn and with His Majesty the Sultan. [191] They formed a pact and united their efforts, thus providing an exception to the general air of divisiveness in the palace. Al-Sayyid Abu al-Huda has the support of "his uncle," as he terms him, and utilizes their unified front to counter the evil influence of the people in Almabayn who are his enemies. Even so, Al-Sayyid Ahmad As`ad will sometimes end up opposing Al-Sayyid Abu al-Huda, all because of the way the latter has of rushing headlong into things. In the course of patching up the tears that Abu al-Huda has caused through his precipitate behavior Al-Sayyid Ahmad As`ad often ends up losing his temper. Clearly Al-Sayyid Ahmad As`ad would much prefer that his "nephew" proceed more deliberately so that they can both achieve the things they want and not be somehow diverted. In the war that prevails among these four shaykhs, these two form a phalanx which confronts Al-Sayyid Fadl Pasha and Shaykh Zafir. Al-Sayyid Ahmad As`ad's rank is Rumeli Qadi `Askar, and he also holds `Uthmani and Majidi Murassa` decorations. Many shaykhs from among the ranks of the *`ulama'* never succeed in achieving the ranks that his sons have; they hold the Istanbul *beyesi* rank, which is at the same level as the *bala* and equivalent to *fariq* (general) in the army. Along with his sons he earns a salary of about five hundred pounds, not to mention the continuous stream of presents and gifts that he gets during the course of the year.

He is an aide to the Sharif of Mecca and plays a central role in their relationship. [192] The Sharif relies heavily on him. In conducting his duties he throws all care to the winds and shows not the slightest consideration for anyone else. He does whatever he wishes. Not even the need to show some respect for the Holy Mosque itself stops him from assaulting the Prophet's own descendants there. As a result, many of them are abandoning the area around the mosque; they can no longer tolerate the harm and insults they are enduring. The Hijaz has been turned into a melting pot for intrigue and a marsh filled with blood. The very obligation to undertake the pilgrimage (*hajj*) has dwindled. Complaints raised by people who have been wronged have been dealt with like wool thrown against a wall. The Sharif meanwhile is hitting the same wall with ingots of gold and silver (not even iron and wood).

Al-Sayyid Ahmad As`ad has managed to convince the Sultan that Arabs will not disobey his instructions or oppose his regime. These very complaints were supposed to be the major reason for his closeness to the Sultan and the prestigious post he now holds. However such feelings have now stopped him traveling to Medina whenever he visits the Hijaz. This happened recently when he went there with Ratib Pasha to meet the Sharif and bring about a reconciliation between the two of them. It is inconceivable that one of the Prophet's own descendants should visit Mecca, but not go to visit his own forebear in Medina, and not carry out his solemn duty to use his pure breaths to ask God to grant His Majesty the Sultan success and victory, to support him, to keep disaster far removed from him, [193] and to grant him aid in solving the problems of the present day. He would thereby be fulfilling his function as an attendant at the Prophet's Mosque and also demonstrate to the people of Medina who have not set eyes on him for many years what liberal gifts have been showered upon him, all with a view to making his friends happy and his enemies resentful. However prestigious a man may be elsewhere, it is in his own homeland and among his own peers and contemporaries that he can give the most pleasure. That is why when `Abdallah ibn Tahir [d. 984] arrived in Egypt as governor and noticed how impressive his retinue was, he said: "If only the old folk in Bushanj could see me today!" In the same way Al-Sayyid would be able see his own people, his relatives, and possessions in Medina. However he is prevented from so doing by the fact that he is well aware that Arabs are waiting for him on the road to Medina. He cannot forget that on one occasion Bedouin robbed him while he was traveling there. In his own claims he has greatly exaggerated the influence he has inside the Arabian Peninsula; to such an extent that he has suggested the Najd be annexed to Ottoman rule. He has sent gifts from His

Majesty the Sultan to Ibn Rashid and opened an ongoing correspondence with delegations coming and going, all of it tied to the hopes that he engenders.

His Majesty the Sultan thinks very highly of him; [194] he even smokes a water pipe in the Sultan's presence.

Al-Muqattam no. 1917, 15 July, 1895[1]

His Majesty the Sultan once sent him to see the English ambassador on a political assignment. When he met the Ambassador, he was afraid of getting into a situation which he would be unable to handle. He therefore started having a fit of coughing so he could get away. The Ambassador was very sympathetic and treated him with great kindness. The reader may perhaps be surprised that His Majesty the Sultan, who is usually so astute, should send on an important political matter a shaykh whose knowledge only includes a very small branch of learning; that is quite apart from whatever the English Ambassador thought. However His Majesty the Sultan has an obvious excuse: these two shaykhs convey the impression of occupying the very highest political positions. The reason is that each one of them has friends in Almabayn who tell him everything that is happening, the merest eye gesture, if it can help the Shaykh's cause. As soon as one of the shaykhs gets to hear of some really important piece of political information, he immediately writes a report to His Majesty the Sultan [195] in which he deliberately refers to the information in a way that conforms with the Sultan's own wishes and intentions. When things hit the right spot, they have a tremendous impact. His Majesty the Sultan thus gets the impression that the Shaykh has mastered the realm of politics. On occasion one of the shaykhs will take things even further and incorporate the political information into a dream he has had. He will then recount it to His Majesty; belief is thus transferred from Earth to heaven.

These shaykhs have assistants, simple and stupid people whom they have managed to attract through promises and mantras of various kinds. Such people pass on to the shaykhs information about His Majesty the Sultan that they then proceed to exploit in their own special way to concoct fresh schemes. This is the duplicitous way they get involved in political affairs, thus superseding ministers and viziers and ensuring that the opinions of such people are devalued and their plans subverted. As an example, I can mention a story which will convey to the reader what I am referring to. Through the endeavors of Kamil Pasha, the Ottoman government agreed with Sir [Henry] Drummond-Wolff to the conditions for the English withdrawal from Egypt within a specified time frame detailed as part of the conditions involved. The whole thing was settled and signed by the Queen of England. All that was needed was His Majesty the Sultan's signature. At this point one of these shaykhs got to hear about it through his spies [196] who were keeping an eye on His Majesty. They learned that His Majesty was not happy about the terms involved. The Shaykh submitted a report in which he claimed that such conditions would bring about the destruction of the empire. There would be a general Arab uprising, and people would refuse to pledge allegiance to the Sultan. The Prophet of God himself—prayers and blessing upon him!—would be aggrieved. When these tactics of intimidation were added to the Sultan's own grumbles, he became yet more determined not to sign the pact, even though the Queen of England had already done so. The thought of what the English government, let alone the English people, might do after such a slight was of no concern to him. All the nights that Kamil Pasha had spent drafting the agreement were wasted. If they had been successfully concluded, there would not be a single English soldier in Egypt today.

This is the way things operate in the political sphere to this very day; they will probably continue to do so till God knows when. As a consequence, grand viziers have no idea of what is happening; everything they plan goes to waste. On the other hand the Shaykh can hit three targets with a single shot. The first is that he appears to His Majesty the Sultan as an astute politician, someone who should be consulted whenever the political situation is intricate. Secondly, he can outmaneuver the Grand Vizier by vetoing whatever the latter has suggested. Thirdly, because he can change the Sultan's mind, people believe him to be important. [197] They fail to realize that His Majesty the Sultan does not like the things that the Grand Vizier plans. With his soothsaying powers the Shaykh simply has to put a word in his ear, and the Sultan will rely on what he hears. But what can His Majesty do when he is surrounded by crooks like these, people who cooperate with each other in their dealings with the Sultan and leave him no time either to check on their activities or make arrangements to get rid of them? Every time they see that he has nothing to keep him occupied, they immediately manufacture something to keep him on edge. This is the way they work, and it is allowed to continue because there is no way of changing things. Until people realize the disease actually exists, how can anyone cure it? And how can anyone find out as long as the Sultan is only to be found behind one wall after another? If anyone yells out from beyond all those walls that the situation looks dangerous, they claim that it is a foreign plot; they interpret the yelling sound in a way that improves their own situation and does harm to the person doing the yelling. Many people have tried to yell, but their voices have been drowned out. Voices from a distance cannot overcome the effect of someone speaking close up. As I write this, I am well aware, were His Majesty the Sultan to read it and become aware of what is going on, that they would even use these words to their own advantage.[2]

AL-SHAYKH AL-SAYYID FADL PASHA AL-MALIBARI AL-MAKKI

This Al-Sayyid is renowned for his links to the Alawis.[3] He is from Malibar. [198] The people of Dhofar chose him to be their amir, and he took over the government of their country. When he started to treat them autocratically, they rebelled and got the English to expel him from Dhofar. He came to Istanbul with a view to requesting that the Ottoman government give him a force of men with which he could regain control of Dhofar. All this happened during the reign of the late Sultan `Abd al-`Aziz. The Ottoman government declined to consider his request. He had also been on good terms with the late `Abd al-Muttalib, the Sharif of Mecca. When His Majesty the Sultan ascended the throne, the Sharif interceded in order for Al-Sayyid Fadl Pasha to be given ministerial rank. He brought his sons from Mecca and settled in Istanbul, but he is still protesting to the British embassy about his dominion in Dhofar and demanding that the Ottoman government help him get it back.

Such was his repute as a shaykh and so renowned his lineage that other shaykhs used to kiss his hand, but all that stopped when they all started hurling insults at each other. His Majesty the Sultan once dispatched Nazim Pasha, the Superintendent of Police, and Al-Sayyid Ahmad As`ad to Al-Sayyid Fadl Pasha's house to convey His Majesty's annoyance at something that the Shaykh had done. He got very angry with Al-Sayyid Ahmad As`ad and spat in his face; they came close to blows. [199] The reason was that the Shaykh got the impression that it was Al-Sayyid Ahmad As`ad who had trumped up some story about him in order to aggravate His Majesty the Sultan. Al-Sayyid Ahmad left the house, and that was the end of that.

Al-Sayyid Fadl Pasha is a plebeian man, but he has written some books; many have been attributed to him, all of them heavily weighted with tales of the glorious feats of his father and forebears. Below I provide detail of some of the more remarkable sections. He claims that the status of Sufi *qutb* is something that can be passed on from one elder to another. That is the cause of the intense hatred between him and Al-Sayyid Abu al-Huda.

He keeps telling His Majesty the Sultan that he will become ruler of India and that America will be converted to Islam. When he received some letters from friends in India, he made full use of them to bolster his own claims and submitted them to His Majesty the Sultan. When Al-Sayyid Abu al-Huda heard that he had submitted a letter from India to the Sultan, he made every effort to downplay its significance. As a ploy to prevent Al-Sayyid Fadl Pasha from claiming India as his own sphere of influence, Al-Sayyid Abu al-Huda sent Shaykh Kamal al-Din who lives in Egypt to India. When the English found out what he was doing there, they expelled him.

Al-Muqattam no. 2010, 30 October, 1895

SHAYKH MUHAMMAD ZAFIR AL-MAGHRIBI AL-MADANI

Shaykh Muhammad Zafir al-Maghribi al-Madani comes originally from Tripoli, but has also lived in Medina; [200] it is from the latter that he takes his name. He traveled to Egypt on several occasions before joining His Majesty the Sultan as a shaykh in one of the Sufi sects; he himself has his own group which he took over from the Shadhilis and for which he proselytizes.

One day he was sitting in Al-Sayyid al-Qasbi's gathering in Tanta. One of the men there was holding a rifle and examining it without realizing that it was loaded. It went off, and the bullet hit Shaykh Zafir; he was under treatment for some time. He is a humble and gentle man who fully acknowledges his lowly origins and puts on an apathetic air. His connection with His Majesty comes about because his brother, Shaykh Hamzah, used to live in Istanbul and frequented some of the gatherings of His Majesty's entourage in the days of the late Sultan `Abd al-`Aziz. While they were talking to Shaykh Hamzah, the topic of people with knowledge of the occult and an ability to predict the future came up. The Shaykh said that his brother had such gifts. When this information was passed on to His Majesty the Sultan, he ordered him to summon his brother to Istanbul from Medina. He came and provided His Majesty with the good news that he would be ascending the Ottoman throne in the year 1293 AH (1876 AD). The Sultan found it hard to credit the information because the time was so close, [201] and Sultan Murad was ahead of him in the order of succession. However, when the Shaykh's prediction proved to be correct and His Majesty did indeed accede to the throne in that year, the Shaykh's prestige rose enormously. Belief in his powers was considerably enhanced. However he maintained his ascetic lifestyle and declined all ranks and decorations. His Majesty the Sultan offered him such things on several occasions, but he always begged permission to refuse them. Eventually His Majesty insisted that he accept at least one, and he did so with some reluctance.

Shaykh Zafir was the intermediary involved when Khayr al-Din was summoned from Tunis and appointed Grand Vizier. His Majesty gave the Shaykh fifteen thousand pounds. All this happened because His Majesty was sick at the time, and the illness scared him. He called in Al-Sayyid Ahmad As`ad and gave him the same amount, telling him to take it so that he would never be in need after the Sultan's death. The Shaykh intoned all the things one should say on such occasions, and His Majesty the Sultan was very happy. The Sultan then ordered the same amount be given to Shaykh Zafir; when he received it, he decided to use it to purchase estates for all his children, some twenty boys and girls. His Majesty built a retreat, a mosque, and some houses for him close to the palace. In fact, His Majesty would occasionally pray the Friday prayer in this very mosque, [202] but then he was told that some dynamite had been placed in it and so he stopped going there (even though they dug down and searched everywhere without finding anything). Shaykh Zafir still performs regular rituals there, and His Majesty will sometimes request that he perform some in the palace as well; in which case the Sultan himself attends and participates. The Shaykh's sons say that the Sultan even kissed the Shaykh's hand on one occasion. If only people realized how incredibly important and prestigious the Islamic Caliphate is, they would be outraged by this. The Caliph is the head of Muhammad's community; no person, religious or secular, can be above him. Even though there may be imams, qutbs, and badals scattered around all over the place,[4] the one unique Imam stands above them all, and they in turn are subject to his injunctions which must conform with the Holy Law (*shari`a*) itself. It is the Caliph's duty to define the penalties against such people if they contravene the regulations of the Holy Law. However shaykhs have now started to boost their own position and that of their own teachers and ancestor at the expense of the Caliphate itself. Indeed they exploit the Caliphate to propagate their own designs. It is almost as though they are bestowing such gifts on His Majesty the Sultan.

When Shaykh Zafir noticed that the palace was so completely convinced by his powers of prediction, [203] he started to expand his sphere of influence. For example, he was once sitting in His Majesty's presence along with Al-Sayyid Ahmad As`ad and Al-Sayyid Abu al-Huda. During the course of the conversation he suddenly stood up and, with tremendous devotion and humility intoned: "To the void and to you be peace! God's mercy and blessings." By this point His Majesty and the other two shaykhs had stood up too. His Majesty asked him about it. Al-Sayyid Zafir replied that Al-Khidr (peace be upon him!) had just passed by and greeted them all, so he had responded.[5] As he was leaving His Majesty's presence, the other two shaykhs upbraided him and threatened him with dire consequences if he did anything like it again. He asked them both for forgiveness, saying that he had been overwhelmed. Once during the Crimean War he told His Majesty the Sultan that he had bought the King of Russia for him for two measures of barley. His Majesty has now joined the Shaykh's sect and given him a pledge.

THE WAY THE SHAYKHS INSULT EACH OTHER

It is now time to discuss the insults that the shaykhs say and write about each other.

About Shaykh Zafir, Al-Sayyid Abu al-Huda says that his grandfather was a Salonika Jew who converted to Islam. Sultan Mahmud had him killed because of his heretical opinions.[204] He also claims that the Shaykh's sect infringes the tenets of Islam, that his writings are a disruptive influence on the faith, and that the prayers he has composed are incomprehensible. If any reader recites them, no one will believe they are of human provenance (such as: Oh He, except Him, concerning Him, from Him). He says that Shaykh Zafir claims that the Shaykh from whom he took over this sect has gone to heaven and is eating rice and lentils (*mujaddara*) in paradise; that he resorts to the actions of the lowest of the low in performing his magic, and then invokes the Qur'an and seeks refuge in God, and the like. All this has been printed, published, and submitted to His Majesty the Sultan and is equally well-known to people in Istanbul.

Some of things he says we will refrain from committing to paper. A man named Shaykh Ibrahim al-Qurbanji has submitted a report, accusing Shaykh Zafir of all kinds of crime and attributing to him various types of infamy. It says that he practices magic, placing his necklet, numbers, and writings into a bag and then leaving them in some deserted spot among the graves at Iskadar. A sultan's decree was issued sending some people to that very spot, and they did indeed bring back a bag [205] containing the things just mentioned. Shaykh Zafir's response is that the whole thing is the work of Al-Sayyid Abu al-Huda. Among evidence they use for saying that he practices magic is that they found a picture of His Majesty the Sultan in the Shaykh's house. For the time being at least, he is going through a period of official displeasure.

Al-Muqattam no. 2013, 4 November, 1895

Anyone with a chance to read the book entitled *Ripping Away the Veil from Deception* (*Tamsiq Niqab al-Taghrir*) should weep for both Islam and the Ottoman government. The book so angered Al-Sayyid Abu al-Huda that he had an official decree published requiring that any copies entering Ottoman domains should be impounded. It contains abuse against Muslims, Shaykh Zafir among them. No one who truly believes in God had ever indulged in such vile abuse against even a tree worshiper, nor indeed has any Muslim engaged in such conduct against an anarchist. Shaykh Zafir's only response is to request that God's gifts be bestowed on Al-Sayyid Abu al-Huda.

WHAT SHAYKH ZAFIR'S FRIENDS SAY ABOUT HIM

Shaykh Zafir's friends say he is a man who never does any wrong, who wishes no one ill, and who never tries to take revenge on those who cause him harm. Modest, pious, reverent, unresentful, zealous in his righteousness, and loyal to friends, he will always visit people, [206] important or not, rich or poor. He is on very good terms with His Majesty the Sultan, often begging forgiveness for someone else who has done wrong, requesting a gift for the needy, or proposing promotion for some deserving person. He is loyal to the Sultan and feels a special affection toward him. These facts are confirmed by all those who have anything to do with him.

WHAT AL-SAYYID ABU AL-HUDA'S FRIENDS HAVE TO SAY ABOUT HIM

The late Qadri Efendi al-Halabi, Second Secretary to the Sultan, who came to Egypt along with Darwish Pasha and Al-Sayyid Ahmad As'ad, wrote a book, *The Enlightening Star Concerning the Life of Professor Al-Sayyid Muhammad Abu al-Huda Efendi Al-Sayyadi al-Rifa'i (Al-Kawkab al-Munir fi Tarjamat al-Ustadh al-Sayyid Muhammad Abu al-Huda Efendi al-'Sayyadi al-Rifa'i al-Shahir*, printed at the expense of one of his followers in Egypt), in which we can read the following:

> My Lord, master, shaykh, and professor; my aspiration, guide, haven, enlightenment; the ladder for my ascent, my inspiration, the great professor and illustrious figure; proof for those who know, star of the 'ulama', mainstay of the Sufi path and true belief; possessor of the twin wings, inheritor of his forebear, [207] the great Imam Abu al-'Alamayn, lord of notables, the descendants of the Prophet, and quintessence of the Banu 'Abd Manaf. He is sword of the Shari'a drawn in the face of innovators, designated saber of truth at the service of our lord and master, our Imam, Commander of the Faithful; model for all shaykhs, deep-rooted mountain and magical treasure endowed with varieties of gift and insight. He is a boundless sea that gushes forth with all manner of extraordinary qualities and political talents; the lord from whose noble ideas intelligent men borrow flashes of brilliance; the craftsman whose sublime and unapproachable gates are the very goal of every student of wisdom and learning. With a firm tread, Hashemite, prestigious and high-minded, our lord, the great Grand Vizier Al-Sayyid Muhammad Abu al-Huda Efendi Al-Sayyadi Al-Rifa'i—may God prolong his life for the sake of all Muslims and myself, and grant to all his followers and myself an abundance of his noble ancestors' blessings and

of his as well, Amen! All this is already widely known, often rehearsed in the regions of empire and spread far and wide. It is fixed in people's hearts and pleases their ears; even those who disagree are unanimous in this fact. Its very light spreads like sunshine even for the blind and reckless. The heads of the Ahmadiyya in both Syria and Iraq have submitted to him, [208] and the fragrant scent of his renown still lingers. His name is to be heard in every region: Rifa'i by descent, Husayni in essence and lineage. The men of his family were notables, lords of the Ahmadiyya who themselves were acquainted with notable lords. His ancestors were Sufi *qutbs* for whom God made an exception to usual patterns; indeed he is the star of the Sayyadi house. Were we to overlook this family, we would find no trace of the glorious feats of the Ahmadiyyah. He is the sun in the firmament of Rifa'i glory; overlook that, and its hallowed past would be unknown.

Among the most amazing of God's secrets is the fact that Al-Sayyid's mother—God have mercy on her!—was an extremely pious woman from whom radiated the gleaming light of felicity. Indeed so pious and upright were both she and her sister that people used to coin proverbs in her name. The revered and devout Shaykh Al-Sayyid Rajab al-Rifa'i Al-Sayyadi, from the village of Sajna', saw her before her son was born—God preserve him!—and gave her his name, all in accord with the insight he possessed and an ability to discern what was hidden.[209] So when the boy was born (God support him!), the Shaykh named him, breathed into his mouth, and prayed for him. He was brought up in the lap of luxury and bosom of piety. His mother swore that she never fed him until she had performed her ablutions. When he was six, he learned to recite the Qur'an in three months; at the age of seven he could chant the text perfectly along with the various readings, all under the supervision of Shaykh Mahmud ibn Hajj Taha, a pious shaykh who was the principal reader in the region. He learned to write very well and read *Al-Ghaya* and its commentary according to the shafi'i school of law with the same Shaykh Mahmud.[6] He then studied with other shaykhs, learning Arabic and jurisprudence according to the school of Abu Hanifa Nu'man (God have mercy on him!).[7] He read a lot in the fields of literature, language, principles of law, tradition, and commentary, and studied widely in the arts. He memorized a large number of texts and delved deep into the disciplines of eloquence, history, genealogy, Quranic sciences, and rhetoric. He made a detailed study of Sufism and through diligent application succeeded in resolving many obscurities and clarifying some of its latent secrets. He has memorized more than a hundred thousand lines of poetry. [210] While on the topic of memorizing poetry, we should mention Al-Sayyid's poetry collection which has been published and warmly applauded by litterateurs. Poets have gone to great lengths in order to describe its eloquence. Among the poems the following lines are to be found:

In trying to draw emotions to me,
How often have I strung out a poem whose bite is worse than a snake's.
On many a day servant will meet master;
Such it is the case in the dominion of the devout.

Another of his poems says:

Following the path of men is good manners;
Plunging into the path of the mystic is to risk harm.
Whoever criticizes a shaykh among his folk
And then hopes for a favor
Is like one who climbs a roof with no ladder
Or seeks knowledge by cutting firewood,
Or traversing Sinai on a needle.
By your life, all you get is exhaustion.
For a people's hands will bar the way
To anyone else who makes a request.
The ways of ignorance are twisted,
And block the path of whoever walks along them.
To follow a road with no purpose is incredible;
Not knowing the path itself is amazement itself.

He extols his own forebear, the Sufi Divine Al-Sayyid Ahmad al-Sayyadi, in these lines:

God protect those days spent in Shaykhun.
And my love for the woes that passed in Matkin.
Nights spent in the shadow of our master
Who brings glory, truth, and faith to Islam.
[211] Glorious warrior, lion-hunter on desert days
When fear strikes the hearts of Sultans.
A great man who bolsters his people's deeds
With a secret revealed by saints in diwans.
A helper when the stranglehold is tight,
Rescuer when cavaliers have hidden in the rocks.
For him the breeze of encounter softens its tone,
While the wine of progress is sweet in the cups.
A man from glorious and generous folk,
Whom all religious folk should love.

And these lines too:

Warrior for God, circle our house for ever
And resolve what is in our minds.
Warrior for God, continue to help us

And honor us with worthy folk and prophets.
Warrior for God, for ever and ever
Strive to fulfill the wonderful hopes for which we long.

His friends claim that his disciples and pupils number in the tens of millions and that the Shaykh could amass 3 million warriors from Arab countries. He himself said as much to a European newspaper editor who is currently in Egypt. If this number were to fall short, then God would make up the full number from among the very angels. Qadri Efendi told a visitor to Almabayn (where he was attending a meeting with some of the palace coterie) that he could not even begin to form a clear idea [212] of the true extent of the Shaykh's power. God had imprinted on his heart knowledge of forty heavenly books. Regarding his hundred or so works his friends say that they are obviously miracles, supernatural phenomena.

The Shaykh is always busy in Almabayn, carrying out His Majesty the Sultan's wishes. When he goes home, he does not even have time to do the necessary chores, sitting with visitors or spending time with his own coterie. No one has ever seen him writing anything on a piece of paper. How then can he have written so many books when years have to be spent on such things? These works are, without doubt, a genuine miracle.

To his closest friends he is the expected Mahdi. As proof they point to the fact that the name "Abu al-Huda," if computed numerologically, comes out to fifty-nine, as does the name "Al-Mahdi." These are the kind of secrets that they will never disclose to anyone else, but they are mentioned in a book which is only given to special disciples—a work which is alleged to contain everything that has happened and will happen to the Shaykh, taken from the records of his shaykh, Al-Qutb Al-Rawwas. They also attribute miracles to his father, Shaykh Hasan al-Wadi. One of these tales relates how, while walking once, [213] he was talking to a man who refused to believe in his mystical gifts. When he reached an oven in which the fire was lit, he made his skeptical companion stop and told him to wait. He rushed over to the oven and put himself in it fully clothed. People started yelling and screaming, but he swore he would only come out when he had eaten the loaf of bread in his hand. Once he had finished it, he emerged laughing from the oven. People prostrated themselves at his feet and started kissing them. Another miraculous tale tells how a man invited him to his house, so he went home with him. When they reached the house, the man went on in to prepare some food. While the Shaykh was sitting by the door, a man with a camel came along bringing some cucumber for the owner of the house. Shaykh Abu al-Huda's father started munching the cucumber and finished almost all of it; there was just a tiny bit left.

When the owner of the house came out, he noticed the camel driver was almost fainting away from what he had just witnessed. The house owner waited till the man had recovered, then asked what the problem was. The man replied that he had just brought eight pounds' worth of cucumber, but the man who was sitting on the ground over there had just consumed them all; he could see for himself how much was left. With that the man swore he would never invite him again, nor would he disbelieve his miraculous powers. When Al-Sayyid Abu al-Huda narrated this miraculous tale about his father at a large gathering, [214] `Abd al-Majid al-Kharadji was seated near the back. He pointed out that the weight of the cucumbers was fifty-eight pounds (in Syrian weights that means four *qantars*, and in Egyptian seventy pounds). Shaykh Husayn al-Jisr, a renowned sage from Tripoli, was also present at this gathering. As the tale spread among the wags of Istanbul, some of them doubted its veracity. When our cucumber-eating Shaykh heard about their attitude, he apparently said that, if they didn't stop, he'd swallow them all up. Another of these miracles tells how he went home to discover there was no oil in the house. He inserted his hand into the empty vat, and it filled up immediately. Oil started pouring out, and everyone in the house had to beg him to remove his esteemed hand from the vat.

Al-Muqattam no. 2016, 7 November, 1895

WHAT AL-SAYYID ABU AL-HUDA'S ENEMIES HAVE TO SAY ABOUT HIM

A ruler of France used to maintain that, whenever an issue was brought before him, "look for the woman" (*cherchez la femme*). Whenever they conducted an investigation, they discovered that a woman was indeed involved just as he had said. Al-Sayyid Abu al-Huda's enemies suggest that the very same charge can be leveled against him; for every disaster and misfortune that has struck the Ottoman Empire or one of its subjects, the word is "Look for the Shaykh." When people have researched the subject, [215] they have found that the root of every disaster has been the above mentioned Shaykh. Some of them even go so far as to state that his relationship to the Sultan is like the Devil to the Merciful Almighty. He afflicts people to such a degree that, if he ever hears of someone saying anything negative about him, you will find him trying to demolish an entire village which was living a peaceful life up to that point; this assumes of course that he can find some way of achieving his goals. He tried his best to exile Shaykh Rashid al-Ma`sarani to Rhodes for something he said.

That is why he hates the Syrian people. He spends all his time destroying other people's lives and wrecking houses and families; to help him implement his plans, he charges other people who are completely dazzled by his jeweled decorations and unfulfilled wishes. When a group of these sycophants realizes what is happening and fall from favor, there is always another cluster of them who are not yet aware of things. For that reason you will find nobody who trusts his word or his friendship. To the majority of people he personifies that brand of faulty logic that benefits no one. There are many, many examples of this.

The speed with which he moved from the rush mats of the Sufi retreat to [216] the plush carpets of the Sultan, and from Sufi cloth to a chest full of medals, means that in his view the rest of humanity consists merely of grains of dust. Whatever fawning lies are propagated about himself he comes to believe. He raises himself over the very stars and despises others to such a degree that they seem like mere reptiles. He yearns for a position just beneath that of Prophet—may God protect His seal! There are those who try to excuse his behavior by saying he himself is being duped. Whenever he lies, hypocrites assure him he's telling the truth; if he does something wrong, they tell him he is acting justly. Should he blame someone, they make amends on his behalf; turn away from someone, they offer excuses. When he smiles, they laugh; when he frowns, they weep; when he moves, they all stand; when he talks privately, they say he's involved in confidential business. The fault, these apologists claim, is not with him but with other people.

People suggest that the way he got to see His Majesty the Sultan was because of his abilities as an interpreter of dreams and as an astrologer. Once he had used all the arrows in that particular quiver—something that denied the very core of our faith, he moved on to a yet broader domain, conspiracy, and intrigue. He used to submit to His Majesty about a hundred reports every day, but in addition he used innuendo and incitement as devices to up the number even further. He has played all kinds of games [217] in order to increase his own prestige with the Sultan. He has claimed that his disciples in the Rifa'i sect number 10 million, that the Arab lands are under his control, that the saints are at his command, that the Prophet—prayers and blessings upon him!—will come to his aid, that God Almighty is at his beck and call, and the fates are in his reach.

He then started playing a new role with the rulers of Islamic countries, saying that they needed the blessing that he could offer them. He asked Sa'idallah al-Baghdadi to inform a certain spy that the Persian Ambassador, Mirza Muhsin Khan, had confided to him that the Shah of Persia would like the Shaykh to pay him a visit in Tehran. The man refused to tell lies about an ambassador. All this brought down on him the wrath of Abu al-Huda; thereafter he shunned the man and caused him all manner of grief, imprisonment, exile, beatings, and threats of death. His eight years of loyal service went for nought.

Having abandoned all hope of subverting this man, he then suggested to the spy that he claimed to have heard the Persian Ambassador noting in confidence that the Shah of Persia had requested that Shaykh Abu al-Huda pay a visit. The spy now submitted a report to His Majesty the Sultan, who ordered an investigation of the matter. The Ambassador and Sa`idallah both denied the report, but the latter did admit that he had been asked by the Shaykh to pass on what was a lie. [218] The Shaykh now swore that he had never spoken to the man, while the spy said he had heard the information from Sa`idallah. Meanwhile the Shaykh made arrangements for His Majesty to hear that the Ambassador could not disclose his Sultan's own commands. Eventually even the Sultan began to have his doubts, and that worked out to Abu al-Huda's advantage.

On another occasion the Shaykh wanted to get someone else to mediate with a different Oriental ruler so that His Majesty the Sultan would be asked to let the Shaykh spend some time in his country. This man did not dare propose what the Shaykh wanted to his Amir, since he was well aware that the Amir was not one to be easily taken in and was far too astute to give any credence to such idiocies. As a result Shaykh Abu al-Huda nurses intense hatreds and takes them out on Muslims as a whole by hatching all manner of intrigue against them, realizing all the while that such things inevitably lead to schism.

The Shaykh will regularly range himself against every Grand Vizier and Shaykh al-Islam once they have assumed office. He has spent his entire life waiting to be appointed to the latter office. And His Majesty the Sultan has promised it to him many times. [219] When Ahmad As`ad al-`Iryanizadeh fell ill, His Majesty the Sultan kept asking how he was, but Shaykh Abu al-Huda asked if he was dead yet. It was the Shaykh who informed the Sultan that the Shaykh al-Islam had in fact died. For a moment His Majesty the Sultan said nothing, but then he summoned `Ali Pasha Qirat al-Trabulsi and instructed him to go to such and such a house (which he described in precise detail), knock on the door, address `Umar Efendi Badrumzadeh as Shaykh al-Islam, and tell him to come immediately to Almabayn. When this appointment was finally accomplished, His Majesty the Sultan informed Shaykh Abu al-Huda that he personally had wanted to appoint him as Shaykh al-Islam, but the Turks had objected; it wasn't usual, they said, for an Arab to be Shaykh al-Islam. From that time onward, Shaykh Abu al-Huda has made a point of spreading hatred of the Turks among Arabs. He has even composed a treatise on the subject, "The Turks and Islam." It is as though, in the Shaykh's own opinion, Turks are not Muslims even though they are renowned for their devout adherence to the faith. He has made a habit of blaming the Turks whenever he meets any Arab who has just arrived in Istanbul. He berates them all in both word and deed; the words come from his tongue, while the deeds take the form of all kinds of intrigue aimed at preventing the new arrival from achieving the goal [220] that has brought him to the capital city. When the visitor cannot get what he wants, he believes everything the Shaykh has told him, failing to realize that the Shaykh's own actions are the reason for his failure. If the visitor does manage to get what he came for, the Shaykh is quick to let him know that he is the one who got the favor for the visitor by bloodying his own fingers. So the Shaykh gets to win this way too.

His enemies claim that one day Sa`id Pasha, the ex–Grand Vizier, brought His Majesty the Sultan some papers containing requests from Shaykh Abu al-Huda for things he needed. His Majesty told the Grand Vizier that he was unable to respond to all of them, and that aroused Shaykh Abu al-Huda resentment against the Grand Vizier. Later on, the Grand Vizier ordered that a room in the Sublime Porte be decorated so that he could receive ambassadors there. The Shaykh told His Majesty that the Grand Vizier had abandoned the room where the holder of the office usually sat, a room, he said, blessed by the presence of Ottoman Sultans and renowned as the very place from which many great victories had been ordained; all this was a very bad omen. His Majesty the Sultan ordered Sa`id Pasha brought in at once and questioned him about the move. The Grand Vizier admitted that it was true, whereupon His Majesty slapped him. Sa`id Pasha was detained in the palace for three days, not knowing whether he was still Grand Vizier or had been dismissed.

[221] Another tale about Shaykh Abu al-Huda tells how `Aziz Pasha, the Almabayn doctor, had said something about him in a context of little significance. This annoyed the Shaykh. It was customary, whenever His Majesty the Sultan paid a visit to the army hospital in Yildiz, for him to stand by the patients' beds and ask them questions. When he came to one particular bed, he asked the patient what his name was, to which `Aziz Pasha replied "Hamid." He asked what the illness was, and the doctor replied that he was suffering from a nervous disorder. Abu al-Huda got to hear about this and told His Majesty the Sultan that `Aziz Pasha was being very disrespectful to His Majesty. The patient's name was Hamid, and the doctor claimed he had a nervous disorder. That made His Majesty the Sultan very angry indeed. He told the doctors to reexamine the patient, and they were able to confirm that he did indeed have a nervous disorder. His Majesty the Sultan nevertheless ordered `Aziz Pasha's banishment.

His enemies also claim that he holds personal grudges against everyone in Almabayn, in government departments, and indeed with every town official. Twenty-one among the `ulama' of Egypt issued a *fatwa* declaring him an infidel and heretic. Now he has this craving to engulf the whole of Egypt. With his deceitful ways he has managed to completely poison the Sultan's view of Egyptians. [222] If he were like everyone else, he would excuse the *`ulama'* in that responses to *fatwas* depend on the nature of the question posed. The *`ulama'* in Egypt were asked: "What is your opinion about someone who glorifies falsehood and considers the Great Refuge and Aid, Imam Al-Sayyid Muhyi al-Din `Abd al-Qadir al-Kilani (may God be pleased with him!), to be an infidel?" To that question they responded that any such person was himself an infidel. The Shaykh's anger should be directed at the person who asked the question, not at those who provided the answer. However God has decreed that no one escape the damage that Shaykh Abu al-Huda causes. That is why he has subjected the shaykhs of Al–Azhar to a veritable torrent of evil.

NOTES

1. The section that now follows is taken from a much earlier episode in the original newspaper articles: *al-Muqattam* no. 1917, 15 July, 1895, column 3.

2. This concludes the inserted section (see previous note), which ends with the words "other details such as these, to make you laugh and weep, will follow shortly."

3. A Shiite sect, also known as Nusayris.

4. These names are given to leaders of communities and holy men within the context of Islam and especially of Sufi sects.

5. Al-Khidr is a legendary figure who appears in Sura 18 of the Qur'an as part of the story of Moses.

6. Presumably a reference to a work of al-Baydawi (d. c. 1286), *al-Ghaya al-quswa fi dirayat al-fatwa.*

7. Abu Hanifa (d. 767) was a renowned theologian and founder of one of the four widely recognized "schools" (*madhahib*) of Islamic law.

• *14* •

Writing *Ma Hunalik*

Al-Muqattam no. 2027, 20 November, 1895

*I*n writing *Ma Hunalik* I have had two goals. The first was to make people in authority realize what was going on and to urge them to prevent the same process from occurring in the second phase of the Ottoman Empire as did with the first; part of it being taken away and annexed to the territories of the great powers and part of it gaining independence. This approach is founded on the fear that an empire may in fact cease to exist, one that held a lofty position among empires and dominions and was of necessity involved in major international issues.

[223] If any further disaster strikes this empire after the events of twenty years ago, then it will not be the fault of Ottoman soldiers or generals. Their courage, fearlessness, and strategic skills are known to the world. Nor will it result from the ignorance of Ottoman politicians, people who have managed to acquire a good deal of political acumen from Europeans and to apply their skills to the solution of knotty problems. No, any collapse now will have been caused by the sheer treachery of a group of spies who have diverted His Majesty the Sultan's attention from the best interests of the state. Such things are now at the mercy of great powers because of the current focus on matters of purely personal interest. That process involves making His Majesty the Sultan scared to death of every single one of his own subjects. This group has succeeded in destroying his peace of mind and diverting his attention from important state policies, to such an extent that a spy's report is now more significant to His Majesty the Sultan than a European pact. The entire structure of the empire has started to crumble. As one politician put it to an Ottoman colleague of his: "I never cease to be amazed at the way the Ottoman Empire manages to survive. The great powers are assaulting it from the outside, while our own rulers are chopping it to pieces from within. Yet it still stands."

[224] The Englishman who said that is correct. Assaults from within and without have not been the cause of its downfall; it's the spies' reports that are to blame—may the All-Powerful God be praised! When the state was armored with mighty sultans, nothing could dominate it. But when the matter was reversed, and state, community, people, Ka`ba, Shari`a, Qur'an, and Sunna, everything had to be employed to offer protection to the Sultan's personage, that was when disaster struck. We were left at the mercy of the great powers; they could do exactly what they wanted with us, and their fleets lingered off Ottoman shores just waiting for orders as to what to do with us. Hasan Pasha al-Jallad once told `Izzat Efendi that he had been talking about an entity called community and people, when in fact not merely community and people but also this world and the next all resided in the Sultan. Al-Jallad was absolutely correct. His Majesty the Sultan is the only entity that remains, along with Shaykh Abu al-Huda who keeps giving him *fatwas* declaring it permissible to lose one-third of the empire in the interest of retaining the other two-thirds. If His Majesty paid attention to everything Shaykh Abu al-Huda was saying and using that same reckoning, only the Shaykh and Al-Jallad would be left in the wake of a series of eighty-eight *fatwas*. It is most unfortunate that we have allowed things to continue to the point that we can now watch the Islamic empire in its death throes, groaning in pain at the hands of these shaykhs who are particularly stingy with their so-called miracles [225] at the most crucial times while filling books with them at others. What we desperately need is to ask Al-Khidr (peace be upon him!)—he being, of course, the one who greets the Shaykh when he is in His Majesty the Sultan's company—to stop for a moment so that we can ask him to help the Ottoman Empire. But then, the Shaykh only manages to invoke the figure of Al-Khidr when money is involved. For this very reason, I myself have despaired of ever achieving this first goal, since there are so many barriers between the people and His Majesty the Sultan, the Caliph and successor of the Prophet. The only response is many executions, even though the Qur'an which enjoins sound counsel should be open on his right side and texts of the Sunna enjoining rectitude on his left.

My second goal in publishing *Ma Hunalik* is that Egyptians and Ottomans should come to realize the true state of affairs in Istanbul and the way in which the empire that managed to withstand Europe on its own for some six centuries is almost on the point of disappearing. A number of people seem eager to keep this fact under wraps so that other people will not be aware of it. Along with the free Ottomans who have all sought refuge in free countries, the Egyptians are trying to convince His Majesty the Sultan to make use of his official authority in order to publish a basic law and convene a council of representatives. Some people who have no idea about the real state of the empire [226] have been accusing us of fanaticism sometimes and of exaggeration at others. In the long run, however, events have proved us correct. Then and only then do they treat us with respect. I am only mentioning here just a few of the many things that I might. God knows that things are far worse than what I am describing here. However, all that said, let me now go back to the things people keep saying about Shaykh Abu al-Huda.

People suggest that there are contrasting phases in his dealings with His Majesty the Sultan. Sometimes the Shaykh will extol him with the words, "Lord protect him; he's in my pocket."

But then at others he will mouth things that are incompatible with any loyal subject of His Majesty who has bestowed so many gifts on him. The Sultan pays him and his two brothers, Shaykh Nur al-Din (who holds the rank of *bala*) and Shaykh `Abd al-Raziq (who holds the rank of Istanbul *beyesi*) and his son, Khalid Bey (who holds the rank of *bey* first-class) the sum of five hundred pounds a month. The Shaykh spends the entire amount venting his enmity on others, harming mankind in general and hatching plots. He often needs more money than this, and in such cases he pawns his jewels. Among the weirder occurrences to report is that His Majesty got to hear that the Shaykh had pawned his jewels in an orphan's account fund for one thousand pounds. The Shaykh was feeling despondent [227] because His Majesty the Sultan had refused to exile someone who had been one of the Shaykh's enemies. His Majesty was anxious to please him, so he had the jewels brought to him, had them put in a basket (the way one does with fruit), put some sheets over them to keep them out of sight, and sent them back to the Shaykh. At first, the Shaykh assumed that they were fruit, but then he uncovered the basket and found the jewels he had pawned.

Every single morning the Shaykh sends his son Hasan Khalid Bey (who is extremely intelligent) to Almabayn. In a short space of time he manages to pass by the offices of all their colleagues and people who agree with their opinions and picks up all available information about the Sultan and everything he has done from evening till morning. He then returns to his father with a complete record of what has transpired, just like a reporter returning to his newspaper's offices. The Shaykh now starts organizing things in accordance with the information he has been given and instructs the spies what to write. He then waits till he is summoned to the palace. When the call comes, he goes to the palace and at the appropriate moment makes his requests. The only things issued from Almabayn are those that conform to his own agenda; he will often use a display of temper to make a particular decision clear. He believes that His Majesty the Sultan does not trust him fully, but is merely scared. Because of the various devices at his disposal and the piles of secret papers he keeps close to his side, the Sultan, he believes, cannot do anything to harm him.

[228] One such episode involves the *fatwa* that 'Iryanizadeh, the ex–Shaykh al-Islam, is alleged to have delivered regarding the deposition of the Sultan. In fact, the late 'Iryanizadeh would never have dared deliver a *fatwa* on the topic. He was afraid of the Sultan and was well aware how generous he had been. However, some schemers arranged with Shaykh Abu al-Huda to pose a question regarding the supervisor of a *waqf*, who has managed to destroy it and lose all the revenue accruing from it. This was duly submitted to 'Iryanizadeh; the reply came back to the effect that the supervisor should be relieved of his duties. Al-Sayyid Abu al-Huda's goal in this scheme was to discredit the Shaykh al-Islam so that he would be removed from office and be replaced by himself. For that particular purpose this *fatwa* was of no direct value, but he nevertheless made use of it in another way by making the Sultan aware that it might be applied to his conduct. People pointed out to His Majesty that this *fatwa* could apply just as much to the issue of his own deposition, since the supervisor of a *waqf* and the rule of a country were essentially in the same category. His Majesty thus became scared of talking about it or any other *fatwa* like it. He therefore surrounded the Shaykh al-Islam with a cordon of spies who restricted his movements and made his life generally intolerable, all this in spite of the fact that the fear was not focused on the *fatwa* that the Shaykh had delivered, since the answer was to be found in the Qur'an itself. The most unimportant *mufti* in the meanest of villages, Abu Hanifa himself, Abu Yusuf the famous judge,[1] and the Shaykh al-Islam, all these people are in one and the same category on such a matter. The giving of *fatwas* is not a matter for disagreement; [229] it is a matter of canon law. It is the canon law that should have worried His Majesty, not the Shaykh al-Islam.

By now people have grown tired of submitting reports about Al-Sayyid Abu al-Huda. All they manage to do is to enhance the close relationship he has with His Majesty the Sultan. I don't believe there is anyone who can topple him from the position he now holds. Nothing that the Sultan utters, night and day, escapes the Shaykh's notice. Actually His Majesty has issued instructions to people at Almabayn and others waiting by the Sultan's door to stand on the other side of the door every time someone enters—no matter who it is—and put their ears to the door so they can be summoned whenever needed. Nothing that is said escapes their notice. As a result news reaches embassies the moment anything happens. This very process has caused the state an enormous amount of damage. The only reason for it is an excessive degree of caution, fear, and lack of trust in anyone and everyone. His Majesty once confided details of something that had happened to a vice minister and then discovered that the story had made the rounds. He blamed the poor man, telling him that he had spread around information that had been confidential; he was therefore most annoyed. His Majesty went on to say that he was the only one who could possibly have spread the information since they were the only two people involved. "But, Your Majesty," replied the Vice Minister, "there were ears at the door."

Al-Muqattam no. 2028, 21 November, 1895

[230] I noted earlier that I had two goals in writing this series of articles: firstly, as a way of informing people in authority about the imminence of the disaster that will strike them and take the state with them; secondly, to inform people about the general condition in which people in positions of authority have left the state. The things I have already seen and heard have led me to despair of ever achieving the first of these two goals.

However, the preceding materials lead me to believe that I have succeeded in the second. As a sign of that, a group of worthy Egyptians has been impelled by a sense of sympathy for the Ottoman state and the Muslim community to request that something be done, this being the only way out of the situation in which the state now finds itself. This involves the publication of a basic law and the convening of a council of representatives. They have begun to draft this in the form of an Islamic advisory text which has been dispatched to the Caliph's residence in Istanbul. Someone with experience warned the group that this action would be inadvisable since it is abundantly clear that the shaykhs in Istanbul can easily subvert any piece of wise counsel to their own ends; some members of the group flinched. The situation he refers to does indeed mean that things get reversed, and everyone's best efforts end up benefiting only the shaykhs whose advice is responsible for the downfall of the empire in the first place.

Here at any rate is the advisory text (God ordains as he sees fit):

Islam, of which you are the Prophet's successor (Caliph) and the allegiance that we have pledged to you, [231] lead us to submit to you this advisory note, devoid of all blemishes that may afflict the mind;

Advising the Sultan is the strongest principle of the faith, particularly at a time when Islam finds itself confronting grave dangers;

Successor of the Prophet, for Islam and its people you are today the sole refuge. They stand before you, hands outstretched, millions of souls beseeching you to save them through your celebrated resolve, famous wisdom, and pure hand;

All Muslims in East and West are at this moment discussing the imminent collapse of the empire—in itself, the very spirit of Islam—if it is unable to find in Your Majesty that helping hand to raise it up again;

The only way whereby kingdoms and empires have been raised up anew and saved is by the process of reform, so that it becomes impossible for foreigners to find ways of interfering in affairs of state;

Mighty ruler—may God grant you prosperity!—you were the first to realize this when you ascended the Ottoman throne. You devised means for solving the situation and embellished your own coronation [232] by promulgating a basic law and convening a council of representatives. This group of loyal subjects, along with the rest of the Sultan's peoples, considers it time to continue with such measures, reinstituting them as a way of preserving empire and community;

As individuals we are obliged to draw attention to these facts, since we can reveal what every Muslim in Istanbul and all the Sultan's provinces are saying, and yet what cannot be said out loud for fear that the truth will be discredited. We can hear the heartbeats of Muslims all over the world pounding in fear of the power center of the empire;

We see no reason why a believer should object to the submission of this plea to His Majesty, describing the painful situation under which Muslims are suffering. God Almighty has said: "Let there be a people made up of you, calling people to good works";[2]

So, on the basis of this explicit text, we submit this note to Your Majesty, expressing thoughts that are continually on the minds of Muslims worldwide. Islam is a single body. So, if one of the limbs is affected, the rest feel it as well. An Egyptian Muslim is hurt when an Istanbul Muslim is, and the same [233] with Muslims East and West. God Almighty has said: "Believers are a brotherhood. So consort with your brothers and fear God."[3]

Al-Muqattam no. 2050, 17 December, 1895

We promised to say some more about the kind of things Al-Sayyid Abu al-Huda's enemies say about him, but we have been sidetracked for fear that some people might disapprove of our going to such great lengths to describe something which does not really concern them, namely talking about someone in whom they are uninterested. They do not care whether his lineage is precisely established or not, whether the Sultan dismisses him or keeps him close at hand, whether poets praise or blame him, whether he gets the better of his enemies or they of him, or whether his own father's alleged miracles are true or not. Even so, I have gained one advantage from this lengthy description, namely the knowledge that the same things happened throughout time even though they may be chronologically separated by centuries.

Sultan Muhammad the Conqueror entered Istanbul in 1454 while the Byzantine authorities were still trying to decide what order of precedence needed to be followed in the debate on how to defend the city against him. This same Istanbul today has the fleets of the great powers at its gates, while

their ambassadors convene and hold complete meetings at which they are discussing various ways of interfering in the Sultan's affairs. [234] The Grand
Vizier rushes off to the British embassy for fear of being watched, and this and
that—all of them things enough to make you weep. Al-Sayyid Abu al-Huda
disagrees with people, argues, spreads falsehoods, curses, deprives himself of
sleep, and heaps blame on the state, and all so that he can force people to believe that his own lineage is genuine. If Moses—peace be upon him!—had
heard someone suggesting that his lineage were false, he would have responded
with "God knows best." Genealogies are things to be entrusted to God. Al-
Sayyid Abu al-Huda has been the beneficiary of so many wonderful gestures
that he really has no need to indulge in such excessive concern about his own
lineage. There must be some other secret reason, and I intend to stay on the
trail till I find out.

Now it is time to finish with the people of Almabayn and talk about His
Majesty the Sultan himself and his private life in the Sultan's palace.

NOTES

1. Abu Yusuf (d. 798) was a pupil of Abu Hanifa, the founder of one of the four
Islamic schools of law, and himself a renowned judge in Baghdad during the `Abbasi
Caliphate.
2. Qur'an Sura 3, v. 104.
3. Qur'an Sura 49, v. 10.

• 15 •

The Sultan

$\int$ultan Al-Ghazi `Abd al-Hamid Khan the Second is the thirty-fourth Ottoman Sultan and Caliph of Islam. He was born on the sixth day of Sha`ban in the year 1258 AH [September 1842] [235] and ascended the throne on 30 August, 1876 "through inheritance and right." This expression is regularly used on such occasions: "inheritance" implies the Sultanate, and "right" the Caliphate. The Caliphate has been associated with this illustrious family which has preserved the purity of Islam for some six centuries now. The practice started in the time of Sultan Selim, the conqueror of Egypt [1516]. The Abbasid Caliph in Egypt paid him allegiance as Caliph after the Sultan had consulted the `ulama' regarding the lack of authority in worldly affairs that characterized the Abbasid Caliphate at that time. Under the Circassian Mamluks who ruled at the time, the Caliph was just like some Sufi shaykh, someone with no real power or authority. The only thing he could say to the person appointed to succeed him was: "I hereby appoint you in charge of what is behind this door." At the time the `ulama' delivered a *fatwa* to the effect that the Caliphate should also have temporal powers, and so the Abbasid Caliph pledged allegiance to Selim as the first Ottoman Caliph. However, he was not addressed as "Caliph" but "Servant of the Two Shrines" (*Khadim al-Haramayn*).[1] The first Ottoman to use the term *Caliph* [236] was Selim al-Qanuni, but thereafter the title Caliph was forgotten among all the other titles appended to the Ottoman Sultan's name. When the Sultan was appointed to succeed, he used to go to the mosque of Abu Ayyub al-Ansari; there the Marshal of the Prophet's Descendants would invest him with the sword, and this was what they term "allegiance." When people in authority wanted to depose Sultan `Abd al-`Aziz and replace him with Sultan Murad, they took the latter to the office of the Army Chief of Staff at night and agreed to carry out their plans by pledging him the proper canonical allegiance as Caliph. Husayn `Awni Pasha detected signs of reluctance in Sharif `Abd al-Muttalib's expression, so he stood up and announced that anyone who refused to pledge allegiance to him (pointing to Sultan Murad) would be beheaded. Acting therefore in accordance with the Qur'an and the Sunna, people pledged allegiance to Sultan Murad.

Readers should not imagine that I have somehow wandered off the point in providing this detail. My aim has been to show that there is an important principle here; people can appreciate that the Caliphate proceeds along canonical lines [237] through Sultan Selim and Sultan Murad.

To return now to our description of His Majesty Sultan `Abd al-Hamid. He is a thin man of medium height or indeed under the average height for men. He is of nervous disposition, but has a firm jaw. He is very quick-witted and fastidious about his own person. It is almost as if he thinks some trap has been set for him with every single step he takes. He has spent most of his time and a large portion of his wealth taking unprecedented measures to protect himself. For this purpose he has adopted a variety of methods that would never even occur to other people. This has reached the stage at which he now regards groups of people as individuals and finds it impossible to think of them as a group. Everyone is just a single person, and the individual implies "them." The divisive methods that his clever mind has dreamed up are such that not even Machiavelli would know about. He has exiled from Istanbul people in authority who have worked in pairs, while retaining those whom he recognizes as individuals. He has made a habit of promising every cabinet member that he will be Grand Vizier, and so no holder of that office can ever relax. Because of all the intrigues, there is no way to plan the Sultan's deposition. That is why grand viziers who have held the office have always been reluctant to accept the position.

[238] He will often summon ex–grand viziers—all with the full knowledge of the current holder of the office—and have private conversations with them, the purpose being to keep an ever-vigilant eye on them. One night, he summoned Khayr al-Din Pasha to Almabayn, took him from one room to another, and ordered his retinue to lock all the doors. The ex-Vizier began to wonder what important matter His Majesty the Sultan was about to reveal to him. He spent a while sitting there with His Majesty, but the conversation was entirely devoted to birds large and small. When Khayr al-Din left, he still had no idea why His Majesty had chosen to conduct the interview in such a peculiar fashion.

People who are aware of his quick-wittedness, resolve, and perception suggest that, if only he would devote to state affairs a tiny portion of the energy he devotes to protecting himself—an amount that would in no way interfere with such protective measures, the empire would not have suffered the series of setbacks that it has. However all the energy that he does devote to state matters is actually intended to protect himself. He does not bother himself about food, drink, and pleasures of that sort; as the French put it, there is no poetry in his life. To the contrary, everything is deadly serious. [239] A minister once told a very funny joke in his presence in the hope of making him laugh, but instead His Majesty turned away and refused to talk to him during the entire audience. He does not drink wine any more (so people say) because he often suffers from headaches and does not wish to be deprived of any time that he might spend protecting himself. His Majesty never sleeps in the same room twice. He has a huge dog that stands guard in whichever room he chooses to sleep. Three times daily he pours cold water on himself, but he never sleeps deeply; some days he only sleeps for four hours.

His Majesty once owned a Circassian slave girl called Malak whose task was to wait on him; she was just nine years old. Sometimes he would stand praying, with a mirror placed in front of him. On one occasion he happened to notice that she had moved one step from her spot. Now it so happens that, before His Majesty had started praying, he had put the revolver that he always carried with him somewhere in the room. He finished his prayers and then made full use of that single step the little girl had made. [240] He ordered an investigation, and the palace went through an upheaval which resulted in the girl being exiled along with fifty others. The palace interior is continually being subjected to incidents like this. When all business in Almabayn is suspended for days, people realize that things are going on inside that make it impossible to keep track of what is happening outside. An astute minister once said that His Majesty the Sultan spends his entire life protecting himself, so he has no time left for either himself or his own people.

His Majesty the Sultan knows only Turkish and a few phrases of Arabic in the Hijazi dialect that he picked up from the Sudanese eunuchs in the Sultan's harem. He can understand some French sentences too because he has heard ambassadors using them in his presence. He is one of the richest rulers on Earth. No Ottoman Sultan has ever managed to amass the amount of wealth that he has, nor collected so many estates. These large estates are one of the many reasons why people are losing their wealth; the people who work there are generally characterized by being exempted from military service and generous princely handouts. These estates have grown, and the country has been destroyed. [241] Supervisors and directors of these estates grab eight-tenths of the revenue, while the treasury gets a mere two-tenths.

So concerned is His Majesty about his own protection that he trusts absolutely no one, near or far. Once he looked out of his window and spotted one of his palm-tree attenders, Salim Efendi, chatting with a soldier. He immediately demanded an investigation which took up a whole week; the two "offenders" were kept in jail during that time. He is very hesitant, but, once his mind is made up, that is the final word on the subject. He always has a big impact on people to whom he is talking; no one will emerge from a conversation with him without feeling delighted. Such delight however only lasts till the person leaving encounters someone else going in and learns what court flatterers have been saying about him during his absence. Delight then turns into anger and resentment. For example, once a vizier was sitting with His Majesty; coffee was brought in, and His Majesty took it and handed it to the Vizier with his own hand. The Vizier stood up, then sat down again, bowing and prostrating himself in gratitude for this gesture. The Sultan treated him most cordially. When the meeting was over, the Vizier met a friend of his who had gone in to see the Sultan after him. [242] His friend mentioned the coffee and told him what X and Y had said during his absence. In reply the Vizier told his friend that he himself had had a thousand apprehensions when he had taken the coffee from His Majesty, but he was delighted to hear that they thought it enough just to make fun of him.

Were it not for the cautious attitude that consumes so much of the Sultan's time and money, he would be the most prestigious and magnificent of all Ottoman Sultans. It is clear that this demeanor of his began in the time of his uncle, who ordered His Majesty and his brother, Sultan Murad, to be kept in custody. This had happened when Napoléon had spoken in a very friendly matter to Sultan Murad in French while they were at table, all in the presence of his uncle, Sultan `Abd al-`Aziz. This made Sultan `Abd al-`Aziz very worried, and he immediately ordered the two princes to be kept in custody and removed from their palaces to small houses where they were surrounded by spies. If you add to that fact all the things the Sultan has witnessed, and especially the deposition of his uncle and brother, then you can appreciate his concern for his own position. Nevertheless, the people do have a right to demand that he do things to preserve their peace of mind. He keeps every aspect of government, big and small, under his own eye rather than hand some things over to the competent officials in the government.

He has given incredible amounts of money away as largesse. On occasion he will give someone [243] five pounds, on another five thousand. He is scared of cholera, because on one occasion a woman called Mahtab (a woman who told fortunes by geomancy) and her daughter, both of whom were residing in the palace at that point, told him even before he ascended the throne that he was going to be Sultan, but there was some fear of cholera. Last year when there were a few cases in Istanbul, doctors were not sure whether it was in fact cholera. His Majesty exiled all doctors who said it was not and gave rewards to all who said it was. This was because the act of saying that it was not implied a lack of the necessary, if somewhat excessive, caution. The evil intentions behind such a denial were, needless to say, obvious. This is what people say. Matters remain the same in Istanbul because it provides a principal method of fawning and flattery.

NOTE

For photographs of `Abd al-Hamid II, see Lord Kinross, *The Ottoman Centuries* (New York: Morrow Quill, 1977), p. 579; and Alan Palmer, *The Decline and Fall of the Ottoman Empire* (New York: Evans, 1993), nos. 5 and 9 between pp. 146 and 147. There are also cartoons of the Sultan in Andrew Wheatcroft, *The Ottomans* (London: Viking, 1993), pp. 242–247.

1. The text has a footnote at this point: "It is told that he used to pray in the sacred enclosure in Mecca and the preacher would pray for him, using the term *Lord of the Two Noble Sanctuaries*. He stopped the preacher and made him say instead: 'Servant of the Two Noble Sanctuaries.' Thereafter it became one of his titles." This title has now been adopted by the King of Saudi Arabia.

· 16 ·

Deposition of Sultans

Al-Muqattam no. 2087, 2 February, 1896

*H*is Majesty the Sultan is keen to be known for his determination, piety, efficiency, and competence. Unlike his predecessors, he has not built enormous
palaces which have depleted the state treasury. He is conservative and prefers
to leave things the way they are. [244] Thus, he does not condone items that
people refer to as modern conveniences: electricity, telephone, and such
things. People say that the reason why he refuses to give a concession for the
telephone is that he does not want communications between his subjects to
be improved. His flatterers have gone to enormous lengths to convey their
fears to him regarding his loyal subjects. This has reached a point where they
have turned cowardice into an embellishment to boast about. When one of
them was in the Sultan's presence, he noticed a sheet of paper with red ink
on it; that made him faint because he thought it was blood.

His Majesty is working on an important project, but he is afraid of re-
vealing what it is until all the necessary precautions have been taken: this is
to make sure that the inheritance is passed on to his eldest son. For the state
and its subjects this is the best thing that could happen. If people took just
a single look at history, they would discover that this is the principle on
which this house has been based since the time of Sultan `Uthman the First.
For three hundred years the inheritance has been passed on this way until
Sultan Ahmad. Fourteen Ottoman Sultans succeeded one another this way,
[245] while the rest of their forebears held government posts. It is this one
great feature that has now been lost. After that time, the crown princes
started living among slave girls, eunuchs, and servants. Their ascent to the
throne became an event like someone emerging from pitch darkness into
gleaming light; at one stroke they were blinded, except, that is, for those to

whom God had given a degree of insight and were thus able to adjust to such an abrupt change. The crown princes continued in this fashion, being trained for government jobs, for about two hundred years, but then some of them rebelled against Sultan Muhammad the Conqueror. With that, he decided to protect himself and his successors. He had a law passed permitting the Sultan to kill his brothers when he ascended the throne. The succession thus passed from eldest son to eldest son, until Sultan Ahmad became Sultan at the age of fourteen and had no son. He therefore kept his brother alive.

Later, however, he did have a son, but he was still in favor of keeping his brother alive. The decision was helped by the fact that the brother was something of a simpleton. When Sultan Ahmad was close to death, he told himself that, if he followed tradition and appointed his son [246] (who was only twelve-years-old at the time), there would be the risk of trouble from the army which at the time was in a state of uproar. He therefore appointed his simpleton brother as his successor. However, before long the army mutinied because of the Sultan's incompetence. As a result things turned out exactly as the former Sultan had envisaged. His own brother, Sultan Mustafa, was on the throne for just a few months before he was deposed.

This was the first deposition of an Ottoman sultan, but since then it has become something of a standard procedure. The number of sultans is thirty-four. Of those, only nineteen have died while still on the throne. The others have died either after their deposition or else as the result of murder or martyrdom. Eleven have been deposed, three have stepped down of their own volition, and one died a martyr. I will now provide details.

THE FIRST DEPOSITION

Sultan Mustafa the First was deposed because he was so naive and unfit to be Sultan. God have mercy on him! He was an excellent example of a spendthrift. Among the more incredible stories is that he used to pass the time staring out to sea, his subjects' money by his side. He used to throw one dinar after another [247] out the window because he enjoyed listening to the splash they made, also—or so he claimed—so that the fish would not go without the things that human beings enjoyed. There are other stories like this one.

As a result, the army mutinied just a few months after his succession. They deposed him and put him in prison.

THE SECOND DEPOSITION

Sultan `Uthman the Second assumed the throne after Sultan Ahmad. He was Sultan Ahmad's son (at the time he was only twelve, as we noted earlier). He was interested in games and pleasurable pastimes and managed to spend prodigious amounts of money. He hated the army and occupied himself with the interpretation of dreams and indulging in fantasies. He was completely under the control of the Agha and his shaykh, Khujah Efendi. He too was fond of espionage, but was too scared to get involved in it himself. He used to visit markets in disguise to see if his regulations on the handling of sweets and tobacco were being flouted. He was unbending in his insistence that neither of these commodities be consumed; if he came across anyone smoking or drinking wine, he ordered them killed instantly as an example.

This regime lasted until he decided to break with his predecessors' practice by taking Circassian girls as concubines. [248] He was keen to marry daughters of amirs according to canonical law, so contracts were arranged for him to wed the daughter of the Vizier and of the Shaykh al-Islam. The army regarded this as reprehensible and made the most of the opportunity. They were about to mutiny, but the Sultan got wind of it. In order to spike their guns, he announced that he was going on the pilgrimage. The army sought the assistance of the Shaykh al-Islam in preventing the Sultan from leaving for the Hijaz. The Shaykh issued a *fatwa* to the effect that the Sultan was under no obligation to go on the pilgrimage. However, the Sultan ignored the *fatwa* and stuck to his plans. He made for Askdar, pitched camp there, and made preparations for his journey to the Hijaz. It was there that the army detained him and proclaimed his deposition because he was intending to go on the pilgrimage. They put him in prison and killed him there.

THE THIRD DEPOSITION

Sultan Mustafa the simpleton was now brought out to assume the Sultanate. At first he thought they had come to kill him, so he bowed down in submission and stuck out his neck. Instead they fell at his feet and started kissing them. When he ascended the throne, the same request was made for blood money for Sultan `Uthman the Second as had been made with his namesake, the third Caliph `Uthman ibn `Affan [d. 655]—God be pleased with him!—many centuries earlier. [249] People in the provinces started demanding blood money for the murdered Sultan; some broke away and declared independence.

So naive was the Sultan that he was not even aware of these developments. He only remained Sultan for thirteen months, then he too was deposed.

THE FOURTH DEPOSITION

When Sultan Ibrahim took over, he began to indulge all his passions. He was a wanton spendthrift, to such a degree that during his reign the state's affairs were in very poor shape indeed. Bribery was widespread in every region of the empire. He himself loved sable coats. Whenever the army returned from a campaign, he never asked about their victories and territorial gains. All he was interested in was the furs they had brought back along with all the spoils. Among many funny stories about his love for furs one tells how a palace cat gave birth, and he put on a big party for it. All the valuable furs in his treasury were laid out in the room where the cat had given birth, all in honor of the cat. On one particular festival day he was on the point of appearing to the populace wearing all the jewels and decorations from his treasury; the only thing that stopped him doing so was a clever ruse on the part of his vizier. The latter observed that, if people feasted their eyes on such an impressive sight, he could not guarantee the Sultan's safety from the effects of the evil eye. With that the Sultan took them all off.

It was this same Sultan who halted a procession alongside a milk seller and asked for a drink then and there. [250] For this action the Vizier engineered the excuse that the Sultan had learned that people drank milk, so a sense of concern for his subjects made him keen—God support him!—to test it for himself. He is also the one who took his baby son away from his wet nurse, struck his head against a marble bath and smashed his skull, all so that he would be the only living member of the Ottoman house. However, God cured him of that habit, and he eventually became one of the longest reigning Sultans after Sultan Sulayman who reigned for forty years.

In Sultan Ibrahim's time the state scored a series of victories. The army conquered Crete, but eventually they grew tired of him and began to intrigue against him. After ten years of rule they deposed him.

Al-Muqattam 2093, 8 February, 1896

THE FIFTH DEPOSITION

After Sultan Ibrahim's deposition he was succeeded by his son, Sultan Muhammad the Fourth, who was four-years-old at the time. He was renowned for his fondness for hunting, spending large parts of his reign indulging his passion in the desert.

People count his reign in months, in spite of the fact that it was a long one. Fortunately, God in His generosity had provided the state with men of virtue and efficiency from the famous Koprulu family: grandfather, father, and son all succeeded each other as Grand Vizier. [251] While the Sultan was off hunting in the mountains of Rumeli, they stabilized state affairs, regulated popular activities, and organized day-to-day business. With the demise of Ahmad Pasha Koprulu [d. 1676], the cornerstone of this prized ring of grand viziers and the most illustrious and devoted of them all (he being the owner of the famous library near their cemetery in Istanbul), state affairs were consigned to people who were not so adept at politics: posts were handed out to undeserving people, and unsuitable governors were appointed. All the while the Sultan carried on hunting, while the state was involved in the famous siege of Vienna, an event without benefit for the Ottoman Empire. For the Ottoman Sultanate this was the first major setback, and it has never really recovered from it. In that way it closely resembles Napoléon's retreat from Moscow.

When the third member of the Koprulu family was appointed Deputy Grand Vizier (the Grand Vizier, according to usual practice, being involved in the war), he gathered all the `ulama' in the Hagia Sophia Mosque and told them how badly things were going and exactly what the empire had suffered. With that they proclaimed the Sultan deposed, but they neither imprisoned nor killed him. Actually, he was left in Edirne to hunt as long as he wished. He stayed there for six years, hunting to his heart's content.

THE SIXTH DEPOSITION

[252] Mustafa the Second now became Sultan. During his reign the war with Russia and Austria occurred. At first victory smiled on the Ottoman Empire, but then it started baring its fangs. England interfered to bring the war to an end, and peace was declared. Terms were agreed at the Treaty of Carlowitz. However, the Ottoman army felt that the treaty was an insult to the prestige and power of the state (what, one wonders, would they have said about the Treaty of Berlin?) and mutinied against the Sultan. The `ulama' proclaimed a *fatwa* deposing him, and they carried it out.

THE SEVENTH DEPOSITION

Sultan Ahmad the Third succeeded and stayed on the throne for almost eighteen years. He was embroiled in the war with Peter the Great and Catherine of

Russia. The campaign was under the direction of the Grand Vizier, Muhammad Pasha al-Baltaji, who managed to encircle Peter the Great and cut off his retreat. He almost managed to take Peter the Great prisoner, but Catherine arrived with a bribe. The siege was lifted, and Peter the Great was saved. That particular rescue had repercussions that last till this very day.

An amazing story tells how the Grand Vizier was questioned about his apparent lack of interest in taking the Czar prisoner [253] and his flippant attitude to the whole thing. "Who else could we leave," he replied, "who could be ruler of Russia and responsible for its affairs?" The army returned in a state of terrible disarray. This scared the Sultan, who decided to get them out of the way by provoking a conflict with Persia. However, the army rapidly deposed him.

THE EIGHTH DEPOSITION

Selim the Third now succeeded and reigned for nineteen years. He was dubbed the second conqueror of Egypt, because it was during his reign that the English pushed the French out. He was keen to introduce European army methods into the Ottoman forces, but the Ankshariyya (Janissaries) refused to accept such a revolutionary idea. They set about getting him deposed by asking `Ata'allah Efendi, then the Shaykh al-Islam, to publish a *fatwa* to that effect. The *fatwa* was duly issued in response to the following question: "Should a Sultan who contravenes the Qur'an be left on the Ottoman throne?" The answer was in the negative, and that was the basis for his deposition.

THE NINTH DEPOSITION

Sultan Mustafa the Fourth now succeeded. Most of the soldiers who supported Sultan Selim the Third, the deposed Sultan, lived outside Istanbul. When they heard news of the deposition, [254] they were on the point of restoring him to the throne. However, Sultan Mustafa found out about it and, before they could move, had his uncle, Sultan Selim the Third, killed. The army entered Istanbul, then deposed and killed Sultan Mustafa. At that point Sultan Mahmud was the only surviving member of the Ottoman family.

THE TENTH DEPOSITION

This involved Sultan `Abd al-`Aziz. The facts are well enough known, so there's no need for detail. Suffice it to say that the *fatwa* issued concerning his deposition was based on the fact that he was insane.

THE ELEVENTH DEPOSITION

This involved Sultan Murad; here too the facts are well known. This too was based on insanity.

Having now dealt with the depositions, we will now list those who have abdicated and the single martyr—God be pleased with him!

THE FIRST [AND SECOND] ABDICATION

Murad the Second was appointed Sultan, but he was a decent man who liked his peace and quiet; he also tended to be lethargic. He therefore abdicated in favor of his son, Sultan Muhammad the Second, and then went to Magnesia where he lived a quiet life. Later he was summoned to become Sultan once again when [255] the army which had started a war against Byzantium ran away, and the young Sultan could not face up to the dangers himself. Thus, father returned, led the army, and directed the campaign. He sent his son to Magnesia in his place till he had won a victory and restored the situation to normal. He then abdicated once again, and his son became Sultan. Murad now returned once again to Magnesia. All this was only possible because of the good relationship between father and son.

THE THIRD ABDICATION

This involved Sultan Bayazid the Second. When he declared his brother Crown Prince, his own son declared war on him. He left the throne because he did not want to see Muslim blood shed. He was anxious to perform the pilgrimage, then return to Magnesia, but three days after he had started his journey, he died while performing the ritual ablutions for afternoon prayer.

THE MARTYR

This was Murad the First—God be pleased with him!—who was killed in battle against the Serbs. Having won a victory, he went out to take a look at the dead and was stabbed by a prisoner. He was brought back to Bursa, which in his name is called "Khudandakar."

Glossary

Almabayn: literally, "what lies between," the name given to the administrative center of the Ottoman government during `Abd al-Hamid's reign because it lay between the Sultan's palace (Yildiz) and the Sublime Porte (Al-Bab al-`Ali)

**Al-Bab al-`Ali**: the Sublime Porte, the office of the Grand Vizier (Al-Sadr al-A`zam), which housed the Ministry of the Interior and the Foreign Ministry

bala: the most senior rank in the Ottoman bureaucracy's award system

damad: son-in-law

diwan: a government department or office

fatwa: an opinion on a legal issue delivered by a religious scholar (*mufti*)

Grand Vizier (Al-Sadr al-A`zam): the senior minister in the Ottoman government

majlis: session, council

ma'mur: a civil official in the Ottoman administration, charged with the supervision of affairs in a province or district

milla: religious community

mirimiran: literally, "supreme commander," an Ottoman military rank, but later used also to designate a senior civil official

mufti: a Muslim official entitled to deliver a legal opinion (*fatwa*)

mushir: field marshal (a military rank)

mutasarrif: governor of a province (in later Ottoman times)

Naqib al-Ashraf: Marshal of the Prophet's descendants

qutb (literally "pole"): a major figure within a Sufi sect

serasker: commander in chief

shari`a: the Islamic code of laws

Sharif (pl. Ashraf): a descendant of the Prophet; also the title of the senior official in Mecca

Shaykh al-Islam: the senior Muslim authority within the Ottoman hierarchy

Sublime Porte: see Al-Bab al-`Ali above

takiyya: a small mosque or shrine

`ulama' (sing. `alim): the religious scholars of Islam

waqf: a religious endowment

yavar, pl. yavaran: a holder of the rank of general in the Ottoman armed forces

yavar akram: senior general

Index

About the Translator

Roger Allen is professor of Arabic and comparative literature and chair of the Department of Near Eastern Languages and Civilizations at the University of Pennsylvania.

He is a specialist on Arabic narrative and has published numerous books and articles on Arab authors, among them Muhammad al-Muwaylihi, Naguib Mahfouz, `Abd al-Rahman Munif, and Ibrahim al-Kuni. His books include *The Arabic Novel*, *Modern Arabic Literature*, and *The Arabic Literary Heritage* and its abbreviated paperback version, *Introduction to Arabic Literature*. He has also translated many works of modern Arabic fiction into English, including novels by Naguib Mahfouz, `Abd al-Rahman Munif, Jabra Ibrahim Jabra, Hanan al-Shaykh, and Bensalem Himmich.